Critical Thinking in Psychology

Personality and Individual Differences

Bere Mahoney

Series Editor: Dominic Upton

LearningMatters

First published in 2011 by Learning Matters Ltd

British Library Cataloguing in Publication Data
A CIP record for this book is available from the British Library.

ISBN: 978 0 85725 114 5

This book is also available in the following ebook formats:
Adobe ebook   ISBN: 978 0 85725 214 2
ePUB ebook   ISBN: 978 0 85725 164 0
Kindle   ISBN: 978 0 85725 294 4

Cover and text design by Toucan Design
Project management by Diana Chambers
Typeset by Kelly Winter
Printed and bound in Great Britain by Short Run Press Ltd, Exeter, Devon

Learning Matters Ltd
20 Cathedral Yard
Exeter EX1 1HB
Tel: 01392 215560
E-mail: info@learningmatters.co.uk
www.learningmatters.co.uk

FSC
www.fsc.org
MIX
Paper from
responsible sources
FSC® C014540

Critical Thinking in Psychology

Personality and Individual Differences

Critical Thinking in Psychology – titles in the series

Contents

Acknowledgements

Many thanks to my mother, Paula, for her limitless reassurance and common sense, and to my sister, Sarah, for her concise and practical advice.

Series editor's introduction

Studying psychology at degree level

Being a student of psychology is an exciting experience – the study of mind and behaviour is a fascinating and sprawling journey of discovery. Yet studying psychology at degree level brings with it new experiences, new skills and new knowledge. This book, one in a comprehensive new series, brings you this psychological knowledge but importantly brings with it directions and guidance on the skills and experiences you should also be developing during your studies.

Psychology is a growing discipline – in scope, in breadth and in numbers. It is one of the fastest growing subjects studied at GCSE and A level, and the number of students studying the subject at university has grown considerably over the past decade. Indeed, psychology is now one of the most popular subjects in UK higher education, with the most recent data suggesting that there are some 45,000 full-time students currently enrolled on such programmes (compiled from Higher Education Statistics Agency (HESA) statistics available at www.hesa.ac.uk), and it is likely that this number has not yet peaked.

The popularity of psychology is related to a number of reasons, not the least of which is its scope and its breadth – psychology is a sprawling discipline that seeks to analyse the human mind and behaviour, which is fascinating in its own right. Furthermore, psychology aims to develop other skills – numeracy, communication and critical analysis, to name but a few. For these reasons, many employers seek out psychology graduates – they bring a whole host of skills to the workplace and to any activities they may be involved in. This book brings together the knowledge base associated with psychology along with these critical skills. By reading this book, and engaging with the exercises, you will develop these skills and in this way you will do two things: excel in your studies and your assessments, and put yourself at the front of the queue of psychology graduates when it comes to demonstrating these skills to potential employers.

Developing higher level skills

Only about 15–20 per cent of psychology graduates end up working as professional psychologists. The subject is a useful platform for many other careers because of the skills it helps you to develop. It is useful to employers because of its subject-specific skills – knowing how people act is pertinent in almost any job and particularly relevant to those that involve working directly with people. But psychology also develops a number of generic and transferable skills that are both essential to effective undergraduate study and valuable to employers. These include higher-level intellectual skills, such as critical and creative thinking, reflection, evaluation and analysis, and other skills, such as communication, problem solving, understanding and using data, decision making, organisational skills, teamworking, and IT skills.

The Quality Assurance Agency for Higher Education (QAA) subject benchmarks for psychology (www.qaa.ac.uk/academicinfrastructure/benchmark/honours/psychology.asp), which set out the expectations of a psychology degree programme, highlight the sorts of skills that your degree should equip you with. The British Psychological Society (BPS), which accredits your degree course, acknowledges that graduate employability is an important area of focus for universities and expects that opportunities for skills development should be well embedded within your programme of study. Indeed, this is a major focus of your study – interesting as psychology is, you will need and want employment at the end of your degree.

The activities in this book have been designed to help you build the underpinning skills that you need in order to become independent and lifelong learners, and to meet the relevant requirements of your programme of study, the QAA benchmarks and the needs of you and your potential employer.

Many students find it a challenge to develop these skills, often learning them out of the context of their study of the core knowledge domains of psychology. The activities in this book aim to help you to learn these skills *at the same time* as developing your core psychology knowledge, giving you opportunities to continuously practise skills so that they become second nature to you. The tasks provide guidance on what the skill is, how to develop basic competence in it and how to progress to further expertise.

At the same time, development of these skills will enable you to better understand and retain the core content of your course. Being able to evaluate, analyse and interpret content is the key to deepening understanding.

The skills that the activities in this book will help you to develop are presented in Table 0.1.

Table 0.1: *Skills developed in this book*

Generic skills	Transferable skills
• critical and creative thinking	• communication: oral, visual and written
• reflection	• problem solving
• analysing and evaluating	• understanding and using data
	• decision making
	• organisational skills
	• teamwork
	• information technology
	• independent learning

In addition to review questions and essay questions, each chapter in this book contains novel learning activities. Your responses will be guided through these activities and you will then be able to apply these skills within the context of personality and individual differences psychology.

Features in this book

At the start of each chapter there are **learning outcomes**. These are a set of bullet points that highlight the outcomes – both skills and knowledge – that you should achieve if you read and engage with the chapter. These bullet points aim to orientate you, the reader, to the content of the chapter before you begin reading it and to demonstrate the relevance of the topic.

We have also included learning features throughout the individual chapters in order to demonstrate key points and promote your learning.

- **Bulleted lists** are used within the chapter to convey key content messages.

- **Case studies** are included as parts of critical thinking activities.

- **Tasks** are a series of short review questions on the topic that will help you assess yourself and your current level of knowledge – use these to see if you can move on or whether you need to re-read and review the material.

- **Critical thinking activities** allow for a review of the text by encouraging key critical and creative thinking of the psychology material presented, and provide for the development of generic skills. Each of these activities is followed by a **Critical thinking review** which unpicks the activity for you, showing how it should have been tackled, the main skill it develops and other skills you may have used in completing the activity.

- **Skill builder activities** use the psychology material presented in the text, but are focused on one particular transferable skill as outlined in Table 0.1. Each of these activities is followed by a **Skill builder review** which may provide further hints and which makes explicit the skills it helps to develop and the benefits of completing the activity.

At the end of the chapter there are also some pedagogic features that you will find useful in developing your abilities.

- **Assignments** in order to assess your awareness and understanding of the topic we have produced a series of questions for you to discuss and debate with your colleagues. You can also use these questions as revision materials.

- **Summary: what you have learned** at the end of each chapter we present a summary of the chapter. We hope that this will relate back to the learning outcomes presented at the outset of the chapter.

- **Further reading** we have included between two and four items that will provide additional information – some of these are in journals and some are full texts. For each we have provided the rationale for suggesting the additional reading and we hope that these will direct you accordingly.

- **Glossary** entries are highlighted in bold in the text on their first appearance in a chapter.

Finally, there is a full set of **references** to support all of the material presented in this text.

We hope you enjoy this text, which is part of a series of textbooks covering the complete knowledge base of psychology.

This book, and the other companion volumes in this series, should provide one place to cover all of your study needs. It will, obviously, need to be supplemented with further reading, and this text directs you towards suitable sources. We hope that you find this book useful and informative and a guide both for your studying now and in your future as a successful psychology graduate.

Professor Dominic Upton
June 2011

Chapter 1

Individual differences
Aims, methods and ethics

Learning outcomes

By the end of this chapter you should:

- *be able to define what is meant by individual differences psychology and to discuss, critically, its aims and fundamental principles;*

- *be able to outline and consider, critically, the main research methods and measurements, or types of data, used in the field;*

- *understand and be able to evaluate the use of the psychometric approach in the study of individual differences;*

- *be able to identify and examine, critically, why reliability, validity, test norms and standardisation are important to the methods and measurements used in individual differences psychology;*

- *through completing a critical thinking activity and a skill building activity, understand some of the ethical challenges involved in using measurements of individual differences.*

Introduction

In this chapter you will consider the scope, research methods and measurements – or types of data – along with some of the ethical challenges faced in individual differences psychology, a field of inquiry within the discipline of psychology. You will do this by attempting to answer the following questions.

- What do we mean by individual differences psychology?

- What are the aims and fundamental **principles** of this **field of psychology**?

- How do psychologists study individual differences?

- What sorts of ethical challenges do psychologists face in individual differences psychology?

- Why are the analysis and evaluation of measurements or data important to the use and study of individual differences?

We need to ensure we have a clear understanding of what the term *individual differences psychology* means before attempting to answer these questions. However, as is often the case in psychology, the terminology we use, and on occasions its misuse and abuse, are important in shaping the discipline. The field of individual differences psychology is no exception to this tendency. For example, some researchers use the term **differential psychology** to denote the field of individual differences psychology (Lubinski, 2000; Revelle et al., 2010). Other researchers focus on specific aspects or domains of individual differences in their terminology. For example, in the USA and to some extent Europe (e.g. Caprara and Cervone, 2000) the terms *personality psychology* and even *intelligence* are sometimes used to describe the field. Indeed, terms such as personality psychology, intelligence, differential psychology and individual differences psychology are related, and are used interchangeably by some researchers (Lubinski, 2000). However, some researchers use these terms in ways that have more distinct meanings. For example, these different terms can indicate the phenomena researchers focus on, or their theoretical and methodological approach to the field.

In this book, a broad and inclusive approach to the field is taken – what has been described as **whole person psychology** (Caprara and Cervone, 2000). This approach assumes that a necessary aim of individual differences psychology should be the identification of *what individual differences look like*, for example by describing their apparent structure. However, this approach also assumes that such a focus on describing individual differences – referred to here as the *what* of individual differences – is insufficient for achieving whole person psychology. What is also necessary is the study of *determinants* – referred to here as the *why* of individual differences – and *functions* – referred to here as the *how* of individual differences. In other words, individual differences psychology should study the what, why and how of individual differences phenomena. We refer to them here as the *3-dimensions* or *3-ds*, and the approach taken here is one that attempts to consider the field as one that needs to be *3-dimensional*. Achieving an understanding of these *3-ds* means focusing not merely on describing individual differences but also on understanding the processes and functions of individual differences phenomena. Therefore, in Chapter 9, once we have examined the main topic areas of the field in Chapters 2 to 8, we will return to this issue and you will be asked to consider, critically, how 3-dimensional individual differences psychology is. It is important that we clarify what we mean by the terminology we use here. The term individual differences psychology and the related term *individual differences* are used here to capture the assumptions about the aims of the field used in this book. The use of these terms is also both *pragmatic* and *descriptive*. These terms have a pragmatic usefulness because they are readily identifiable in the content of the British Psychological Society's syllabi for undergraduate and postgraduate courses it accredits. Furthermore, the terms also feature heavily in undergraduate and graduate level textbooks, journal articles and journal titles, and are therefore useful search terms. Finally, the terms have descriptive value as researchers often refer to *individual differences* within domains considered in the field, such as individual differences in personality, intelligence and motivation.

The overall goal of this chapter is to set the scene for the remainder of this book by developing your understanding of some of the fundamental conceptual and methodological issues that shape individual differences psychology and, to some extent, give it characteristics distinct from other fields. These are the starting points for the fundamental purpose of this book – which is to encourage you to think critically about the field generally and about the topics we will consider. This book attempts to take a broad, inclusive and whole person psychology approach to the study of individual differences, and this is a challenging position to take. For example, this book is inevitably selective in its content. Exhaustive coverage of the vast domain of research in individual differences psychology is beyond its scope. It could be argued that using selective content actually makes it impossible to consider the field using a *3-d* approach. However, it is important to understand that the particular broad, inclusive and whole person psychology approach to the field used here is not fundamentally quantitative – in other words, it is not simply achieved by exhaustive coverage of the greatest number of topics within the field (Caprara and Cervone, 2000). Rather, it is fundamentally *qualitative* – it is about a particular perspective or way of thinking about individual differences psychology that entails recognising the value of considering how *3-d* the field actually is, based on the premise that such an approach could ultimately provide the fullest understanding of individual differences (Lubinski, 2000). Furthermore, judging the actual 3-dimensionality of the field is an intellectual activity that involves thinking critically about a range of 'taken for granted' assumptions used in the field (Yanchar and Slife, 2004). Exhaustive coverage of individual differences topics is therefore not necessary to achieve the fundamental purpose of this book – which is to encourage you to think critically about key topics and issues in individual differences psychology.

Nevertheless, it is impossible to avoid both the complex range of psychological phenomena that characterises individual differences psychology and the sheer breadth of psychological phenomena it encompasses. This alone presents students of the field (and, indeed, those writing textbooks in the field) with a challenge. In this book, students are presented with the additional challenge of trying to approach the field of individual differences psychology by considering critically how *3-d* it is. This whole person psychology approach requires the holistic and integrated study of the full range of psychological phenomena – affects, behaviours, cognitions and desires (Caprara and Cervone, 2000) – but without exhaustive coverage of topics in the field. To help you meet this challenge we will spend some time considering what makes individual differences psychology distinct from other fields in the discipline. The affects, behaviours, cognitions and desires it considers are, of course, of interest to psychologists in general. However, what makes individual differences psychology distinct from other fields when studying these phenomena emerges partly from how the field typically goes about studying these phenomena – its predominant aims, and the principles and methods it uses. These give the field a distinct identity or approach, albeit a controversial one, as the field is far from unified in its approach to individual differences. In particular, not all of those working in the field support the predominant methods it uses, and specifically the approach of choice by the majority – the *psychometric* approach. This means that researchers are also reflecting on the very fundamentals of the field in terms of the **theory**, **research paradigms**, methods and measures currently synonymous with individual differences psychology. For example, some researchers are considering critically how psychometrics – so prototypical of the methods used in the field – are faring as the approach of choice in individual differences psychology (Boorsboom, 2006; Lamiell, 2007), along with the consequences of the dominance of psychometrics for the psychological landscape of the field. This also means that researchers are questioning which aspects of individual differences the field actually focuses on. Despite discussions about these issues, the focus of the field remains fixed strongly on describing the nature and structure of individual differences in the domains of personality and intelligence, along with the predictive usefulness of these structures – the *what* of the *3-dimensions*. There is still rather less attention focused on the determinants – the *why* – and even less attention focused on the functions – the *how* – of individual differences in the field. Determinants and functions of individual differences can be referred to as the process mechanisms (Revelle et al., 2010) of individual differences or what can also be described as **inter-** and **intra-individual processes** (Cervone, 2005). This relatively narrow focus has, to some extent, been aggravated by the effects of specialisation – or separatism – in the field, a trend that some regard as problematic because:

> a much richer picture of humanity and psychological diversity is brought into focus when constellations of individual-differences variables are assembled for research and practice.
>
> (Lubinski, 2000, p407)

In Chapter 2 you will therefore consider how the relationship between individual differences psychology and other fields in psychology is increasingly being questioned (Sternberg et al., 2001). Nevertheless, the psychometric approach remains dominant in the field, meaning that the integrity of individual differences psychology continues to depend on the soundness of this approach.

The term *psychometrics* literally means the measurement of psychological phenomena or mental processes (Bartram and Lindley, 2005), and in individual differences psychology this means the measurement of psychological phenomena we refer to as individual differences. Measurements or measures of individual differences we collect in the field are therefore central to the psychometric approach. Measures of individual differences, or individual differences data, are used in real contexts to make important decisions about individuals or groups of individuals (Lubinski, 2000; Revelle et al., 2010). Consequently, the measurements we use in individual differences psychology, along with the methods we use to collect the data that form these measures, have social significance. This is because they are used in real contexts to make important decisions about individuals or social groups (Lubinski, 2000; Revelle et al., 2010). The field's contribution to such high-stakes decision making about individuals and groups in the domains of education, work, mental health and the criminal justice system remains unabated and substantial (Revelle et al., 2010). Thus the theoretical and empirical findings of the field have both academic and real world significance. The reality is that the access of individuals and social groups to certain resources and opportunities in the domains of education, training, work and within the criminal justice system involve the collection and interpretation of individual differences measures and data. This means that when working in the field – whether as academics, practitioners or students – our conduct is of *ethical* and *professional* importance. In this chapter we will therefore also consider some of the ethical and professional responsibilities we have in the field. Our overarching responsibility is to ensure that we competently and respectfully uphold the highest possible standards of quality in the methods of data collection we use, the data we collect and our interpretation of such data, or its analysis and evaluation. The importance of these issues means we will return repeatedly to these issues throughout this book. Ethics and professional conduct are also issues that are an important part of your **reflective critical thinking** about the field.

Finally, you are studying individual differences psychology at an interesting time in its development. The tasks and activities in this chapter are designed to encourage you to think critically about such issues. At the end of the twentieth century researchers reflected on the so-called *vision of the future* of individual differences in the twenty-first century in light of over 100 years of activity. Currently, we are seeing the resurgence of old debates about what the scope and aims of the field should actually look like. Indeed, Lubinski's (2000) view cited earlier was far from new at the start of the twenty-first century. Such a broad and inclusive approach to individual differences psychology can be found in the earlier writings of classic researchers in the field such as Thorndike and Cronbach in the 1940s and 1950s (Ackerman, 1997). Currently, debates about the apparent narrowness of the focus and methods of much of contemporary individual differences psychology are not necessarily creating intellectual tidal waves through the field – there is a quality of déjà vu about some of the current controversies. Indeed, there have been many apparent intellectual tidal waves in the field, and they tend to come and go with some degree of cyclical regularity. In fact, it is difficult to find a topic or domain in individual differences psychology that has not witnessed the boom and bust of a major theory or empirical finding. Rather, it appears that current debates are presently sending gentle ripples of controversy through the field. However, these more controversial issues can often be overlooked (e.g. Boorsboom et al., 2004), as undergraduates are often encouraged, quite rightly, to focus on key studies and general trends in the discipline and in its various fields of inquiry. Nevertheless, in this chapter you will be encouraged to consider both general, or mainstream, trends *and* more controversial issues in individual differences psychology. Considering the more controversial issues in the field should also help to develop your critical thinking skills.

The scope of individual differences psychology

Identifying the scope of individual differences psychology – how we define the field and its aims – is important because it will help you understand the particular characteristics of the field, and this is, therefore, the first task we will attempt. We will then examine how research on individual differences is conducted – by considering the **concepts** and fundamental principles of the field. Remember that the issues covered have been selected because of their importance rather than to provide comprehensive coverage.

Defining individual differences psychology

What is meant by *individual differences psychology* and what are *individual differences?* Defining these terms is an important task because it will help clarify the scope of the field, and the range of psychological phenomena that is studied. One way of understanding this scope is to try to identify the sorts of questions that might be asked in individual differences psychology about different psychological phenomena.

Task

Below is a scenario (Norton, n.d.) that describes the situation of a fictional character called Justine. Your task is to read this scenario and then, either individually or in groups, to identify the sorts of comments, issues and questions you think might be asked in individual differences psychology about the scenario. Remember, at this stage all you need to do is to base your answers on what you believe or already know about individual differences psychology. There are no right or wrong answers in this task and it is acceptable to include your personal beliefs and experiences here – do not feel compelled to make your responses appear 'academic' at this point unless they actually are.

Justine is a bright, attractive and likeable 19-year-old in her first year at university and studying for a degree in psychology. She has been advised to see a student counsellor by her personal tutor, who is very worried about her. Apparently, after a good start Justine has been missing lectures, seminars and workshops and is now falling behind in her coursework. When she went to see her personal tutor she said she had been feeling 'down' and 'miserable', and then broke down and appeared extremely distressed. She could not stop crying and shaking but refused to say what was wrong. In her first meeting with the student counsellor, Justine looks unwell and finds it hard to speak. After a long silence, she eventually blurts out that she is terrified of public speaking and simply cannot face the psychology workshops. She says she has been completely thrown by an essay that she is supposed to be writing on phobias because every time she tries to read up on the subject, she is reminded of her own fear, which now seems to be generalising to a fear of going out to public places. In the last few weeks this has become so bad that she has practically stopped going out altogether unless it is absolutely necessary, in an attempt to avoid the **anxiety**. Justine says she want to give up her degree, but cannot stop because her parents are so proud of her and would be terribly disappointed if she did not graduate. She also says she cannot carry on with psychology because of the course requirements for participation.

Comment

Everyday life is replete with situations in which we have to make judgements about ourselves or others, and scenarios such as this are far from unusual. Generally, people are often interested in the *sort of person they are* or *someone else is*. In fact, there is evidence that students are often drawn to study psychology at university because they believe it is the study of people, their problems and people fixing (Wallwork et al., 2007). To some extent this is the essence of much of the discipline. The fact that you are reading this textbook could indicate that you are likely to be a psychology undergraduate, and gaining a place on your course of study is likely to have involved the assessment of the sort of person you are in various ways. For example, measures of your cognitive ability through your performance on some form of test and your self-reported interest in the discipline are standard sources of information you have to provide when completing your UCAS form (currently the predominant method for gaining entry to university in the UK). Actually starting your university career can also lead you to ask questions about yourself in comparison to others. These are all phenomena of interest to individual differences psychology; and in the scenario about Justine there are both direct and indirect references to many of these and other psychological phenomena or individual differences typically studied in individual differences psychology. What follows is a list of some of these phenomena along with general comments, issues and questions that you might have in your responses.

- *Cognitive abilities*: Justine has completed certain tests that measure her cognitive ability to gain entry to university, and her tutor judges her as 'bright'. What does this mean, and how has this judgement been made?

- *Aspects of personality*: Justine is described as 'likeable'. What does this mean? Can we use this characteristic to judge other individuals? Do individuals vary on this characteristic? How could we measure this characteristic and capture how individuals differ in this? Are there differences between individuals on this characteristic? Are such differences enduring or stable characteristics or dispositions of individuals?

- *Aspects of motivation, emotion and mood*: Justine appears to be experiencing unpleasant **emotions** but what are these emotions more precisely? How has this been judged? How does this differ from feeling 'blue'? Is this typical of Justine or out of the ordinary for her? How 'blue' or 'distressed' do other people feel? Do some individuals experience such unpleasant emotions or **moods** most of the time? Justine describes herself, or self-reports that she is highly motivated and wants to do well at university, but she also appears motivated by external pressures. What do we mean by *motivation*? What motivates individuals? How can we measure motivation, and are there different types of motivation?

- *Behaviours that seem 'out of character' or unusual in some way*: Some of Justine's behaviour is described as unusual and not typical of other individuals in her cohort of students. How do we make such judgements? What is *typical*? What is typical of Justine? For example, does her behaviour vary from situation to situation, in other words, what do we know about the **intra-individual variability** of Justine's behaviour? How do individuals vary in this behaviour in general or what is the **inter-individual variability** between individuals? Do social groups vary systematically in this behaviour, such as men compared to women; in other words, is there inter-individual variation between groups?

- *Observations of behaviour* and *self-reports of behaviour*: How accurate are the observations of Justine by others? How accurate are Justine's self-reports of how she feels and behaves? Are behaviours observed by others and Justine's self-reports related? Can we use these sources of information to understand other aspects of Justine, or what we could describe as *underlying characteristics* or *dispositions*?

The scenario describes aspects of Justine's characteristic affects, behaviours, cognitions and desires as perceived by both others and herself, and some aspects seem out of character for her. The scenario also contains both explicit and implicit references to the aims, methods and measurements used in the field of individual differences psychology. For example, certain terms are used to describe Justine's typical characteristics that have relatively general meaning, such as likeable and bright, and these are the sorts of **constructs** that individual differences psychology attempts to study more formally, systematically and scientifically. Your list of answers will be returned to in subsequent tasks in this chapter, so keep these at hand and make sure you mark them as your first answers.

The task should draw your attention to a number of issues. First, the sheer scope of individual differences psychology means that it is not exclusively about one topic such as personality or intelligence. Second, individual differences psychology aims to study the whole person, and this means it considers psychological phenomena of interest to other fields within psychology. Third, individual differences psychology typically involves operationalising constructs we cannot observe directly, or what can be called latent variables (Biesanz and West, 2000; Boorsboom et al., 2004; Caprara and Cervone, 2000). Frequently, this involves describing *surface features* or *observable* and *measurable traits* that tell us something about the enduring underlying characteristics or *dispositions* of individuals. These characteristics might be typical of individuals or demonstrate their best or maximum performance on some task. The use of surface features and underlying characteristics as concepts to describe individuals' differences is a controversial issue and one that we will return to in this and subsequent chapters. Fourth, as stated at the start of this chapter, terminology is important in the field. This terminology includes terms used to describe the psychological phenomena typically studied in individual differences psychology. These phenomena can be grouped to form domains of psychological phenomena or individual differences. Cronbach's (1957) four principalities of correlational research continue to provide a useful rubric for organising the domains of psychological phenomena considered in individual differences psychology (see Figure 1.1), and later in this chapter we will consider why the term *correlational* is central to the field. Finally, measurement and assessment are important features of the field. Self-assessments or self-report data, test data and the assessments of others, including **sociodemographic information**, are used as sources of data about individual differences. In addition, the interpretation of such measurements is a central issue in individual differences psychology. Consequently, the field is concerned with how we use such data about individuals, and the different methods we use to collect data.

These topics and issues will be considered in more detail in this and subsequent chapters. However, at this point we can specify the working definition of individual differences psychology and individual differences used in this book. It draws heavily on the work of Caprara and Cervone (2000, pp2–7) and states that the field is concerned with the study of the *structure and determinants of enduring psychological characteristics as perceived by the individual and those around them.* Specifically, these enduring characteristics are *collections of behaviours, feelings and thoughts* that *systematically typify how individuals and groups of individuals appear to be similar or different.* These psychological phenomena also have *consequences for how individuals react* and therefore *regulate themselves across a range of life domains,* and the relationship between these person and situation variables is complex and reciprocal.

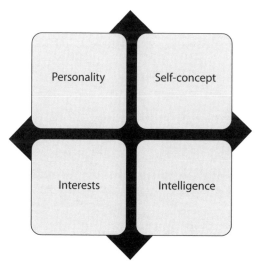

Figure 1.1: Cronbach's (1957) principalities of correlational research

Personality

Self-concept

Interests

Intelligence

Aims of individual differences psychology

Having defined individual differences psychology and individual differences, we now turn to consider the aims or purposes of the field. Earlier, we stated that other fields within the discipline are, ostensibly, interested in the same phenomena and the same issues, so we still need to identify more precisely what distinguishes individual differences psychology from other fields in psychology. For example, the field of developmental psychology is also concerned with the study of the structure and determinants of behaviours of individuals and social groups over the **life course**, and the identification of typical or general patterns or trends in such phenomena. Likewise, social psychologists are interested in how individuals interact in different situations, and general patterns or trends in such interaction. However, if we analyse our working definition of individual differences psychology, we see that it contains ten features that capture a little more precisely some of the features of field that *distinguish* it from others in the discipline. These features are shown in Figure 1.2.

Structure and determinants summarises the broad aims of many working in the field, which are to systematically describe both the structure and determinants – or the causes – of individual differences. This typically involves the development of formal frameworks or taxonomies that list particular aspects of individual differences. These serve two functions. First, they provide individual difference dimensions that can be used to describe individuals in general, such as traits that describe personality and different dimensions of intellectual or cognitive ability (e.g. verbal and mathematical ability). In this sense, these dimensions are used to capture similarities between large numbers of individuals. Attempting to make such general statements about large numbers of individuals is a characteristic of the **nomothetic** approach to research. Second, these dimensions can be measured, and this measurement enables us to compare individuals and how much they differ from one another. A final point here is that the identification of these dimensions across domains of individual differences is a fundamental feature of the field, and one that has shaped the field for over a century. However, some researchers argue that the field has become too focused on this activity, which has tended to involve the study of what individual differences

Figure 1.2: *Features of individual differences psychology*

Structure and determinants	Enduring	Perceived and experienced	Characteristic behaviours, feelings and thoughts
Typify individuals and groups	Similarities and differences	Consequences	Self-regulation
	Life domains	Person-environment reciprocal interaction	

actually look like. In other words, the focus of the field tends to be the study of the surface features or tendencies of dispositions – the *what* of the 3-dimensions – and the study of the origins of such differences is neglected (Cervone, 2005). To some extent, this debate is a red herring. It can be argued that we cannot usefully attempt to understand the determinants of domains of individual differences if we have yet to identify their actual structure. Clearly, the search for determinants of individual differences and how they work – the *why* and *how* of the 3-dimensions – presupposes we have a good understanding of *what* these differences are in the first place. However, the issue in this debate is about the balance of research in individual differences psychology, and how research on the structure of individual differences is interpreted. Specifically, the latter research is simply that and does not necessarily help our understanding of the determinants and functions of individual differences. This is an important and technical debate in the field and one that we will return to because it has implications for both the extent of our understanding of the nature of individual differences, and how 3-dimensional the field actually is.

The second feature – *enduring* – describes a fundamental principle that runs through much of individual differences psychology. The field is interested in variations between individuals that are relatively enduring rather than momentary changes in behaviours, feelings and thoughts. The issue of the stability of dispositions is something psychologists have considered at various points in the history of the field, such as with the *person-situation debate* (see Chapter 2) and when considering how dispositions change or remain stable across the life course (see Chapter 2). Mainstream research on individual differences tends to differentiate stable dispositions from other more changeable aspects of individuals such as mood, motivation and emotion. However, increasingly the links are being considered, hence their inclusion in Chapter 8.

The third feature – *perceived and experienced* – indicates that individual differences psychology attempts to study inter-individual variation that is perceived and experienced as meaningful to individuals. For example, the field has developed *taxonomies* – lists of features – for describing individual differences using terminology that reflects our everyday expressions of differences by which we judge others and ourselves. This is the basis of the lexical hypothesis that underpins many trait approaches to personality (see Chapter 2). The lexical hypothesis is not without controversy, and there are different versions of this used in the research. However, whatever variant of this we are considering, the critical issue here is that we use these expressions to make inferences about psychological phenomena or constructs that, technically, have not been observed directly. In this sense, these underlying constructs are, to some degree, hypothetical.

The fourth and fifth features – *characteristic behaviours, feelings and thoughts that typify similarities and differences between individuals and groups of individuals* – highlight a major aim of the field – to identify and understand a range of psychological phenomena or typical behaviours, feelings and thoughts of individuals or groups of individuals. Thus the unit of analysis in the field appears to be the individual or groups of individuals – in fact, the language used in the field refers to differences between individuals. Moreover, an aim of the field is to find ways of comparing individuals so that we can then judge the similarities and differences between them, and this is the sixth feature. This typically involves constructing taxonomies of characteristics that can apply to individuals in general, or what can be described as a *nomothetic* approach. This is usually contrasted with the **idiographic** approach that focuses on the relatively unique characteristics and experiences of particular individuals. An important caveat should be made here. At the start of this chapter attention was drawn to the importance of terminology in the field, and this applies to the use of the term *individuals*. Technically, much of contemporary individual differences psychology uses *aggregate data*. Aggregate data is a general term that can have several meanings. For example, it can be used to describe a composite test score of an individual that is the sum, or mean, of their responses to a number of items on a test. The term can also be used to describe data collected from a group, or groups, of individuals drawn from specific populations that are then combined in some way to produce aggregate group data. The important issue here is that when researchers and writers in the field refer to how one individual or individuals differ from one another or are similar, they are often referring to research results that are essentially some form of aggregate data. This is an important technical issue, and one that can make it difficult at times to interpret the research in the field.

Although listed separately, features seven, eight and nine – *consequences for self-regulation across life domains* – are closely related. A fundamental principle in the field is that individual differences, however conceptualised, have consequences for individuals. For example, individual differences can be used to predict how individuals react to events in their environment, and how individuals are likely to manage themselves psychologically – what can be called their self-regulation. These consequences of individual differences themselves can then be regarded as another type of individual differences data (see Chapters 3 and 4). Importantly, individuals vary in how successfully they regulate themselves, and individual differences in personality and cognitive ability appear to be related to this self-regulation across a range of life domains (see Chapters 3, 4, 6 and 7). The measures of individual differences we use can also have consequences for individuals because, as stated earlier, such measures are used in occupational, educational and clinical contexts.

The tenth feature – *person-environment reciprocal interaction* – signifies that ultimately the relationship between individuals and their environment is complex and reciprocal. Individuals can influence their environment and we can use individual differences to predict how individuals influence their environment through their particular and typical behaviours, feelings and thoughts. In turn, the environment can influence individuals. Individual differences are part of this complex reciprocal process of person-environment interaction.

As stated earlier, a challenging feature of the field for psychology undergraduates is the sheer breadth and volume of theory and empirical research encompassed under the banner of individual differences psychology and individual differences. Generally, researchers tend to focus on *some* of the features listed in Figure 1.2 rather than all of them. Likewise, they also tend to focus on some rather than all of Cronbach's (1957) four principalities of correlational psychology in Figure 1.1. The list of features is a useful **heuristic** for making sure you do not miss key aspects of the field.

A final heuristic that might help you understand the scope of individual differences is the way in which the field is generally organised in the literature. These groupings are far from exact and there is a good deal of overlap across the field. However, you will often encounter individual differences psychology literature that falls into the following groupings.

- Research that focuses on *general academic* aspects of broad domains or principalities (Cronbach, 1957) of individual differences, such as the structure and determinants or personality or intelligence.

- Research that is generally academic but that focuses on more *specific aspects* of the broad domains of individual differences such as research on how certain aspects of individual differences appear to be related to physical health (see Chapter 3) or mental disorder (see Chapter 4). This sort of research also includes a focus on a particular measure or test of some aspect of individual differences.

- *Practitioner work* that focuses on the nature, measurement and consequences of individual differences in applied professional areas of the discipline, such as occupational, educational and clinical psychology.

Task ── Now that we have identified some of the psychological phenomena and questions considered in individual differences psychology, examine your answers to the first task and check whether these are indeed the sorts of questions asked in the field. This time, work through all ten features in Figure 1.2 and use this figure to map your responses on to the ten features that it lists.

Comment

What this task should demonstrate is that although the phenomena considered by other fields in psychology are similar to those considered in individual differences psychology, the aims, methods and measures of the field have some distinct qualities.

Fundamental principles: dispositions and psychometrics

Individual differences psychology also differs from other fields in the discipline because of the *principles* it uses. Currently, individual differences psychology is dominated by the use of principles about the nature of dispositions and psychometric principles. These principles underpin much of the theory development and empirical research in the field of contemporary individual differences psychology.

Currently, the field can be regarded as one that focuses on the scientific measurement of dispositions, and a number of important principles about the nature of dispositions dominate the field's approach to the study of individual differences.

- Stable or enduring dispositions that are *measurable* can be used to formally and systematically measure inter-individual variation. Typically, this means assessing – measuring – how individuals react to certain tasks or events through observing these reactions or through the reports of such reactions by others or individuals themselves.

- These self-reported observations, or observations made by others, or performances on some task or test have *meaning* – they tell us about individuals' fundamental qualities, or dispositions. However, we cannot necessarily observe these dispositions *directly*. Instead, we infer these *hypothetical constructs* from these various observations or data. Also we attempt to identify general patterns in these observations from which we can develop systematic ways of describing large numbers of individuals or the *nomothetic* approach. The *accessibility debate*, that is, the issue of how directly, or indirectly, we can observe fundamental dispositions is a critical and as yet unresolved issue in the field (Cervone, 2005).

- Through the application of scientific methods of measurement referred to as psychometrics, we can not only develop these general ways of describing inter-individual variation, or taxonomies, but also make *predictions* about individuals and groups of individuals using measures of these dispositions. This is because taxonomies are essentially descriptions of dispositions that are fundamental qualities of individuals in general, such as cognitive abilities or characteristic ways of behaving, feeling and thinking – that is, personality.

These principles draw on *psychometric principles*. Psychometrics is a branch of mathematics that itself uses specific principles and statistical techniques to measure observable phenomena and to develop statistical models of these phenomena. Four key features of psychometrics drawn on in individual differences psychology are shown in Figure 1.3. First, psychometrics, as the scientific measurement of mental processes (Bartram and Lindley, 2005), assumes that complex phenomena can be transformed into quantities or numerical data, and this is known as *scaling*. Quantities or numerical data are assumed to represent real differences in the physical world, such as the height and weight of animate or inanimate objects. As such, these numerical data are assumed to be more or less linear representations of the quality being measured. For example, a centimetre as a measure of length is assumed to represent a real quality of the object or objects being measured. In this example, the quality being measured – length – can be measured or observed *directly*. It is assumed that the same principles can be applied to more complex phenomena, such

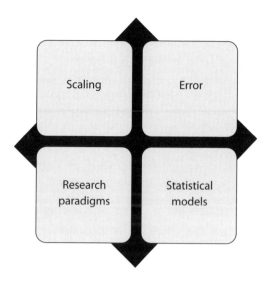

Figure 1.3: *Four key features of psychometrics*

as the behaviours, feelings and thoughts considered in psychology, even if we accept that we cannot necessarily measure or observe them directly. This is a fundamental and at times controversial issue in individual differences psychology because researchers in the field do not agree on how appropriate such scaling is for psychological phenomena. The controversy is also aggravated by what can be described as the *accessibility debate* – there is disagreement in the field about the extent to which enduring dispositions are accessible or observable directly, or can be inferred from phenomena we observe and measure. Despite the existence of these controversies, there is some apparent agreement in the field that relatively complex psychological phenomena can also be transformed into quantities – numbers – or scaled. Moreover, such numerical data are often used in the field to represent real differences in complex psychological qualities, such as dispositions and abilities. Such a use implies that such numerical data are linear with the psychological phenomena they are used to represent, although researchers do not always clarify their precise stance on this issue. Finally, the use of scaling in the field implies that we can conceptualise individual differences as dispositions that are *continuous dimensions*. Using our *3-d* approach, this means we can refer to the *what* of individual differences in terms of continua along which individuals can be placed (e.g. personality dimensions or traits, and dimensions of intelligence) depending upon their score on some measure of that dimension (e.g. score on a measure of the personality trait of extraversion, or score on a test of verbal ability). Second, measurement per se always contains random and systematic error. Therefore, the actual measures or scores we collect are not true scores or 100 per cent accurate because they are never free of error. Instead, actual measures or scores represent the true score plus random error and systematic error, a premise taken from *reliability theory*. Third, we therefore need to use specific methods or *paradigms* to minimise error and maximise the relationship between a true score and the actual measures or scores we collect. Finally, we can use statistical techniques to achieve this and to develop statistical models of complex psychological phenomena.

Task — Return to Justine's scenario and think about how some of the characteristics of Justine have been assessed in the description. What sorts of measures have been used to make judgements about her? Simply use language you feel comfortable with and do not attempt to make this technical or academic unless it actually is. Make a note of when your responses appear to contain quantitative or qualitative information and how accurate these observations might be.

Comment

This task should encourage you to think about the challenges involved in measuring or operationalising individual difference constructs, and how the nature of the measures we use influences the accuracy of our measures. The task should also encourage you to start reflecting on what we mean by accuracy.

What distinguishes individual differences psychology from other fields in the discipline is, to some extent, its scope, aims and principles. These characteristics are most evident in the methods, designs and measurements used in the field, and we will consider these next.

Methods, designs and measurements

As described in the previous section, the psychometric approach as used in contemporary individual differences psychology entails using the principle that we can measure quantitatively meaningful but essentially hypothetical or latent constructs that we refer to as individual differences. Given the dominance of the psychometric approach in the field, the methods and designs it uses to collect measurements are of central importance. We will therefore consider these next.

Methods and designs

Technically, the term *methods* refers to the tools used to run research and the ways in which data are collected, although conventionally – for instance, in research reports using the American Psychological Association (APA) format – the Methods sub-section includes all the main aspects of how a research study has been run – the design, participants, materials and procedure. In individual differences psychology, individual differences data are often collected using *paper and pencil tests* – these are the main tools or methods or means that are used to collect data. Technically and conventionally when writing research reports, *design* refers to the manner in which participants are considered in the research. For example, participants might be considered in comparison to other participants, or the relationship between different aspects of their data might be considered. In individual differences psychology, researchers often use *correlational designs* because they are usually interested in examining the relationships between the data collected from individuals. The methods and designs used by researchers also tell us about the explicit and implicit *assumptions* the researcher is making about the nature of the phenomena being studied, and here that means their assumptions about the nature of individual differences. These assumptions can be wide ranging, such as whether the psychological phenomena in question can be controlled or determined or whether they are naturally occurring. We can identify these various assumptions in the research paradigm or in the overall research approach used. This is the case in individual differences psychology. The research paradigm of choice by many psychologists working in the field reflects their assumptions made about the nature of individual differences – specifically, that individual differences are complex psychological phenomena shaped by multiple variables that we cannot control or manipulate using experimental designs and methods. They also reflect the psychometric principles we have outlined. Therefore, although other methods such as experimentation and observation are used in the field, the majority of research on individual differences uses correlational designs and paper and pencil methods for three broad purposes.

- To *develop and test theories* of individual differences or related psychological phenomena.

- To *develop and test tools* that can be used to collect measurements of individual differences, or individual differences data.

- To *make predictions about individuals*, including predictions that can be applied to a range of real world domains, such as education, work and health.

Experimental methods have been, and continue to be used in individual differences research. However, the field remains dominated by research that uses correlational designs.

Correlational designs and statistical tests of correlation are important in the historical development of individual differences psychology. Cronbach (1957) referred to psychologists working in the field as *correlators* whose goals are distinct from experimental psychologists. Specifically, he describes their respective methodological and design traditions as follows.

Individual differences have been an annoy rather than a challenge to the experimenter. His goal is to control behavior, and variation within treatments is proof that he has not succeeded. Individual variation is cast into that outer darkness known as 'error variance'. For reasons both statistical and philosophical, error variance is to be reduced by any possible device . . . your goal in the experimental tradition is to get those embarrassing differential variables out of sight . . . The correlational psychologist is in love with just those variables the experimenter left home to forget. He regards individual and group variation as important effects of biological and social causes. All organisms adapt to their environments, but not equally well. His question is: what present characteristics of the organism determine its mode and degree of adaptation?

(Cronbach, 1957)

Thus individual differences psychology aims to *predict variation* that we can observe or measure by asking *how much people vary*. Cronbach (1957) goes on to state that the statistical analysis of correlation, namely Spearman's correlation coefficient, has shaped the fundamental nature of contemporary individual differences psychology because *what began as a mere summary statistic quickly became the center of a whole theory of data analysis*. In particular, the use of statistical tests of how two continuous variables are related, and the testing of partial correlations, has given the field methods for what Murphy (1928 in Cronbach, 1957) referred to as *the mathematical 'isolation' of variables which cannot be isolated experimentally*. The development of advanced statistical techniques that enable the statistical analysis of the relationship between more than two variables has enabled those in the field to become more than *mere observer(s) of a play where Nature pulls a thousand strings . . . his multivariate methods make him equally an expert, an expert in figuring out where to look for the hidden strings* (Murphy in Cronbach, 1957). However, the advantages of using correlational designs should not be oversimplified. To some extent, even in 1957 the field focused heavily on the statistical analysis of data or the description of the structure of individual differences rather than the development of theories explaining the *why* and *how* of individual differences (Cronbach, 1957). Such a focus was regarded as problematic by Cronbach (1957), who argued that:

> *The correlational psychologist was led into temptation by his own success, losing himself first in practical prediction, then in a narcissistic program of studying his tests as an end in themselves. A naive operationism enthroned theory of test performance in the place of theory of mental processes.*

At the heart of these methodological debates is the issue of how we can and should go about most accurately understanding human variation. In terms of contemporary individual differences psychology with its psychometric focus, this means making sure that our methods or the tools we use to produce measurements or data are as accurate as possible. Another way of describing this is to say that our methods and measurements need to be as *reliable* and *valid* as possible. Thus the measurements we use and the concepts of validity and reliability are important to the field, and we will consider these next.

Measurements

Four main types of measurement or data tend to be used in individual differences psychology. These are shown in Figure 1.4.

S-DATA – self-report data – is the most frequently used type of measurement of what can be described as non-ability aspects of individual differences. Such data are often collected to assess the three principalities of personality, self-concept and interests identified by Cronbach (1957 – see Figure 1.1). For example, the majority of measures of personality use this type of data. The data are usually collected using *self-report scales* or *inventories*. Individuals completing such scales are

Figure 1.4: *Types of data used in individual differences*

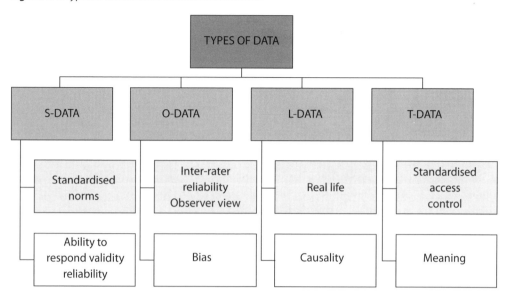

asked to make a judgement about some aspect of themselves by responding to a stimulus item or items using a *forced choice response format*. Individuals completing the scale – the respondents – select a response from a range provided in the scale or inventory, so in this sense the individuals' responses are forced because they are forced to select from responses they are given. Respondents are usually invited to respond to statements in terms of how well these describe themselves typically, and these statements can describe various behaviours, feelings and thoughts.

According to Bartram and Lindley (2005) these are:

> *Measures of TYPICAL PERFORMANCE . . . designed to assess disposition, such as personality, beliefs, values and interests and to measure motivation or 'drive'. Measures of typical performance are usually distinguished from measures of MAXIMUM PERFORMANCE which are designed to assess how well people can do things and measure ability, aptitudes or attainment.*

Researchers can use variants of typicality in their research. For example, instead of asking respondents to judge the extent to which they agree or disagree that a statement is typical of them, they could be invited to self-report how frequently they behave in certain ways, or have certain thoughts or experience certain feelings. Some scales use single words rather than the *statement approach* (see Chapter 2). Forced response options formats can differ as well. For example, often some form of *bipolar numerical rating scale* is used, in which respondents self-report their response to the statement by selecting the appropriate number on the scale, and the numerical scale is mapped onto qualitatively distinct response options. Technically, these are ordinal data. However, some scales provide respondents with a smaller number of forced choice response options, for instance when the options are merely *yes* or *no*. These are examples of *nominal scales* producing *nominal data*. The assumption underlying these variants is a psychometric one – that such responses provide meaningful numerical data about individuals. You will also encounter the term *scale* to describe these tools because *it is common to talk of measuring characteristics along a scale. Ability, for example, being a scale which goes from low to high scores. Thus scores obtained on a TEST of some characteristic are generally referred to as SCALE SCORES* (Bartram and Lindley, 2005) or the sum or aggregation of the individual's answers or responses. For example, when we attempted to define what we mean by individual differences psychology, we used the case of Justine. In her scenario, she reported to a counsellor that she was terrified of public speaking and could not face the psychology workshops. She went on to describe in more detail how certain social situations and activities reminded her of her own fear which seemed to be generalising to a fear of going out to a public place. As a consequence of these feelings that had become so bad she reported that her behaviour had changed to the extent that she had practically stopped going out altogether unless it was absolutely necessary, in an attempt to avoid the anxiety. Justine appears to be self-reporting characteristics of *social anxiety*, a characteristic of *social phobia*, a clinical disorder in which the individual experiences anxiety and fear in social situations. A number of self-report scales have been developed to measure more systematically the characteristics Justine was experiencing, such as the Fear of Negative Evaluation (FNE) Scale (Watson and Friend, 1969). The FNE Scale is a 30-item self-report scale that uses a true-false response format to collect self-report data on a specific characteristic of social anxiety – the extent to which the individual fears negative evaluation by others. The 30 items describe a range of behaviours, feelings and thoughts, and the respondent is invited to judge how typical – *true* – or not – *false* – each is of them. For example, *I am afraid that others will not approve of me* and *I often worry that I will say or do the wrong things* are items that one might expect Justine to identify as typically *true* of her. In contrast, *I rarely worry about what kind of impression I am making on someone* and *If I know someone is judging me, it has little effect on me* are items one would not expect Justine to identify as true of her. Instead, we would expect her to describe them as typically false of her. In principle, self-report inventories such as the FNE Scale have the following advantages.

- They enable a *standardised* method of assessment and scoring to be used, thus minimising the effects that differences in these might have upon the individuals' responses.

- They produce *numerical data* that can be analysed using statistical tests and enable comparisons to be made between individuals.

- They enable the description of complex data.

However, such data have disadvantages. We cannot assume that individuals can easily describe or access their responses to certain self-report test items, and we also have to make assumptions about the way individuals interpret both test items and forced-choice response options. These problems can be aggravated if a self-report inventory has a large number of items – lengthy inventories can lead to respondents becoming fatigued when completing the scale. Response bias can also influence how individuals complete such scales – the situation where individuals tend to produce acquiescent responses that endorse the *agree* or *yes* response options is called *response acquiescence* or *response set*. Given the transparency of many self-report inventories, it is also possible that individuals completing the scale will respond with socially desirable answers rather than their actual and most honest responses. In fact, many characteristics of self-report inventories can influence how individuals respond to them, and these include the order in which items are presented and the use of positive and negative sentences. Such factors can make the interpretation of test scores difficult. In other words, self-report inventories or scales do not always produce *accurate* measurements or data of individual differences. It is also worth remembering that while accurate self-report inventories can be challenging to develop, some of the problems associated with their use result from researchers' inappropriate interpretation of the data they produce. It is therefore important that we have methods to ensure that S-DATA are as accurate as possible, and we will consider these when we examine reliability and validity.

Task

It is worth spending a little more time examining self-report data and the different ways in which they are used by practitioners to measure individual differences because they are widely used in the field. The British Psychological Society runs the Psychological Testing Centre (PTC; www.psychtesting.org.uk), and it has produced a range of guides for both test users and test takers. Your task is to go to its website and examine the document *Psychological testing: a user's guide*. To access this document you will need to enter their website and search for the guide using their search site option. When you have found this guide, use its contents to answer the following questions.

– How does the document define *psychological tests*?

– What are the differences between tests that measure *typical* as opposed to *maximum performance*?

– How is self-report data used in measures of typical performance?

– Are you surprised by the variety of different ways in which self-report data are used to assess typical performance? Why were you surprised?

Comment

This task should draw your attention to the complex nature of S-DATA. We make certain assumptions when we collect such data as measurements of individual differences, and the usefulness of such data depends on how accurate such data are.

The term *O-DATA* refers to *observer data* or the judgements and evaluations of some aspect of an individual made by someone other than the individual themselves. Such data can be diverse and range from structured observations of individuals in relatively controlled research contexts to observations made in less structured or real contexts. The relationship between the observer and those being observed can vary. The observer might be unfamiliar with the observed, as is typically the case in structured research contexts. Alternatively, the observer might be known to the observed – for example, they might be a friend, family member or colleague. Likewise, the observation might occur in real time – as it is happening – or retrospectively. In the case of Justine, her personal tutor reported retrospectively that she appeared extremely distressed, and this judgement appears to have been based on the tutor's observations of Justine. The tutor noticed that there had been a change in her behaviour, that her attendance had become poor and that she was falling behind in her coursework. Some of the advantages of O-DATA are that they do not rely on the perspective of the individual being observed and that it is possible to confirm whether self-reports of the observed are consistent with those of others observing them. We can also examine the inter-rater reliability of observers. O-DATA are also useful when assessing psychological phenomena that are not suitable to assess using self-report inventories, or for individuals who might have difficulty completing such scales. In the case of Justine, we suggested that we could use the FNE Scale to systematically measure her level of social anxiety, but social phobia and social anxiety are also observed in children as young as eight years of age, which makes the use of lengthy self-report inventories difficult (Beidel et al., 1995). When assessing social phobia in pre-adolescents, therefore, a clinical assessment is conducted that uses the observations of clinicians and parents of the children, as well as some self-report scales, to provide the most accurate measure of the condition. However, O-DATA can be difficult to collect and interpret. Although we can check that observers agree, there is scope for observer bias in the interpretation of others' behaviours.

L-DATA are *life data*, which are typically data that describe the social, economic and more general demographic characteristics of individuals. Such data are typically sociodemographic, and include publicly available measures of the individual's life situation or circumstances, such as their marital status, educational achievement, employment and housing. Such data have the advantage of not relying on the individual's potentially biased self-reports, and they are frequently collected using standardised formats enabling large amounts of standardised data to be considered. In the case of Justine, her entry to university might be regarded as such a measure and, potentially, her educational failure as a form of L-DATA that can be used as a measure of the consequences of her social anxiety. However, such macro-level data cannot be assumed to provide meaningful information about the causes of individual differences or their direct consequences – and methods used to collect sociodemographic data also have their own biases.

The term *T-DATA* refers to test data, or data collected from an individual's performance on some form of task or activity. Unlike self-report data, test data assess individual maximum performance.

These data are most frequently used to assess ability, in particular intelligence or intellectual ability, but they can also include physiological measures, such as tests of reaction time or other more explicitly physiological measures of reactivity. These can be described as scalar (Bartram and Lindley, 2005). In the case of Justine, she appears to show characteristics of social anxiety and possibly social phobia (SP), and researchers have attempted to explain the onset and maintenance of SP as the result of underlying neurophysiological differences between individuals. For example, Kimbrel (2008) argues that individuals with SP have a more sensitive autonomic nervous system (ANS), and that we can measure this sensitivity using measures of ANS reactivity, such as galvanic skin response (GSR). However, although T-DATA can be collected using standardised methods and are potentially data that cannot either be assessed directly or by other means, the interpretation of such data is complex.

Reliability and validity

Reliability and validity are important concepts in individual differences psychology for a variety of psychometric reasons. We will consider these concepts now and the main methods used to test them in measures of individual differences.

Reliability is the extent to which a measure assesses a characteristic as accurately as possible. According to the British Psychological Society European Test User Standards Glossary of Terms (Bartram and Lindley, 2005), reliability is:

> *The extent to which one can rely on the obtained TEST score being an accurate measure of a person's TRUE SCORE, rather than a measure of incidental random factors. RELIABILITY is usually assessed either by means of INTERNAL CONSISTENCY, EQUIVALENCE or STABILITY.*

There are different types of reliability, but they all share a common feature: we use means or methods to assess reliability to ensure we collect *true scores* or scores as near to their true score as possible. Here we will consider three types of reliability, and these also refer to different means or methods (see Figure 1.5).

It is important to note here that individual differences psychology uses statistical techniques and concepts drawn from psychometrics to ensure that their tests are as accurate as possible. This has meant that considerable value is placed on *internal consistency* or *coefficient alpha* as an indicator of test quality. An important psychometric principle is that the measures one uses should be as accurate as possible because the field is essentially about the measurements of stable characteristics that typify individuals, or measurements that indicate maximum performance or how well individuals can do certain things. For psychometric reasons, therefore, it is important that our measures assess these with as little *random error* or *systematic error* as possible. Aspects of reliability theory are used to explain and minimise both of these types of error using the premise

Figure 1.5: Types of reliability

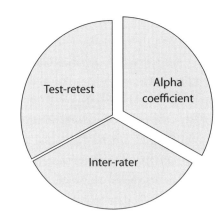

shown in Figure 1.6. When measuring any object or construct there will be some unwanted random error in the measurement. This means that the measurement is as likely to be an over-estimate as an underestimate of the true measure. However, if we repeatedly measure the construct, the overestimated and underestimated measures will cancel out the effects of the random error on the true score. This method of maximising the accuracy of measurement works well on unidimensional constructs, but psychological constructs are far from that. In fact, if we repeatedly took the same measure, for example by using the same item on a self-report scale, we would introduce a different type of error, known as systematic error. Psychological constructs suffer from this for other reasons. For example, when responding to self-report items on per-sonality inventories and solving problems on cognitive ability scales, responses will be influenced by factors other than the target construct – such as the mood of the individual or their familiarity with the terminology in the item. The solution is to use *domain sampling*. This means selecting items or tasks that represent the broad domain of the target psychological construct. In the case of Justine, the FNE Scale is a measure that could be used to assess her apparent social anxiety, and this scale contains multiple items that reflect the different aspects of the complex construct social anxiety. The assumption here is that if the domain of the target behaviour is sampled adequately, then the range of systematic errors will also be sampled and these will cancel each other out when item responses are combined to produce a test score.

In the case of both random and systematic error there is a difference between the individual's true score, free of error, and their actual test score, which is always a combination of some form or degree of error. However, the goal is to make sure the relationship between test score and true

Figure 1.6: Basic premise of reliability theory

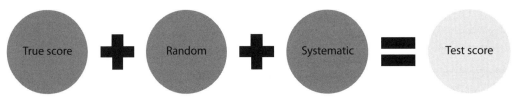

score is as close as possible. This is tested by calculating the *alpha coefficient*, also referred to as coefficient alpha, a statistical technique based on calculating the *internal consistency* of a multi-item test. The statistical details of this technique are not the central issue here, and these issues have been dealt with by other writers (Boorsboom, 2006; Cooper, 2002). What is important here is the principle of the alpha coefficient.

- It is used as a measure of the relationship between the individual's test score and their true score.

- Its calculation involves the statistical analysis of the relationship between the overall test score and scores on individual items, hence the term internal consistency – the consistency or relationship between each item that comprises the test and the overall test score.

There are other means or methods for testing the accuracy of our measurements. *Test-retest* reliability refers to the consistency of a measure or test over time and is usually calculated by correlating test scores at time 1 with those collected with the same measure and participants at time 2. This measure of test accuracy is relatively important in individual differences psychology if the researcher is attempting to assess stability in a disposition or trait. Likewise, *inter-rater* reliability is a method used to establish the accuracy of measurements taken by different observers, typically when using some sort of inventory of categories of behaviour. In this sense, inter-rater reliability tells us about the consistency with which observers rate or categorise the behaviours being observed. To some extent it also provides us with some information about the validity of the behaviour categories we are using. For example, observers might fail to agree on how they categorise behaviours resulting in low levels of inter-rater reliability. Now this could suggest that the observers are not using consistently the descriptions of behaviour they have. However, it might also suggest that the descriptions judges are using are not valid descriptions of the target behaviours.

A number of points can be made. First, self-report inventories appear relatively easy to construct but reliable ones are not. Second, we use psychometric principles to tackle the issue of reliability. Third, individual differences psychology places great store in the alpha coefficient as an indicator of the accuracy of a scale or test. However, the alpha coefficient is a statistical phenomenon that uses theoretical or hypothetical principles. Thus, ultimately, alpha coefficients provide us with statistical information about how responses to items on a scale are related and not necessarily anything else. Finally, a measure can be reliable but lack validity – in other words, a measure can assess consistently the same construct, but this consistency can be observed even if the measure does not actually measure what it claims to. Thus the validity of a measurement is also central to its accuracy.

Validity is the extent to which a test measures what it claims to. According to the British Psychological Society European Test User Standards Glossary of Terms (Bartram and Lindley, 2005), the validity of a test *tells the user what inferences can be drawn about the person who has produced the score on a test and what is being measured by a test – that is, what is it a test of.*

Thus the accuracy of our measurements in individual differences psychology in terms of validity is important because if a measure assesses what it claims to, then given the known characteristics of this phenomenon or phenomena, we should be able to make predictions about other aspects of the individual related to this construct. As is the case with reliability, each type of validity entails a means or method of assessing validity. If a measurement fares well with a specific method of assessing validity, it is said to possess that particular type of validity. The main types of validity we consider in the field are shown in Figure 1.7.

According to the BPS (Bartram and Lindley, 2005) *face validity* is *the superficial appropriateness of a test or what the test appears to measure*. As such, this type of validity does not ensure that a measure actually assesses what it claims to. However, two forms of criterion-related validity are important types of validity. According to the BPS (Bartram and Lindley, 2005), when we use an individual's test score to *predict or anticipate how they will perform on types of task not directly sampled by the test but which have been shown to be correlated with test performance*, we are engaging in a process described as *criterion referencing*. According to Cronbach and Meehl (1955), when we obtain this other measure at the same time as the measure in question, it is referred to as *concurrent validity*, but if the other measurement is collected some time after the measurement in question, it is referred to as *predictive validity*. Both concurrent and predictive validity are types of criterion-oriented validation procedures. These should be distinguished from what Cronbach and Meehl (1955) describe as *content validity*, which is the extent to which *the test items are a sample of a universe in which the investigator is interested. Content validity is ordinarily to be established deductively, by defining a universe of items and sampling systematically within this universe to establish the test.* In addition, when a measure accurately assesses what it claims to, then

Figure 1.7: *Types of validity*

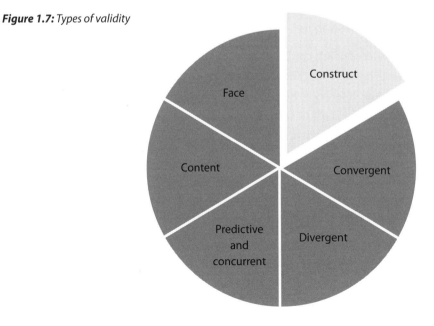

the data from such a measure, such as test scores, should *converge* with scores on related or equivalent measures and *diverge* with scores on unrelated measures. We usually calculate convergence and divergence using statistical tests of correlation, and if measures converge as predicted, we can say that the measurements in question have *convergent validity*. If measures diverge as predicted, we can say that the measurement in question has *divergent validity*. The final and perhaps most important type of validity is *construct* or *theoretical validity*, which, according to Cronbach and Meehl (1955), is a more complex concept than the other types of validity:

> *[Construct validity] is involved whenever a test is to be interpreted as a measure of some attribute or quality which is not 'operationally defined'. The problem faced by the investigator is, 'What constructs account for variance in test performance?' Construct validity calls for no new scientific approach. Much current research on tests of personality . . . is construct validation, usually without the benefit of a clear formulation of this process.*

Two further constructs important to the psychometric approach to measuring individual differences are *standardisation* and *norms*. In individual differences psychology we often use the term standardisation to refer to the manner in which a test or measure is *administered*. This can include: the use of standardised instructions that are followed by all individuals completing a scale; the standard mode of completion required when using a test such as self-completion that enables a test to be completed by large groups of individuals in a single sitting; and a test that requires a test administrator who helps the individual to complete the test on a one-to-one basis. Standardisation is also used to refer to the transformation of test scores into a standard measure or one with *known characteristics* (Bartram and Lindley, 2005) such as a Z score or a correlation coefficient because these statistics have known properties that enable us to make meaningful comparisons between individuals' scores and between measures with different scales. Such standard scores help us to interpret test scores – as do *norms*. Norms are statistical information about the distribution of scores on a particular test from a known population. In this sense norms are also test scores that have been transformed. However, norms include information about the proportion of a known population that achieve less than a particular test score, and this percentile rank is expressed in the following format. If we return to the FNE Scale mentioned earlier, let us imagine that this scale might have established norms and that this hypothetical norm table might show that the 60th percentile rank corresponds to a score of 8. This means 60 per cent of a sample of individuals drawn from that particular population will achieve a score of less than 8. Test norms are important to the use of individual differences tests in applied contexts where they are used to make important high-stakes decisions about individuals. However, it is important to remember that the construction of such norms and thus their accuracy for such decision making is influenced by the samples used to construct the norms in the first instance.

Task ── Using the information we have considered thus far, construct a checklist of criteria that could be used to judge whether a measurement of individual differences is *accurate*.

Comment

This task should draw your attention to the complexity of assessing the accuracy of measurements of individual differences. It should highlight the different ways in which we can assess the accuracy of our measurements, as well as the need to identify which types of accuracy are most important to the task at hand.

To conclude this section, it is important to remember that the concept of accuracy that dominates individual differences psychology is based on psychometric principles. However, some researchers have argued that what this has really meant is the inappropriate application of such principles. For example, the testing of validity in individual differences psychology has been questioned by Boorsboom et al. (2004; see the Further reading section) who argue that the field has misused the concept of validity. The use of psychometrics in individual differences is controversial, despite their widespread use.

Critical thinking activity

Reliability and validity of measurements

Critical thinking focus: analysis and evaluation of data

Key question: *How can we analyse and evaluate conflicting data?*

In this activity you will take the role of a research assistant working on a project studying the way in which social anxiety is related to friendship formation. Social anxiety is a characteristic of social phobia, a clinical disorder in which the individual experiences anxiety and fear in social situations. According to *The International Classification of Diseases-10*, also referred to as *ICD-10* (World Health Organization, 2007, p112), social phobia is one of a group of disorders known as *phobic anxiety disorders*, and individuals diagnosed with one of these disorders have the following characteristics:

anxiety that ranges in severity from mild unease to terror . . . is evoked only, or predominantly, by certain well-defined situations or objects (external to the individual) which are not currently dangerous . . . these situations or objects are characteristically avoided or endured with dread, and mere contemplation of entry to the phobic situation usually generates anticipatory anxiety . . . a focus on individual symptoms such as palpitations or feeling faint and is often associated with secondary fears of dying, losing control, or going mad . . . their anxiety is not relieved by the knowledge that other people do not regard the situation in question as dangerous or threatening.

Social phobia (SP) (World Health Organization, 2007, pp113–14) is a type of phobic anxiety disorder, and has the following more specific characteristics.

- Onset is usually in adolescence and the prevalence of the disorder is equally common in females and males.

- Anxiety and fear are centred around a fear of scrutiny by other people in comparatively small groups (as opposed to crowds), usually leading to avoidance of social situations.

- The disorder may be discrete (i.e. restricted to eating in public, to public speaking, or to encounters with the opposite sex) or diffuse, involving almost all social situations outside the family circle.

- Fear of vomiting in public may be important, and direct eye-to-eye confrontation may be particularly stressful in some cultures.

- Individuals often have low self-esteem and fear criticism.

- The disorder may present as a complaint of blushing, hand tremor, nausea, or urgency of micturition, the individual sometimes being convinced that one of these secondary manifestations of anxiety is the primary problem.

- Symptoms may progress to panic attacks.

- Avoidance of scrutiny by others is often marked, and in extreme cases may result in almost complete social isolation.

This can be *generalised* across most social situations, a disorder referred to as *general social phobia* (GSP; *Diagnostic and Statistical Manual of Mental Disorders-IV-Text Revision [DSM-IV-TR]*) or *diffuse* (*ICD-10* [World Health Organization, 2007]) or *specific* to certain situations, a disorder referred to as *specific social phobia* (SSP; *DSM-IV-TR*) or *discrete* (*ICD-10* [World Health Organization, 2007]; Kimbrel, 2008). Epidemiological research in the general population using both diagnostic criteria from the two main classification systems – the *DSMs* and the *ICD* – and more specific self-report scales suggests that both clinical and sub-clinical manifestations of the condition, such as social anxiety associated with public speaking, is relatively prevalent in general populations. Unlike the characteristics of sufferers described in *ICD-10* (World Health Organization, 2007), this research has also shown that in the general population, SP and its associated symptoms are more prevalent among women, and among those with low levels of educational achievement and social support (Furmack et al., 1999; Furmack et al., 2000; Wittchen and Fehm, 2003). For example, Furmack et al. (1999) conducted a postal survey in Sweden. They developed a four-part self-completion questionnaire using diagnostic criteria from both *DSM-IV* and *ICD-10*. From their original sample of 2,000 participants, a total of 1,202 responded – 541 men and 661 women with a mean age of around 42 years of age and a standard deviation of around 14 years. Furmack et al. (1999) found that 15.6 per cent of respondents met their criteria for a diagnosis of social phobia: these respondents rated themselves as experiencing high levels of distress in at least one of 14 social situations (e.g. speaking or performing in front of a group of people, maintaining a conversation with someone unfamiliar, eating/drinking in public, using public lavatories, attending a party or a social gathering), and they consistently confirmed that this situation or situations triggered SP symptoms. Finally, these respondents self-reported poor functioning and distress as a result of that fear in at least one of three life domains – work or academic life, leisure, or social life.

The project you are working on has been using different measures of social anxiety with samples drawn from the general or non-clinical population. The measures were chosen because the existing literature shows that scores on these scales converge and therefore both *could* predict friendship formation. However, in the project this has not been found. The measures being used on the project are:

- the Brief Fear of Negative Evaluation (BFNE) Scale (Leary, 1983);

- a measure of trait introversion-extraversion taken from the Eysenck Personality Questionnaire;

- four measures of friendship formation: observer rating of levels of co-operation on a group task;

- three self-report items participants respond to using a five-point bipolar scale (1 = not at all, through to 5 = very much): *I like the people I am completing this task with, I believe most members of the group like me, I felt anxious when completing the group task.*

Your task is to try to explain why the scores on the BFNE and on the measure of introversion–extraversion are not converging as expected, and why neither of these scores predicts performance on the four criteria used to measure friendship formation.

Worked example

The BFNE Scale used might have questionable psychometric properties and it would be useful to check the construct validity of the measure. The criteria used to measure friendship formation might not be a valid way to assess this complex construct. We also do not know how performance on this task was actually measured.

Critical thinking review

This activity requires you to analyse the constructs being measured in the project and the concepts of validity and reliability. There are a number of controversies in the research on SP that make it useful for examining the methods and measurements used in individual differences psychology. In particular, there is a debate in the literature about how to most accurately measure social phobia and its characteristics. You should analyse and evaluate how the researchers have selected their measures and the possible sources of error that might be influencing their results. You should also analyse the possible ways in which the measures used might not be either valid or reliable measures of social introversion, and identify what the researchers could do to check the reliability and validity of their measures and to improve this if possible.

Other skills likely to be used in this activity: this activity also requires you to use problem-solving skills to identify the possible sources of 'error' in the research, and make decisions about how research literature can be used to inform the research process. You are required to test your knowledge and understanding on concepts, and you could also use IT skills to search for research on the constructs and measures used.

Ethics

Given the potential uses of individuals' test scores in a range of applied contexts, there is scope for misuse and abuse of psychometric measurements of individual differences. It is unsurprising that many tests developed do appeal to those outside psychology as tools for assessing, predicting and evaluating individuals in occupational, educational and health contexts. Such measurements have face validity and appear relatively easy to administer. However, as you should be aware by now, the development, administration, scoring and interpretation of test scores is complex. This means that the use of test scores for high-stakes decision making can be controversial and requires the consideration of *ethics* and *professional conduct*.

In an attempt to limit the misuse and abuse of measurements of individual differences, access to many tests is restricted to those who have undergone specific training and had their competence

Figure 1.8: *Levels of competency*

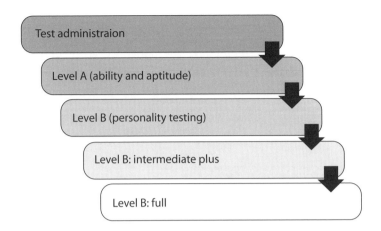

Test administraion

Level A (ability and aptitude)

Level B (personality testing)

Level B: intermediate plus

Level B: full

assessed. In Great Britain the British Psychological Society runs the Psychological Testing Centre (PTC; www.psychtesting.org.uk), which provides guidance, information and resources on the construction, use and taking of tests, along with information about the different levels of competence and training required for access to different psychometric tests in two applied areas – occupational testing and educational testing. Figure 1.8 summarises the five levels of competence used in occupational psychology.

An important issue here is that we must be cautious about how we use data from tests because of the ethical and legal implications of the decisions we make based on this information. The BPS issues a range of documents to advise both test users and takers of their rights and responsibilities, and their 12-point *Code of good practice for psychological testing* (British Psychological Society, 2007) sets out clearly that those using psychological tests have a responsibility to ensure that they:

- are competent to administer the tests being used;

- follow the required procedures for administering a specific test;

- keep test results securely, in a form suitable for developing norms, validation, and monitoring for bias;

- protect the welfare of those completing tests, and this includes gaining informed consent, clarifying what the test data will be used for and what will happen to their results, including where the information is stored and who has access to it.

Poorly constructed tests, poor test administration and the poor interpretation of test scores can undermine the academic and professional integrity of psychology.

Skill builder activity

Ethics

Transferable skill focus: understand and use data

Key question: *What challenges do we face when using self-report data to make decisions about individuals?*

The owner of a large bar employs seven students as part-time bar staff. However, for the past 18 months the owner has employed students who appear to perform well in interview but who subsequently are unreliable, for example not turning up for their shifts or arriving late. The owner believes he has developed a 'test' comprising six questions that applicants can be asked in order to measure what he describes as 'applicant reliability', and he intends using this as part of the application form, or administered in a telephone or face-to-face interview. He intends using the data to make predictions about which applicants will be reliable if employed and thus select individuals based on these data. The six questions are shown below. The owner reports that either he asks applicants to 'write down' their answers in their own words or, if administered in an interview, he himself records their responses.

- Have you had a job before?

- Why do you want this job?

- If you were unable to make your shift, what would you do?

- What are your interests?

- Do you play sports?

- Do you have a car?

However, having used his 'applicant reliability' measure for around three months, the owner still seems to be employing individuals who are unreliable despite appearing to be 'reliable' using his measure. The owner has also been unable to administer the measure to all applicants because he has either forgotten to include this during interviews or applicants have refused to complete this part of the interview process. Your task is to examine the ethical issues raised by the owner's decision to use this method of selection to make decisions about potential applicants. Your task is to compile a list of infringements made by the owner against the relevant BPS Psychological Testing Centre guidance documents (see www.psychtesting.org.uk). Your list should be no longer than one side of A4 and presented in a manner that would be relatively accessible for the owner and in a format that he could use to make changes to his method. You can complete this activity individually or as a group discussion.

Worked example

The 12-point *Code of good practice for psychological testing* (British Psychological Society, 2007) states clearly that the test user – the owner – is responsible for ensuring that they are competent to administer and interpret test scores, and most importantly that the test used is valid. There is no indication in the scenario that the owner has considered issues of test validity and reliability. It is likely that some applicants might perceive the test as 'unfair' because there is no indication that the owner has explained why the test is being used. The reluctance of some to complete the 'test' suggests that test takers perceive the test as questionable, and there is no evidence that the owner has considered how he will store the information. There is also little information on how the test is actually scored.

Skill builder review

This activity requires you to understand how tests are developed and their data used, and especially to understand the responsibilities of those developing 'tests' and the rights of those taking such tests. The BPS Psychological Testing Centre website at www.psychtesting.org.uk would be a useful starting point for this activity and you should use whatever documents you feel are most relevant to this task.

Other skills likely to be used in this activity: the activity also requires you to use problem-solving and decision-making skills to identify the documents relevant to the scenario and to reflect on the ethical dilemmas such an approach raises.

Assignments

1. To what extent is individual differences psychology nothing more than the study of hypothetical as opposed to valid constructs?

2. The primary aim of individual differences psychology is to describe what individuals *have* rather than what they *do*. Critically consider this view.

3. Critically evaluate the contribution of psychometrics to individual differences psychology.

4. Discuss, critically, why and how psychologists try to ensure their measurements of individual differences are as 'accurate' as possible.

Summary: what you have learned

Individual differences psychology aims to scientifically identify the structure, determinants and consequences of differences between individuals and groups of individuals. Currently, psychometric principles and techniques are used to achieve this by systematically measuring a range of dispositions. Ensuring these measures are reliable and valid is central to theory development in individual differences, and its application both within the field, other fields in psychology and in real-world contexts, such as work, education and health settings. Through completing a critical thinking and skill building activity you will have started to develop an understanding of why understanding, using and evaluating data are important to individual differences, along with the ethical challenges faced when developing measures and using the data they produce.

Further reading

Boorsboom, D, Mellenbergh, GJ and van Heerden, J. (2004) The concept of validity. *Psychological Review*, 111(4): 1061–71.

This paper challenges mainstream approaches to validity in individual differences and provides a thought-provoking critical approach to many taken-for-granted assumptions in the field.

Cronbach, LJ and Meehl, PE (1955) Construct validity in psychological tests. *Psychological Bulletin*, 52: 281–302.

This is a classic paper that demonstrates that the current debate in individual differences about its use of psychometric principles is far from a recent development.

Vul, E, Harris, C, Winkielman, P, Pashler, H (2009) Puzzlingly high correlations in fMRI studies of emotion, personality, and social cognition. *Perspectives on Psychological Science*, 4(3): 274–90.

This paper is a useful discussion of the challenges involved with using physiological measures of aspects of individual differences such as personality. In particular, it draws attention to the need for caution when interpreting correlation coefficients between different types of data.

Useful websites

http://psychclassics.asu.edu/ (Classics in the History of Psychology)

This is an invaluable web resource containing many original classic early papers that provide a useful coverage of the history of individual differences.

www.psychometrics.ppsis.cam.ac.uk/page/217/first-psychometric-laboratory.htm (First Psychometric Laboratory: Cambridge 1886 to 1889)

This website describes the early research on psychometrics conducted at Cambridge University by James Cattell. This is part of the web pages of the Psychometrics Centre, Cambridge University, and contains resources, articles and tutorials, and provides access to a number of useful resources including tests and publications.

www.psychtesting.org.uk (BPS Psychological Testing Centre)

In Great Britain the British Psychological Society runs the Psychological Testing Centre (PTC), and this website provides invaluable guidance and resources for students and researchers alike using tests.

Chapter 2

Personality

Learning outcomes

By the end of this chapter you should:

- *be able to define personality and discuss, critically, how psychological research on personality has developed historically;*

- *understand how theories of personality differ in their focus on its determinants, structure, processes and relationship to behaviour;*

- *know and be able to evaluate the main biological and trait approaches to personality;*

- *be able to discuss the importance of the Five Factor traits to personality research;*

- *develop critical and creative thinking skills by completing an activity integrating personality theories, and develop problem solving skills by using personality research to explain behaviour across different situations.*

Introduction

This chapter will examine an important aspect of individual differences – personality. We will consider how psychologists have attempted to describe and explain its structure, determinants and functions by focusing on four questions.

- How have psychologists attempted to define personality, and how has their research and theory developed?

- What are the main philosophical and conceptual debates in personality research?

- What are the main approaches to personality, and how convincing are they as explanations of inter-individual variation, intra-individual variation and intrapsychic personality processes?

- To what extent is contemporary personality research on course to achieve its mission *to provide an integrative framework for understanding the whole person* (McAdams and Pals, 2006, p204)?

The overarching purpose of this chapter, therefore, is for you to develop your knowledge of core issues in what can be called personality psychology. However, you will do this while attempting to take a critical stance towards mainstream approaches. This stance includes reflecting on the sort of person theorist you are and how this might influence your interpretation of theory and empirical evidence on personality. The critical thinking and skill builder activities are also designed to develop your critical creative thinking about personality theories by attempting to integrate them using a process known as theory knitting (Sternberg et al., 2001). You will also attempt to use academic research to problem solve – by using it to explain consistency and inconsistency in behaviour.

Definitions of personality

Task — In everyday talk about ourselves and others we use the term *personality*. To some extent, therefore, you are likely to already have ideas about what the term means simply because of the various uses you make of it. Either individually or in groups, list some of the ways in which you use the term *personality* both when thinking about yourself and others, and in your everyday talk with other individuals. Make sure you list some examples of these uses, such as illustrative sentences or phrases, situations or individuals. When completing this task make a note of the different *meanings* you ascribe to the term.

Comment

This task should draw your attention to your everyday definitions of personality, and such definitions also contain implicit assumptions about the nature of this aspect of individual differences. For example, you might use personality to refer to the type of person you or someone else appears to be, for example, a *strong personality*. You might also describe someone you know as having a *good personality* or even refer to others you know as *not having much of a personality*. These sorts of everyday uses contain implicit assumptions about the nature of personality. For example, the term *type* implies that we can classify individuals using categories of personality. Likewise, using the phrase *strong personality* implies that personality can be conceptualised as some form of one-dimensional quantity that someone has more or less of. The use of evaluative terms such as *good* to describe personality also implies that we can clearly identify better or worse aspects of personality. However, everyday uses of the term *personality* are not necessarily the same as formal academic uses of the term, and it is important not to confuse everyday and academic uses, especially in your studies and when completing academic assessments. Confusing some terminology in personality psychology, such as the use of the term *personality type* when this is not actually meant, can be particularly problematic because terminology underpins a number of important theoretical debates in the research. Keep your answers to hand and as you work through this chapter check how your everyday use of terminology about personality is similar and different from formal academic terminology.

We will now clarify what we mean by personality in the academic literature by examining a number of definitions of the term, and considering critically how these relate both to our working definition of individual differences psychology and its scope, and also to individual differences per se. In Chapter 1 we defined individual differences psychology and individual differences, and identified personality as one aspect of this field studied by psychologists. We also stated that there is not universal agreement about what precisely constitutes the field. This pattern of differing definitions is repeated when defining personality – psychologists differ on what the term means. To some extent there is a degree of *broad* agreement about the key features of personality – nevertheless, the *differences* between definitions of personality are important to acknowledge because they highlight critical debates in the field.

To start, let us return to our definition of individual differences (Caprara and Cervone, 2000) described in Chapter 1. This states that the term *individual differences* is the study of the *structure and determinants of enduring psychological characteristics as perceived by the individual and those around them*. Specifically, these enduring characteristics are *collections of behaviours, feelings and thoughts* that *systematically typify how individuals and groups of individuals appear to be similar or different*. These psychological phenomena also have *consequences for how individuals react* and *therefore regulate themselves across a range of life domains*, and the relationship between these person and situation variables is *complex and reciprocal*.

If personality is one domain of individual differences, then it seems reasonable to assert that any definition of personality should at least contain these features. To examine this assertion we will use three definitions of personality. The first definition is a classic definition, while the second and third are relatively general contemporary definitions.

Allport and Allport (1921) provided a classic definition of personality as *the definitely fixed and controlling tendencies of adjustment of the individual to his environment*, and continued:

> it is necessary . . . to determine tentatively the fundamental traits (or) . . . deeper and more pervasive tendencies . . . character is the interplay of fundamental personality tendencies in the social and economic environment . . . it is superficial in that there are deeper currents beneath it.

Allport (1927) went on to define traits as *a tendency to reaction which when measured with reliability demonstrates an independence of other variables*. According to Allport, personality is a fixed quality of individuals that shapes how they interact with their environment. Importantly, he argued that *fundamental traits underlie personality*, whereas *personality is observable* in the individual's *character*. In other words, there is a difference between what we can access or observe of personality and the fundamental traits that it is comprised of. Another feature of this definition is that these traits are, in principle, independent and not influenced by other variables. Thus Allport (1927) draws attention to the distinction between what is observable about personality and the unobservable processes that underlie personality. In this sense, these unobservable but more fundamental aspects of personality can be regarded as a latent variable. The term *latent variable* is one you are likely to encounter when considering some statistical analysis tests when it is used to denote a specific inference made from the analysis of quantitative data. Here, it is used more broadly to denote a psychological variable – or individual difference construct – that we infer from observable variables. Allport (1927) uses the term *trait* to denote the latent or unobservable fixed aspects of personality that we might also refer to as disposition. Importantly, Allport regards the observable aspects of personality as the individual's character that results from the interaction of the fixed traits of individuals with their social and economic environment.

Cooper provides our second, relatively general and more contemporary definition of personality (Cooper, 2002, p11). Cooper's definition is based on the assumption that *all* individual differences, such as personality, can be conceptualised as *traits* – specifically, personality traits:

> *Reflect a person's style of behaviour . . . These are broad generalizations, since how we behave is obviously also influenced by situations . . . Nevertheless . . . these traits may be useful in helping us to predict how individuals will probably behave most of the time.*

This definition identifies personality as broad and something that can be described nomo-thetically, using traits. In other words, this definition implies that we can use traits to describe the personalities of large numbers of individuals, using *general* traits that capture how they behave *typically*. To some extent, Cooper's (2002) use of the term *trait* appears more similar to Allport's (1927) use of the term *character*. Cooper implies that personality can be described using traits as observable units of behaviour that apply to individuals in general. This definition also suggests that we can use traits to capture *inter-individual variation* – traits can be used as the unit of analysis for identifying similarities and differences between persons. An important feature of this definition is that personality traits are not the only determinants of behaviour and that *intra-individual variation* is the result of interaction between the individual and the situation they find themselves in. This view has been called *interactionism* and the debate over the predictive link between measures of personality traits and actual behaviour has been controversial for over 40 years, and was considered most obviously in the person-situation debate associated with Mischel (1968). Although some argue that interactionism is now regarded as a truism in personality psychology and the person-situation debate as defunct, we will return to these issues later in this chapter. However, in Cooper's (2002) definition the psychological truism of interactionism is accepted because behaviour is not always predicted by traits. Nevertheless, prediction is an important issue in personality psychology because, with some caveats, measures of personality traits should enable us to make some meaningful predictions about how individuals behave *most of the time*. This predictive value rests on the assumption that in some ways personality traits are decontextual. In other words, personality traits tell us something meaningful about individuals in general in ways that are not *wholly* context-dependent. An important feature of Cooper (2002) is that this definition focuses on the *observer perspective*. This is a relatively general focus in many definitions of personality, and is relatively typical of the focus on psychometrics in the United Kingdom and the USA (Lubinski, 2000). The focus is, however, an ironic one given that much of what we know about personality is based on self-report data or individuals' descriptions of *themselves*.

In Chapter 1 our definition of individual differences psychology drew attention to other features of individual differences that can be used to clarify what we mean by personality. Indeed, our third definition of personality from Caprara and Cervone (2000, p3) is closer to this broad definition of individual differences psychology and individual differences per se. Caprara and Cervone (2000) state that personality *can be thought of as a complex, dynamic system of psychological elements that reciprocally interact with one another*. These researchers acknowledge that from the observer's perspective, personality is indeed *a set of psychological characteristics that distinguish individuals from one another* (p11) or what individuals *have*. However, Caprara and Cervone (2000, p11) also define personality from the perspective of the individual themselves as:

> *The psychological system that emerges from the interaction of the individual with the environment and that mediates intrapsychic functioning and person-environment interactions ... a self-regulating system with the capacity to serve individual development and well-being.*

This definition of personality contains a number of important features absent from but not precluded by Cooper's (2002) definition. It implies that personality:

- encompasses the *whole person* or all aspects of their psychology, and as Caprara and Cervone (2000) argue, this makes personality psychology difficult because of the scope and complexity of such a task;

- is a *process* involving mechanisms that are both internal and external. However, these are not deterministic mechanisms because we have purposes and intentions. This view draws on the **agentic approach to personality** developed by Bandura (1999);

- can be conceptualised as having *surface tendencies or characteristics* but that these are not necessarily identical to underlying mechanisms. In other words, we infer underlying or latent aspects of personality from what we can observe of personality, but surface tendencies might not be the same phenomena. We can use a house metaphor here: in some respects the term *house* is used to describe dwellings that people live in, and many have similar appearances. However, this basic structural similarity does not mean that the interiors of all houses are the same or that they serve the same functions or uses for all inhabitants of houses. Likewise, surface tendencies or traits or character can be described in general, but the underlying processes and functions might differ between individuals and groups. We cannot assume that the observable similarities of personality correspond identically to the mechanisms underlying personality;

- is a *dynamic and potential process* – this dynamic quality of personality is evident in the ways personality varies over time, in different contexts, and in the ways it can influence how we interact with others – our interpersonal relationships. Personality processes are also dynamic in the sense that they are about *potentials* – to some extent individuals are agents of their own destiny and can influence and interpret their environment. Therefore personality is about *potentials* or what individuals might possibly achieve or ways in which they might possibly behave, feel and think. Importantly, personality traits are not deterministic and thus personality is not seen as fixed and controlling, as implied to some extent by Allport (1927);

- develops or *emerges* over time. Personality involves change over time and development across the lifespan. Personality as a potential of the person also means individuals have vulnerabilities – there is a risk that these complex processes can work more or less successfully. Furthermore, the influence of culture and the environment is reciprocal. For example, individuals can select certain environments and experiences, and these in turn influence the individual. These sorts of process have been described using concepts such as trait coherency and trait activation.

This definition has a methodological implication: psychology should study the whole person, and given the complex reciprocal relationship between these elements of personality, the study of personality should therefore be integrated rather than segregated to enable us to understand all these processes. This is a point made by Sternberg et al. (2001) about psychology in general when they argue that the discipline would better understand many psychological phenomena if it was more integrated in its approach to research and theory rather than segregated as it appears to be currently. The view that personality psychology should focus on the whole person and take an integrated approach is far from new, and can be found in the writings of researchers in the middle of the twentieth century such as Thorndike and Cronbach (Ackerman, 1997; Lubinski, 2000; Revelle et al., 2010).

Although we have considered merely three definitions of personality, it is relatively clear that important differences exist between the ways in which individual differences researchers define personality. Nevertheless, it is possible to identify some general points of agreement about what personality actually is.

Task ─┐ Identify general points of agreement about what we mean by *personality* from the definitions we have just considered. To do this you could compare and contrast these definitions or simply analyse each and list their main features. Whatever strategy you use, make sure you include the concepts they use to define personality.

Comment

Analysing definitions is one way of thinking critically about psychological phenomena because it encourages you to focus on the conceptual and technical details of the constructs being considered. Some of the similarities between these definitions include the conceptualisation of personality as both manifest and deeper – or intrapsychic. They acknowledge that the internal and external are linked, and that both influence how the individual interacts with their environment. They use the concept of self-regulation or adjustment as functions of personality. Differences between the definitions are subtle. For example, Caprara and Cervone (2000) refer to personality as a system that emerges from the interaction of various other systems. Allport describes personality as the interplay of personality factors and the environment.

Across these definitions the following concepts are used to define personality, and these represent general points of agreement across these definitions:

- inter-individual variation;
- intra-individual variation;
- intra-individual process;
- biopsychosocial construct;
- development across lifespan;
- mediation by interpersonal relationships between the individual and the social structures around them;
- dynamic process;
- potentials;
- determinants;
- mechanisms;
- agentic process;
- observer and self-perspective.

Personality is a complex system of agency and construction, coherence and continuity. It involves the whole person, and focusing on single acts of behaviour on single occasions will not provide us with an understanding of the whole person. Instead, we should study affect, behaviour and cognition across the lifespan and incorporate the goals of personality processes.

Task — What kind of person theorist are you?

The previous task involved examining three definitions of personality. Each contains some implicit theoretical assumptions about the nature of personality. You also have implicit theoretical assumptions about the nature of personality and you will identify yours here using the lay theory approach. An important part of many definitions of personality is that personality involves making perceptual judgements of ourselves and others, and for the first task in this chapter you started to think about this issue by identifying your everyday uses of the term *personality*. According to Dweck et al. (1995) scientific theories of persons such as those we will consider later in this chapter contain certain *explicit assumptions* about the person. Likewise, they argue that we all have assumptions about ourselves and other persons that they call naive or lay theories. These *guide the way information about the self and other people is processed and understood* (p267). However, despite these lay theories having important functions for individuals, they are implicit and are not expressed easily. Dweck et al. (1995) have developed relatively simple measures of these implicit lay theories that can be used to identify an individual's assumptions about specific attributes or individual differences, such as intellect or morality, or persons as a whole. From their research it appears that these lay theories tend to focus on either the malleability of people or their personal attributes, forming two types of person theories: the entity theory judges persons or their attributes to be non-malleable or fixed; the incremental theory judges persons or their attributes as malleable or changeable.

For this task, you will first need to identify what sort of person theorist you are by completing the following measure (Dweck et al., 1995).

We are interested in *your own personal views and experiences* about people. Please indicate your views on the following using these response options: 1=strongly agree, 2=agree, 3=mildly agree, 4=mildly disagree, 5=disagree and 6=strongly disagree. Write the number of the response that best describes your view against each statement.

1. The kind of person someone is, is something basic about them, and it can't be changed very much.

2. People can do things differently, but the important parts of who they are can't really be changed very much.

3. Everyone is a certain kind of person and there is not much that can be done to really change that.

Your person theory score is the mean score for the three items. A mean score of 3 or lower classifies you as an entity theorist and a mean score of 4 or higher classifies you as an incremental theorist. Dweck et al. (1995) describe a range of research that suggests that entity and incremental theorists differ systematically in their judgements of the behaviours of themselves and others. This influence is especially evident when considering socially unacceptable behaviours such as harming another person and when judging how likely someone is to behave in a consistent manner.

Now, ask yourself the following questions.

– Do you believe your person theory accurately reflects your assumptions about people and how fixed or changeable they are in general and on specific attributes?

– Do you think your person theory stance has or will influence your objectivity when examining personality theory and research?

– What sort of person theorists do Allport (1927), Cooper (2002) and Caprara and Cervone (2000) appear to be?

Comment

This task is about making your implicit theoretical assumptions explicit. According to Yanchar and Slife (2004, p85), implicit theoretical assumptions are *taken-for-granted ideas . . . – that provide the intellectual background for contemporary theories*. Importantly, we all possess implicit theoretical assumptions, and while these are not formal theories, they *shape theories* (Yanchar and Slife, 2004, p85). Here, you have identified your implicit theoretical assumptions about the fixed or changeable nature of persons using a lay theory approach. Identifying your assumptions is a useful device for developing your critical thinking. It can enhance your awareness of different perspectives and be a starting point for considering where these perspectives come from. Importantly, this process involves reflecting on the evidence base for your implicit theoretical assumptions. We will return to these issues throughout the chapter so please keep your responses to this task close to hand.

Approaches to personality

Fundamental issues

Given the sheer scope of personality psychology, students can find the field difficult to grasp, and as said earlier, personality psychology has been described as difficult (Caprara and Cervone, 2000, p2). One way of getting to grips with this difficulty is to consider the fundamental issues that shape personality psychology. Caprara and Cervone (2000) identify three fundamental issues, and these are shown in Figure 2.1.

These fundamental issues are the source of much debate in personality psychology, and to some extent they divide researchers, who tend to align themselves with one issue or another. For example, historically, work on personality tended to focus on describing and explaining the functions of personality, and in particular the *functions* of personality as individuals adapt to their environment and circumstances. However, contemporary personality psychology has tended to move away from such functionalism towards focusing on describing the *structure* of personality and the discrete elements that we can use to capture general differences between individuals. Such a focus necessarily leads to different research paradigms or concepts to operationalise the psychological phenomena of interest. Such structuralist approaches tend to use hierarchical frameworks in which certain constructs such as dispositions, temperaments and traits capture general behaviour patterns at their highest level, with specific behaviours appearing lower in this hierarchy as expressions of these. Those taking a functionalist focus tend to use conceptual

Figure 2.1: *Fundamental issues in personality psychology*

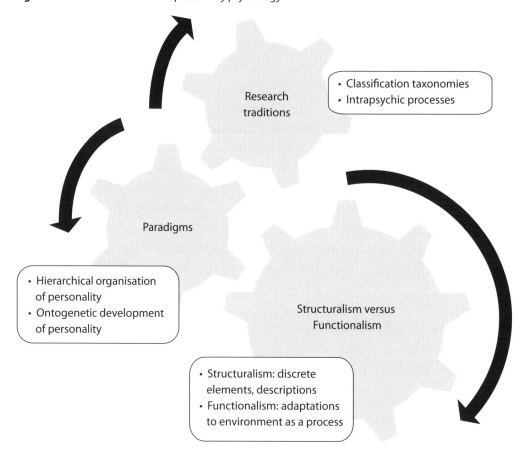

frameworks that capture the interactive nature of personality processes. Finally, as structuralist and functionalist approaches use different research paradigms, they also tend to have different ways of conducting research or research traditions. For example, structuralism focuses on describing the elements of personality that are observable and how these are organised hierarchically, and thus has a tradition of conducting research focused on the classification of individuals and the development of personality taxonomies. Those taking a more functionalist approach, being interested in how personality processes help adaptation to the environment, tend to use inter-actionist paradigms to capture the relationship between the individual and their environment. This has led to a tradition of using research examining intrapsychic personality processes of individuals, often using idiographic research methods.

Early approaches

The roots of many of the fundamental issues in contemporary personality psychology can be traced to specific historical, intellectual, philosophical and social trends. Importantly, very little about contemporary research on personality is actually new, and many ideas have their origins in ancient writings by academics and philosophers rather than contemporary psychologists. Figure 2.2 shows some of these historical trends.

The background to the development of contemporary approaches to personality can be found in the writings of philosophers in ancient Greece and Rome (Anastasi, 1937; Revelle et al., 2010). Early historical writings suggest that ancient Greek societies conceptualised the individual in terms of their relationships with others and the wider community (Caprara and Cervone, 2000). Hippocrates wrote about the nature of individuals being different depending on which of the four humours was predominant (an idea developed further by Galen in the second century AD) (Smith, 2002; Stelmack, 1997). Ideas among ancient Roman philosophers such as Plato and Aristotle shifted to more practical matters and to some extent reflected the ethos of ancient Rome that the individual was in charge of their own destiny.

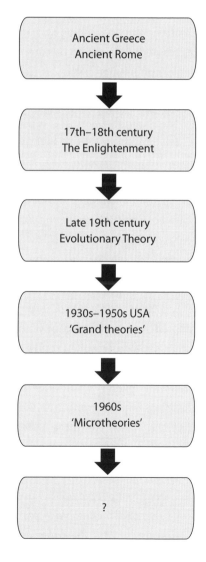

Figure 2.2: Historical trends in personality psychology

Much closer to the present day, Kant's ideas (Kuehn, 2001) and the Enlightenment was the period in the seventeenth and eighteenth centuries when philosophers, writers and other artists began to consider issues such as individuals' emotions and moral character in this so-called age of reason (Caprara and Cervone, 2000). Kant wrote of individuals being governed by general temperaments that could be found in all individuals and by their moral character, something the individual could control (Kuehn, 2001). From the late nineteenth century, psychology began to develop as a distinct discipline (Caprara and Cervone, 2000), and the ideas of Darwin (Boyce and Ellis, 2005; Buss, 1991; Nettle, 2006) and others gave rise to notions of individuals' characters resulting from their biology in interaction with the environment. The work of researchers in the early twentieth century, such as Galton and Pearson's work on correlational research, broadened the scope of research on individual differences, and there was a growth in the emphasis on applying this work outside laboratory settings (Lamiell, 2007). From the 1930s to the 1950s specialisms began to develop in the field of psychology, and to some extent the segregated nature of the field that typifies contemporary psychology emerged. For example, there were those who described themselves in terms of their favoured research paradigm or epistemological position on the nature of psychological phenomena, such as experimental psychologists, and those who used the principles of humanism (Lamiell, 2007). Consistent with this trend towards segregation in the discipline, the 1960s also saw the emergence of many microtheories in personality psychology.

Critical psychologists challenge the ways in which we tend to trace the origins of the field to ancient philosophy and thought. Parker (1999) regards situating the history of individual differences psychology within ancient history as a *trap* because *when Psychology tries to include all of the times and places that people have ever spoken about themselves, we are surely witnessing a grandiose and colonising impulse in the discipline*. In fact, Parker (1999) identifies two traps – the tendency towards over *inclusivity* and the tendency to over *exclusivity*. He called for an alternative approach in which psychology should examine how it is situated within popular culture, how we think about ourselves in everyday life and how we cope with the problems life throws at us.

Freud (1936) is regarded as the founder of the psychodynamic approach to personality. This approach uses the concept of unconscious processes to explain the development and structure of personality. Despite Freud's ideas being closely associated with the concept of personality, mainstream personality research does not feature his ideas consistently (Westen, 1998). However, there has been a resurgence of interest in Freudian concepts and theory, and the legacy of his ideas is often implicit within contemporary psychology, including personality psychology (Westen, 1998). To some extent this illustrates the cyclical nature of ideas in personality psychology. Westen's five tenets or propositions of psychodynamic theories in general (1998) are:

> [first] much of mental life – including thoughts, feelings, and motives – is unconscious, which means that people can behave in ways or develop symptoms that are inexplicable to themselves . . . [second] mental processes, including affective and motivational processes, operate in parallel so that, toward the same person or situation, individuals can have conflicting feelings that

motivate them in opposing ways and often lead to compromise solutions ... [third] stable personality patterns begin to form in childhood, and childhood experiences play an important role in personality development, particularly in shaping the ways people form later social relationships ... Fourth, mental representations of the self, others, and relationships guide people's interactions with others and influence the ways they become psychologically symptomatic. Finally, personality development involves not only learning to regulate sexual and aggressive feelings but also moving from an immature, socially dependent state to a mature, interdependent one. (p335)

These tenets can be identified in other more contemporary approaches to personality. For example, Westen (1998) emphasises the links between research on the self and relationship formation as fundamental to both psychodynamic theory and contemporary personality research. In fact, when we considered definitions of personality, the differences between the observer's and the observed's perspective on personality was an issue we highlighted as distinguishing researchers' conceptions of personality. In addition, the functions of personality for how individuals adapt to their everyday circumstances, or their self-regulation, bear some broad resemblance to these generic psychodynamic propositions. Importantly, contemporary researchers are recognising the need to return to these issues and integrate them with contemporary trait approaches. This can also be linked to the call for personality psychology to be the psychology of the whole person (Caprara and Cervone, 2000).

Task ⌐ Figure 2.2 provides a brief and incomplete schematic representation of the progression of early approaches to personality. However, the last box is empty and the figure lacks some detail. Your task is to develop this diagram into a mind map of the early history of personality psychology. Mind maps are essentially diagrammatic representations of your thinking about an issue, question or topic. In this task, your mind map should capture your ideas about the history of personality psychology that we have considered and any other knowledge you have acquired from further reading. In your mind map you should also try to notice and indicate how certain ideas, issues and concepts appear and reappear, and influence the development of the work of others.

Comment

This task should develop your awareness of the explicit and implicit theoretical assumptions and therefore the fundamental issues that have shaped personality psychology. Certain assumptions remain robust. It should also help you to identify how the sociocultural context influences the development of intellectual ideas. For example, some ideas about personality fall out of favour because they do not fit the intellectual zeitgeist of an era. Importantly, the rise and fall of ideas is not necessarily marked by a seminal moment or turning point. Often, the process is more complex and subtle.

Biological approaches

Three strands dominate biological theories of personality. Increasingly these are interlinked as researchers attempt to integrate the theories and methods from one strand with another (see Figure 2.3). They are described as *approaches* because each encompasses a range of theoretical ideas and methods rather than a single theory. However, each approach tends to focus on the structure or process of personality and currently some key themes dominate each.

Behaviour genetics is the study of the degree to which observable characteristics of an individual – known as phenotype – can be accounted for by the inherited genetic make-up of the individual – known as genotype – *and* their environment (Plomin and Caspi, 1999). Essentially, this

F*igure 2.3:* *Biological approaches to personality*

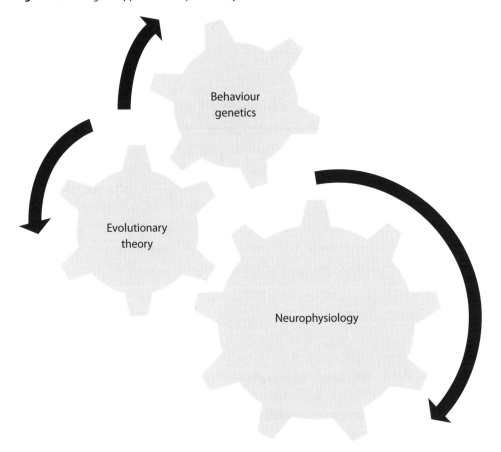

approach attempts to separate out the amount of *observable variance* that we see in characteristics of individuals that we can attribute to their genetic make-up inherited from their parents (their biological heredity) rather than to their environment. Observable variance typically refers to variation in scores on self-report inventories used to measure personality traits, and essentially refers to *statistical variation*. Studies that relate the personality trait scores of twins, including those adopted, is the most widely used method in behaviour genetics research (Loehlin et al., 1990; Loehlin et al., 1998; Plomin and Caspi, 1999) because it enables researchers to separate these influences statistically. Researchers tend to use the schematic equation shown in Figure 2.4 to structure their research and thus enable the separation of influences.

It is worth clarifying that interpreting behaviour genetic research is complex. Researchers vary in how they operationalise the basic premise (shown in Figure 2.4), and in how they identify **zygosity** – whether twins are identical or monozygotic (MZ) or non-identical or dizygotic (DZ). Importantly, the process from genotype to phenotype is complex. Genetic material is coded in DNA or deoxyribonucleic acid, which is the chemical basis of heredity located in the nuclei of 23 pairs of chromosomes that each individual inherits from their parents. These form a total of 46 chromosome cells that are surrounded by cytoplasm, and this cytoplasm contains RNA or ribonucleic acid, which transports DNA into the cell cytoplasm. The process through which this genetic information contributes to phenotypic variance is complex and known as polygenic inheritance – we inherit different genes and these can have an additive or non-additive effect on phenotype. It is important to remember that the relationship between DNA and RNA is reciprocal. Phenotype results from a complex process in which the environment can influence the genotype we observe. For example, the environment influences body biochemistry (e.g. through diet and other lifestyle factors) that in turn influences the *expression* of genotype. Genotype is technically, therefore, a *potential* and this is why in behaviour genetics researchers refer to gene expression. Importantly, the complex processes that link inherited genetic make-up and observable characteristics of individuals contain many opportunities for factors other than DNA to influence phenotype (Plomin and Caspi, 1999).

Researchers have used behaviour genetics to answer the question *Is personality inherited?* Using the logic of behaviour genetics, we can quantify how much of the variance we observe in the phenotype of personality that can be attributed to biological heredity *and* separate this statistically from the contribution of the environment to this variance. Twin studies enable us to compare individuals with identical genotypes – MZ twins – with individuals who have less similar genotypes – DZ twins and other siblings. If MZ twins are reared together, then any variance we see

Figure 2.4: *Basic premise of behaviour genetics research*

in their personality is *technically* the result of shared genes and environment, whereas MZ twins reared apart only share genotype. However, the environment can itself provide individuals with both common and unique experiences even when individuals are raised in the same family. This means that we cannot assume that MZ twins reared in the same family experience the same environment or what is often referred to in the literature as the shared environment. For example, we cannot assume that parents and caregivers treat identical (MZ) twins identically and such twins may experience non-shared or unique environments.

There is compelling evidence that certain personality traits are, to *some extent*, inherited. Plomin and Caspi (1999) summarised the behaviour genetics research on personality up to 1999 and identified six patterns in the empirical evidence.

- Twin studies using self-report personality measures show *moderate* heritability. Much of the research has focused on the heritability of the traits neuroticism and extraversion-introversion, which are two of what are known as the Five Factor personality traits. We will consider the Five Factor traits in more detail later in this chapter.

- Twin studies using methods other than self-report measures of personality also show moderate levels of heritability.

- Adoption studies show less heritability than twin studies.

- *Non-shared* or *unique* aspects of the environment, sometimes referred to as *measurement error*, rather than shared environments have the greater influence on personality.

- Measures of environment are typically measures of behaviour that themselves show heritability.

- There is some evidence that specific collections of genes might be linked to certain aspects of personality. This research – called quantitative trait loci (QTL) research – has shown that a group of genetic markers known as DRD4 appears to be linked to individual differences in novelty seeking (e.g. impulsivity, exploratory behaviour, excitability and extravagance).

At the time, Plomin and Caspi (1999, p296) were optimistic about the contribution of behaviour genetics research to personality psychology and stated: *we predict that in the 21st century, as observers look back on personality research during the 20th century, they will see behavioural genetics as a source of some of the field's most novel and important discoveries.*

Bergeman et al. (1993) used participants from the Swedish Adoption/Twin Study of Aging (SATAS) to assess the heritability of three of the Five Factor traits – openness, conscientiousness and agreeableness. They argue that researchers have tended to focus their work on personality traits that have the highest levels of known heritability, namely, neuroticism, which appears to have a known heritability of around 31 per cent, and extraversion, which appears to have a known heritability of around 41 per cent. They found that both openness and conscientiousness had moderately high levels of heritability. Loehlin et al. (1998) used participants in the USA National Merit Twin Study to assess the heritability of the Five Factor traits with three different measures of personality traits. They found that correlation coefficients between MZ twins were around twice as large as those among DZ twins, with the highest coefficients being observed for the traits of extraversion, neuroticism and conscientiousness. Loehlin et al. (1990) used panel members from the Texas Adoption Study in a 10-year longitudinal study. Their aim was to test the effects of shared environment. They argued that *if shared environment is important, family members, genetically related or not, would be expected to show similar changes. With the effects of shared environment, or with measurement error, the changes for any two individuals would be unrelated* (p222). Their results show that over time genes and shared environment are not the most important predictors of between-person variability in personality; unique environmental experiences predicted more inter-individual variation. They also found that over the ten years that participants were studied, both adopted children and those reared by their natural biological parents tended to develop personalities similar to their genetic parents. In a more recent study, Kandler et al. (2010) used a similar paradigm to Loehlin et al. (1990). They used the NEO Personality Inventory, a measure we will consider later in this chapter when examining the Five Factor personality traits, to gather self and other assessed personality data over 13 years. They found that genes accounted for the long-term stability of personality, but that changes in personality scores were best accounted for by environmental factors in both early and middle adulthood. Behaviour genetics research has also shown that the influence of genetics declines across the lifespan, that genetic inheritance accounts for much of the stability we observe in personality, and that the environment accounts for the changes we observe in personality (including Kandler et al., 2010; McGue et al., 1993). Finally, there is evidence that shared environment does not increase the similarity of MZ twins, as MZ twins reared together appear no more similar than those reared apart.

However, it is important not to oversimplify what this research *actually* shows.

- Genotype influences the environment that an individual experiences, thus making it difficult to separate the effects of these factors (see Plomin and Caspi, 1999).

- The focus on single genes is naive, and the link *is probabilistic rather than deterministic* (McGuffin et al., 2001).

- This research focuses on estimating the quantitative influence of genotype on phenotype and generally has not actually explained the mechanism that leads from genotype to phenotype. Molecular genetics is attempting to address this using QTL research. However, behaviour genetics research generally provides another level of analysis that is about describing variance patterns rather than explaining personality mechanisms. There is evidence that some personality *processes* associated with the Five Factors are inherited. Wolf et al. (2009), using behaviour genetics methods, found that the self-monitoring aspects of personality have some degree of heritability.

- Phenotypes in personality are measured predominantly through self-report measures and do not necessarily address the issue of personality as a process.

- Heritability coefficients increase when environments are relatively uniform, and given the nature of research, it seems likely that many participants are drawn from populations with relative uniformity.

- We can estimate the heritability of anything observable – including your clothes – but we would not claim that there is a car choice gene or front-door colour gene. Likewise, we need to take a cautious approach when interpreting this research. As Caprara and Cervone argue (2000, p167), *There can be no doubt that genes play a role in shaping psychological phenotypes. However, it is unlikely that we inherit personality traits or behaviours as such.*

Increasingly, researchers are drawing on evolutionary theory to explain the patterns of genetic inheritance we observe. Evolutionary approaches to personality attempt to explain personality variance using evolutionary concepts (Buss, 2009). Personality therefore reflects universal social adaptation to the environment as we evolve personality characteristics that enable reproductive fitness, and those aspects of personality that do not serve this function disappear (Michalski and Shackelford, 2010; Nettle, 2006; Webster, 2009). Increasingly, researchers are integrating evolutionary and behaviour genetics to develop evolutionary genetic accounts of personality (Penke et al., 2007). This work uses the following proposition: personality reflects social adaptation, and behaviour genetics research provides evidence of the natural selection of certain aspects of personality. If personality has evolved principally in response to environmental pressures and reflects the most successful outcomes of social adaptation, then it is difficult to understand how some aspects of personality and individual differences are observed if they do not appear to offer individuals any form of selective advantage. However, the work of researchers such as Belsky has attempted to use evolutionary concepts to explain aspects of individual differences that do not appear to offer any advantages (Belsky, 2008; Belsky et al., 1991).

Task | Earlier you identified the sort of person theorist you are. Based on your score from the first task, how convinced should you be by behaviour genetics research on personality? For example, an entity theorist should be more convinced and an incremental theorist less convinced – how accurate is this for you?

Comment

This task should encourage you to reflect on how your implicit theoretical assumptions can potentially influence how you judge academic research. It should also highlight the importance of theoretical assumptions to approaches of personality.

The final group of biological approaches attempts to explain personality in terms of neuro-physiological processes. The work of Pavlov (Paisey and Mangan, 1982), Eysenck (Eysenck et al., 1992) and Gray (1970) illustrates this approach. Although there are some important differences between them, all these approaches use the following broad concepts.

- Nervous system sensitivity underlies personality.

- Observable variances in personality are underpinned by differential sensitivities of individuals to environmental stimuli, and this can be observed and thus measured in the **conditionability** of individuals.

- When these neurophysiological systems become *unbalanced* or one becomes more *dominant*, this has consequences for how the individual functions.

Pavlov's (1927) ideas, although most closely associated with classical conditioning and associative learning, have also influenced ideas about personality. In particular, he used the concept of *temperament*, a concept with ancient origins that featured in the writings of Hippocrates in the fifth century BC. Temperament is a term originally used to describe the innate characteristics of individuals, but used by early twentieth-century personality researchers, such as Allport (1937), to refer to the individual's emotional characteristics. Pavlov (in Corr and Perkins, 2006; Ruch, 1992) studied the physiological mechanisms that underlie these observed differences in temperament. He identified *conditionability* as central to explaining different temperaments. His approach to personality was derived from his observations of dogs used in his experimental research. Their differential sensitivity to conditioning was referred to as empirical evidence of their different personalities (Paisey and Mangan, 1982; Ruch, 1992).

Subsequent research and theory from Eysenck (1992) and Gray (Gray, 1970, 1979; McNaughton and Gray, 2002) has been influenced by Pavlov's early research on the neurophysiological basis of temperaments or personality (Ruch, 1992).

Eysenck's biological theory of personality straddles both biological and trait approaches. His tripartite trait structure of personality is underpinned by biological mechanisms. The theory uses the concept of personality *superfactors*, namely psychoticism (P), extraversion (E) and neuroticism (N), to describe the structure of personality, and it is usually referred to as the PEN or tripartite model of personality. Each of these superfactors is the result of different *neurophysiological sensitivities* that lead to cortical arousal. Although much of the research on PEN has focused on the superfactors or traits of E and N, a fundamental principle of the model is that personality is hierarchical and consists of three superfactors, with *primary traits* and *habitual acts* appearing lower down in the hierarchy respectively as more specific manifestations of traits. Each superfactor, or trait, is underpinned by a particular neuro-anatomical structure, neurophysiological system or particular neurochemistry, and these shape how the individual responds to certain stimuli. Namely, E is linked to the **ascending reticular activating system (ARAS)**, N is linked to the **limbic**

Figure 2.5: *The PEN model of personality*

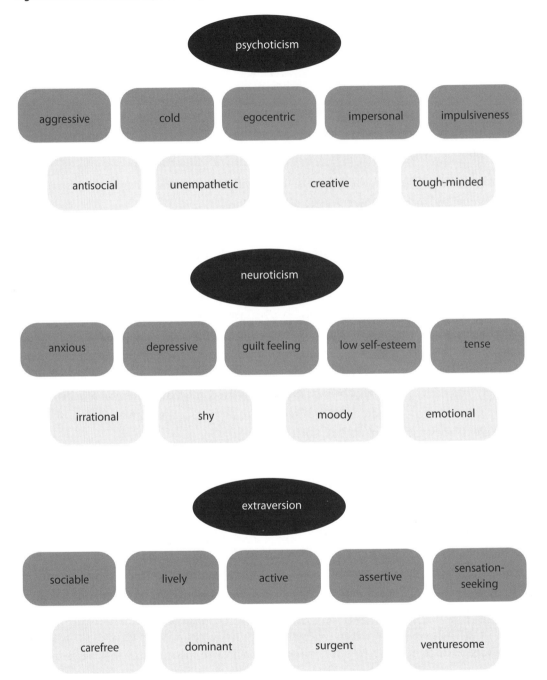

system and P is related to neurochemistry, specifically **androgens**. Observable behaviour or personality is linked to high or low levels of cortical stimulation in these systems, which, ideally, should be *balanced*. In other words, each system's optimal condition is equilibrium or moderate levels of activity, and the primary traits and habitual acts we observe in individuals reflect those individuals' attempts to restore balance.

Gray's (1970, 1987, 1990) theory is related to Eysenck's work but is distinct in certain important ways. Gray's theory proposes that personality can be conceptualised in terms of the dimensions of anxiety and impulsivity, and these dimensions have Eysenck's PEN superfactors or traits of neuroticism and extraversion as their subcomponents. Individuals who are highly *anxious* are described as *neurotic introverts* and are sensitive to stimuli associated with punishment, whereas those who are highly *impulsive* are described as *neurotic extraverts* and are sensitive to reward stimuli. An important component of Gray's theory is that three systems shape behaviour: the behaviour inhibition system (BIS) that is sensitive to environmental punishments and non-rewards; the behaviour approach system (BAS) that is sensitive to environmental rewards and non-punishments; and the flight–fight system. The behaviour of anxious individuals is dominated by their BIS and that of impulsive individuals by their BAS because of their differential sensitivities to rewards and punishment. These systems are interrelated and their output – those aspects of personality we can observe – is also influenced by:

- general arousal;

- decision making so that the motor system produces the correct response;

- comparators that compare actual to expected responses.

Matthews and Gilliland (1999) identified three problems with Eysenck's and Gray's theories of personality.

- *Methodological* the measurement of the exact neural systems and mechanisms underlying personality is difficult and has produced mixed results;

- *Conceptual* unambiguous predictions from these models are not achievable;

- *Empirical* when robust research methods are used, research often fails to find the physiological differences the theories predict.

Taxonomies and traits

The *trait approach* (see Figure 2.6) describes a variety of approaches to personality research that share common features but differ in other ways (Caprara and Cervone, 2000). A number of important points can be made here. First, original trait psychology can be traced to Allport (1937) who emphasised the importance of studying the determinants and underlying mechanisms

Figure 2.6: *Features of trait and taxonomic approaches to personality*

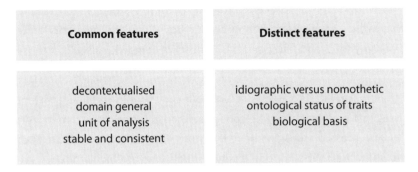

Common features	Distinct features
decontextualised domain general unit of analysis stable and consistent	idiographic versus nomothetic ontological status of traits biological basis

associated with traits. Second, contemporary approaches to trait psychology are shaped substantially by the statistical techniques now available to researchers. The process through which trait approaches have developed is shown schematically in Figure 2.7.

Trait psychology generally focuses on describing hierarchical taxonomies of personality. To some extent the proliferation of *different* taxonomies has been both a hindrance and a help to personality

Figure 2.7: *The development of trait approaches to personality*

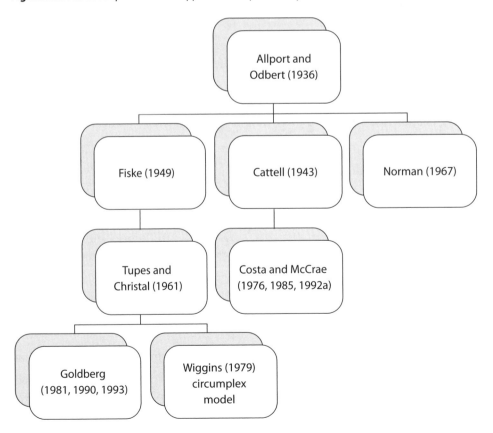

psychology (John and Srivastava, 1999), and the search for a single **taxonomy** of personality traits is important in order that *large numbers of specific instances can be understood in a simplified way* (John and Srivastava, 1999, p102). The search for taxonomies of traits using the lexical hypothesis is an important feature of this work. The lexical hypothesis states that ways in which we have come to distinguish one person from another should be evident in our natural language, so collections of natural language, such as dictionaries, are a starting point in the search for these terms (Goldberg, 1993). Allport and Odbert (1936) are cited as some of the earliest psychologists using this approach. Importantly, the lexical hypothesis is actually based on the assumptions that:

- important personal characteristics are encoded in the adjectives we use in natural language;

- searching the vocabulary of natural language should produce a comprehensive and finite set of such characteristics;

- natural language is meaningful because it is important to interpersonal relations – we use everyday language to regulate our interactions with others. Therefore, the lexical hypothesis is essentially grounded in the importance of social interaction (Goldberg, 1981).

Allport and Odbert (1936) used 18,000 terms from an English dictionary that they identified as relevant to distinguishing people's behaviour, and they organised these terms into four categories.

- Personality traits or generalised and personalised determining tendencies – consistent and stable modes of an individual's adjustment to their environment.

- Temporary states.

- Evaluative judgements of conduct.

- Physical characteristics.

Norman (1967) subsequently reworked their data into seven categories (see Figure 2.8). According to these categories, personality encompasses a range of characteristics for the whole person. Importantly, these categories are claimed to be independent.

Cattell (1943) used Allport and Odbert's (1936) work to develop his multidimensional model of personality using a subset of 4,500 of their trait terms. This was reduced to 35 using a mixture of semantic and empirical clustering and literature reviews, and these 35 were further reduced to the 12 factors assessed in his 16PF questionnaire. Cattell's (1943) use of *dimensions* to organise traits stimulated further research using this approach, most notably by Fiske (1949) and by Tupes and Christal (1961). The latter reanalysed Fiske's data and found that the *trait adjectives* could be grouped into *five factors*, later described as the *Big Five* by Goldberg (1981). Researchers were clear to point out that the term Big Five indicates the way in which these factors capture different aspects of personality and not to denote that all characteristics could be reduced to five factors.

Figure 2.8: *Norman's seven categories (1967)*

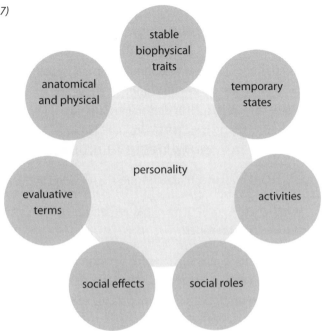

Research using the Big Five or the *Five Factor traits* (FFT) grew substantially from the mid-1980s onwards. Cattell's work from the 1940s has been important in shaping contemporary trait psychology. This original strand of trait psychology was developed further by Goldberg (1990) who partially repeated Cattell's original process using 1,710 adjectives that individuals use to rate their *own personality* characteristics. Research has repeatedly found that these adjectives form groups that resemble the Big Five or FFT (Goldberg, 1990; Saucier and Goldberg, 1996). However, researchers have used different methods to assess the FFT. Goldberg's trait descriptive adjectives (TDA) approach is methodologically distinct from the questionnaire statement approach epitomised by Costa and McCrae's NEO Personality Inventory (1985) and the revised version, the NEO-PI-R (1992b), which uses statements rather than single words to assess the FFT. At this point, a number of important points can be made about how this research has developed.

- Two strands exist in the measurement of the FFT – the adjectival and the questionnaire statement methods – although both methodological strands derive from a specific set of research data.

- Researchers worked in parallel using different scales and theories but often producing converging results. For example, Eysenck's tripartite model includes the superfactor traits of E and N that are also two of the FFT despite the noticeable lack of intellectual dialogue between these two camps of researchers.

- It is simplistic to assume that the FFT are owned either theoretically or methodologically.

Costa and McCrae's work dating from the 1980s is most closely associated with the FFT. This is partly due to the measures they developed. Originally, these researchers did not include agreeableness and conscientiousness in their measure, hence their scale measuring these traits was originally named the NEO-PI, indicating the personality traits of neuroticism, extraversion and openness it assessed. However, following further analysis using Cattell's 16 PF questionnaire and working collaboratively with Goldberg, the factors of conscientiousness and agreeableness were included in a revised version of their original scale, hence the NEO-PI-R (1992). The influence of their work has led some researchers to use the phrase the NEO-PI Five Factor Model (see Figure 2.9).

The FFT and particularly the work of Costa and McCrae have had a significant impact on personality psychology. To some extent the identification of the FFT has addressed John and Srivastava's (1999) call for a taxonomy of personality traits that has some degree of universality and parsimony. The contribution of the FFT and in particular the development of a standard measure has been substantial, and the regularity with which we will refer to the FFT in subsequent chapters is a testimony to this. For example, Chapters 3, 4 and 5 include consideration of how the FFT have been used to predict and explain physical health and well-being, mental disorder and health, and inter-individual variation in personality across cultures and nations and between the sexes, and all with some degree of success. Importantly, the FFT appear to offer more than simply a universally applicable taxonomy for describing personality. Researchers are now using them to *explain* personality processes, such as the mechanisms that link the FFT to mental health and disorder (see Chapter 4). Comparative research suggests that the FFT can be used to describe personality in non-humans and in particular among apes (Gosling, 2001; Mehta and Gosling, 2008; Pederson et al., 2005). Such research, along with research on the evolutionary basis of the FFT and behaviour genetics research suggests that the ubiquitous status of the FFT is to some extent justified.

However, the FFT approach to personality is not without controversy. Here we will consider two broad issues: *methodological and conceptual issues* and those that emerge from the debates surrounding the *trait versus situationist approaches*.

Not all researchers agree with the methods used in the development of the FFT or the conceptual framework of five traits that has emerged from this work. For example, Tiliopoulos et al. (2010) argued that the way in which factor analysis (FA) was used to develop the NEO-PI-R is questionable. Specifically, they question how new the FFT can be regarded, given the known similarities with Eysenck's PEN model. In fact, Eysenck's (1992) scepticism about the conceptual distinctiveness of the FFT relative to his tripartite model includes the proposition that the PEN superfactor traits of N and E are equivalent conceptually with those of the FFT, while trait agreeableness (A) and conscientiousness (C) he regarded as subsumed under his superfactor trait of P Eysenck argued that the FFT's conscientiousness is actually an aspect of intellectual ability or intelligence (see Chapter 6). Tiliopoulos et al. (2010) also question the manner in which the NEO-PI-R was developed, and in particular the way in which factor analysis was used. They question the methods

Figure 2.9: *Costa and McCrae's NEO-PI Five Factor traits (FFT)*

openness versus closedness to experience	conscientiousness versus lack of direction	extraversion versus introversion	agreeableness versus antagonism	neuroticism versus emotional stability
Ideas (curious)	Competence (efficient)	Gregariousness (sociable)	Trust (forgiving)	Anxiety (tense)
Fantasy (imaginative)	Order (organised)	Assertiveness (forceful)	Straightforwardness (not demanding)	Angry hostillity (irritable)
Aesthetics (artistic)	Dutifulness (not careless)	Activity (energetic)	Altruism (warmth)	Depression (not contented)
Actions (wide interests)	Achievement striving (thorough)	Excitement-seeking (adventurous)	Compliance (not stubborn)	Self-consciousness (shy)
Feelings (excitable)	Self-discipline (not lazy)	Positive emotions (enthusiastic)	Modesty (not show-off)	Impulsiveness (moody)
Values (unconventional)	Deliberation (not impulsive)	Warmth (outgoing)	Tender-mindedness (sympathetic)	Vulnerability (not self-confident)

of statistical analysis used to develop the FFT. Specifically, they argue that when conducting FA it is usual to include a greater number of test items than is used in the final version of the scale being developed. They also suggest that the results of their FA suggest that some of the FFT are not independent, and they describe the process used to identify the FFT as a *somewhat arbitrary process*. While such criticisms of FA are not specific to the work of Costa and McCrae, this issue has fundamental conceptual implications for the FFT. Specifically, Tiliopoulos et al. (2010) argue that if we accept that a correlation coefficient of 0.3 between trait scores is sufficient to suggest that the traits actually constitute a larger trait, then the correlation coefficients cited by Costa et al. (1991) suggest that the FFT *could be more parsimoniously accounted for by fewer dimensions*. Namely, as N and E appeared to be correlated (–0.49), and as E and openness (O) appeared to be correlated (0.43), and if conscientiousness is, as Eysenck argued, a dimension of intelligence, then the PEN model is a more economical taxonomy of personality traits. Indeed, Tiliopoulos et al. (2010) confirmed this in their study of 384 adults who completed the NEO-PI-R. They analysed the results using both FA and an alternative method of statistical analysis known as Nonmetric Multi-dimensional Scaling (NMDS). The details of these different statistical techniques are not the central issue here, but the method-sensitive nature of the FFT *is*. Tiliopoulos et al. (2010) found that using FA they confirmed the FFT structure among their participants but that this was not confirmed when using NMDS, which produced a trait structure more similar to Eysenck's PEN model. The method-sensitive nature of the FFT raises questions about the conceptual robustness of the FFT, and there have been other conceptual doubts raised about it. For example, Saucier (2003) found eight factors when using a *lexical noun approach* similar to Goldberg's trait descriptive adjectives (TDAs). To some extent the circumplex approach to the structure of personality, although derived from the adjective approach (Hofstee et al., 1992) has produced circumplex models of personality that, although derived from the NEO-PI-R model, are distinct from it (Backstrom et al., 2009). Using nouns rather than adjectives has also produced alternative models of the structure of personality such as Lee and Ashton's (2004) HEXACO model (see the Further reading section), and the work of Musek (2007) who suggests that in fact there is actually one personality superfactor or the *g of personality* rather than five or three traits. This sort of research has led some researchers to state what Paunonen and Jackson suggested in the title of their 2000 paper: *What is beyond the Big Five? Plenty!* (Paunonen and Jackson, 2000).

Another fundamental issue that challenges trait approaches per se is whether traits, and trait scores, enable us to predict how individuals behave. This issue underpinned the person-situation debate and the work of Mischel in the 1960s (Fleeson, 2004; Mischel, 1968) when the relationship between personality trait scores and actual behaviour – the personality coefficient – of between 0.2 and 0.3 was cited as the evidence that *interactionism* was a more appropriate way to conceptualise behaviour. This debate has led to the development of numerous alternative interactionist-like approaches to conceptualising the link between personality traits and behaviour. For example, Fleeson's (2004) density distributions approach proposes that people vary in their range of behaviours in different situations, but that this range is relatively consistent and shows inter-individual variation. Funder (2009) has developed the *personality triad approach*, in which we can distinguish persons, their behaviours and the situations they find themselves in. Funder (2009, p125) refers to this approach as *post-interactionism* because:

> A complete analysis of person–situation-behaviour main effects and interactions is not an end in itself. Rather, it is a means towards understanding something deeper and more mysterious: the nature and workings of personality. What I mean is not the group of traits (or set of types) with which personality is usually described or through which it is usually assessed, but the mysterious entity within the mind which is the source of all the behaviours and feelings that make up psychological life. The reason we put so much effort into puzzling through all of our data and the complex interactions among persons, situations and behaviours is to move, ever-so-gradually, towards an understanding of this underlying entity.

Other researchers have also developed the issues most clearly associated with the person-situation debate of the late 1960s to produce approaches to personality that do more than focus on describing the structure of personality. Indeed, the focus on personality structure rather than personality processes has been a major criticism of the trait approach, and of the FFT in particular. It would be simplistic to demonise the FFT and its developers as the principal purveyors of a strictly structural approach to personality; and this accusation is itself not strictly accurate (see Chapter 4). However, irrespective of the causes, the widespread use of the FFT and the focus on testing and developing the NEO-PI-R appears to have coincided with a heavy emphasis on describing personality rather than attempting to understand personality processes. However, there has been a consistent interest in refocusing personality psychology onto such processes, and much of this work has drawn on aspects of the person-situation debate. For example, Mischel and Shoda (1995) have developed more fully the ideas they first touted in the late 1960s into an *interactionist approach* that considers the cognitive-affective mechanisms of personality. Subsequently, they have also developed methods for capturing this interactionism, such as situation-behaviour profiles to describe inter-individual variation (Mischel et al., 2002). Such variation is a combination of stable general differences between an individual's behaviour and *distinctive and stable patterns of situation-behaviour relations (e.g., she does X when A but Y when B)*. These if . . . then . . . profiles constitute behavioural 'signatures' that provide potential windows into the individual's underlying dynamics. Theirs is a processing model that bears some relation to Biesanz and West's (2000) account of *traitedness*. Biesanz and West (2000) argue that personality research has focused on consistency rather than coherency, even though the latter they regard as closest to everyday conceptions of personality. Moreover, they state that we can use the notion of *traitedness* to explain why the link between personality and behaviour is not always supported empirically. According to Allport (1937), traits vary in their *traitedness* or relevance to individuals, and he defines traitedness as *how strongly, if at all, that trait influences each individual's behaviour* (p.426). This is the basis of their moderator variable approach – traitedness moderates the trait-behaviour link. The focus on consistency rather than coherency assumes a nomothetic equality in traitedness – we all have the same range of behaviour, but this approach does not always capture those aspects of personality that are not of functional significance for behaviour (see Furr, 2009, for an outline of how personality research can integrate idiographic and nomothetic approaches).

Integrative approaches to personality

McAdams and Pals (2006) *A New Big Five* is an attempt to *consolidate the gains personality psychology has made in recent years and to bring its many rigours together within an elegant theoretical frame . . . an integrative science of the person* (p205). Some argue that McAdams and Pals (2006; also McAdams, 1996) do not go far enough because they still regard trait psychology as the most influential approach but without qualifying this (Lamiell, 2007). However, the views of McAdams and Pals (2006) are not new (Diener and Scollon, 2002). Allport (1927) argued that most personality research has *centred upon some trait in isolation*, rather than the personality as a whole. He also stated that *the definition of the unit of personality is one problem pressing for a solution,* and set out an agenda (1927) for personality psychology.

- Traits should be used as the unit of personality.

- Traits form a hierarchy.

- We should acknowledge limits of what we can know from comprehensive traits.

- A major synthesis of ideas is required in personality psychology and must include apparent inconsistencies in behaviour or *dissociated acts*.

- Personality is a process and includes the individual's *subjective values*. This is the core of the synthesis of the New Big Five approach to personality, and we cannot complete objective evaluations of personality, or character, from purely psychological methods.

This approach can be linked to Bandura's (1999) agentic approach to personality that conceptualises individuals as *self-organising, proactive, self-reflecting, and self-regulating, not just reactive organisms shaped and shepherded by external events* (p2). Lamiell (2007, p169) captures the fundamental ethos of this approach when he argues that *knowledge about the differences between individuals cannot properly be regarded as knowledge about individuals.* In fact, Lamiell (2007) does not believe McAdams and Pals (2006) go far enough because they still see traits as the fundamental construct of personality. This is all about engaging in the sort of disciplinary reflexivity in individual differences psychology that Parker (1999) called for over 10 years ago.

Critical thinking activity

Theories of personality

Critical thinking focus: critical and creative thinking

Key question: *What is Sternberg et al.'s (2001) theory knitting approach, and can this be used to integrate different theories of personality?*

According to Sternberg et al. (2001) psychology is characterised by divisions between different fields using different methods, and they describe this state as *segregated*. They also argue that segregation in psychology prevents researchers from developing a full and useful understanding of psychological phenomena, such as personality, that are of common interest across the discipline. They propose that instead of focusing on differences between fields, methods and theories, psychology would benefit from integrating the most successful aspects of these as applied to common phenomena, a process they call *theory knitting*. For example, research and theory on personality traits such as the FFT and research and theory on human development across the lifespan share a common interest in many psychological phenomenon – they are concerned with enduring characteristics of individuals that lead some individuals to cope better than others with certain life events, such as parenthood, bereavement or chronic illness (see Caspi et al., 2005, for example). However, in general, research across these two fields uses different research paradigms, methods and theory. Although not all researchers agree that theory knitting is either desirable or achievable (Sternberg and Grigorenko, 2001), for this activity you will try to knit two theories of personality using Sternberg et al.'s (2001) approach.

Please select two theories of personality that you regard as different in their approach to describing the structure and function of personality. Your task is to produce a series of diagrams illustrating your theory knitting process applied to these two personality theories, by doing the following.

First, identify those parts of the theories that have empirical support. You will regard these as *successes* of the theories. Second, identify and then compare successes of each theory and attempt to specify any similarities between their successes. Third, develop terms to describe these common successes.

At each point in this process use a diagram to illustrate the critical thinking you have done about each theory and to demonstrate how creative you have had to be throughout this process. Also consider how this integration has advantages over the segregated approach typical of much personality psychology. Finally, ask yourself the following questions.

How feasible is this approach?

What are its advantages and disadvantages?

What have you learnt about your knowledge of personality theories from this activity?

Critical thinking review

This activity requires you to think critically about the evidence supporting particular personality theories and to evaluate the strength of this evidence. The task also requires you to be *creative* in your critical thinking – you have to think not only about similarities and differences between theories but to synthesise these into an integrated 'new' theory, something that requires you to think not only about theory and evidence but about your own understanding of personality research.

Other skills likely to be used in this activity: this activity also requires you to use decision making and problem-solving skills, to make sure you select two theories that are sufficiently different but also have some common features. You also have to reflect on your own understanding and how you communicate this with diagrams. You have to use your knowledge and understanding of theoretical concepts, and if you choose to conduct a literature search on your chosen theories, you have to use research and IT skills to identify the empirical success or evidence that supports your chosen theories.

Skill builder activity

Personality stability

Transferable skill focus: problem solving

Key question: *How can we use the research of Fleeson (2001) to explain our own behaviour and that of others?*

Fleeson, W (2001). Toward a structure- and process-integrated view of personality: traits as density distributions of states. *Journal of Personality and Social Psychology*, 80(6), 1011–27. Available online at www.personalitytheory.com/revelle/syllabi/class readings/fleeson.2001.pdf

This activity is about using academic theory and empirical evidence to help us make sense of the following workplace scenario. Imagine you work part-time as a volunteer at a local community centre. Your duties include dealing with individuals' queries face to face and over the telephone on a range of services and activities run at the centre. However, most of your work involves working as part of a team of around ten other volunteers with special responsibility for parent support groups, and most of your work involves explaining to parents the services that are available to them and how they can access them. At a recent team meeting the team leader reported that some centre users were remarking on the variability of friendliness among staff – some staff were always perceived as cheerful, bright, talkative and generally helpful. However, users had remarked that some staff appeared to be more difficult to talk to sometimes. One parent had noticed that she did not know where she was with some of the team because they appeared to be more unpredictable in their behaviour. The team leader did not see this as a problem because centre users were happy with the service overall, and she accepted that *people vary and that's fine*. However, she did want to know what could be going on. Perhaps something could be done to make users more understanding of different behavioural styles among staff and perhaps staff awareness of user perceptions could be enhanced.

Knowing you are a psychology undergraduate the team leader asks you if you know anything about these sorts of things. Being wary of the ethical problems that could arise because of how your comments could be used, you instead offer to give a brief ten-minute presentation at the next team meeting about how we perceive personality and behaviour stability and variability. Your task is to use Fleeson's (2001) research as a basis for your ten-minute talk. Remember that your goal is to enhance people's awareness of issues drawn from Fleeson (2001) in a relevant, accessible, brief and ethical manner. You can complete this activity individually or as a group.

Worked example

You might choose to solve this dilemma by using other resources as the basis for your presentation, such as a web resource that contains relevant information about such issue – and this could become your presentation. If you decide to solve this dilemma by developing your own presentation, you will need to make sure you present general information to your team and make it clear that you are not making judgements about individuals but simply outlining what the research shows about people in general. You could also decide to use personality inventories as part of an activity to show how challenging it is to use our impressions of others to predict their behaviour in different contexts.

Skill builder review

This activity requires you to apply academic theory and research on personality to a workplace issue. The activity not only uses problem-solving skills to identify and communicate relevant aspects of the paper by Fleeson (2001) but also presents you with an ethical dilemma about how you should respond to your team leader's request: you should show caution because the request could have implications for individual team members, and you might well believe you should decline the request. However, as a student of psychology you might believe that you have a duty to explain some general principles about personality and behaviour within the limits of your competence in order to correct any misunderstanding that might arise if the situation is not discussed openly.

Other skills likely to be used in this activity: the activity involves the use of decision making, data analysis and evaluation skills, and also the understanding and use of academic information to a real situation. The activity also requires you to reflect on your knowledge, oral communication skills and ethical responsibilities.

Assignments

1. How has the trait approach contributed to our understanding of personality?

2. Critically evaluate the importance of biological approaches to personality psychology.

3. Critically discuss the extent to which the contribution of behaviour genetics to our understanding of personality is limited to the quantification of sources of variance rather than *causes* of personality.

4. Critically consider the relevance of the person-situation debate to contemporary personality research.

5. To what extent is contemporary personality psychology the study of differences between persons and not *the* person?

Summary: what you have learned

Personality psychology has a long history, and some of its fundamental ideas and debates have their origins in both ancient philosophy and disciplines other than psychology dating from the nineteenth and early twentieth century. These ideas continue to shape researchers' pursuit of understanding the structure and determinants of personality. Despite its diverse origins, contemporary personality psychology is dominated by research on inter-individual variation using the trait approach, with self-report inventories being the preferred method of collecting data that are used in theory development and in the design and testing of scales. However, the ascendancy of this approach, seen most clearly in research on the relatively ubiquitous FFT, is a trend criticised by some as far removed from the original mission of differential psychology (Lamiell, 2007) and early trait psychology (e.g. Allport, 1937). Currently, researchers are discussing how more clearly integrated research on personality can take personality research closer to its original mission – what has been described as whole person psychology. The critical-thinking and problem-solving skills you use to complete the activities should help your understanding of some of the fundamental questions in personality psychology by examining the similarities and differences of personality theories and applying academic research on personality to a real situation. Considering how your own person theory might influence your approach to personality research should also enhance your critical thinking skills by encouraging you to reflect on your implicit theoretical assumptions about the fixed or changeable nature of people.

Further reading

Cantor, N (1990) From thought to behaviour: 'Having' and 'doing' in the study of personality. *American Psychologist*, 45(6): 735–50.

This older paper outlines a fundamental issue that continues to concern personality psychology – the tendency for researchers to focus on describing the structure rather than the processes of personality.

Caspi, A, Roberts, BW and Shiner, R (2004) Personality development: stability and change. *Annual Review of Psychology*, 56: 1–17.

This is a comprehensive paper that provides a useful summary of the main issues surrounding personality development and stability across the lifespan.

Fleeson, . (2004) Moving personality beyond the person situation debate: the challenge and the opportunity of within person variability. *American Psychologist*, 13(2): 83–7.

This is a readable paper that summarises the classic research and main issues to emerge from the person-situation debate. It argues that both sides in the classic paradox of personality are 'right' and that personality research should consider both stability and variability.

Gosling, SD (2001). From mice to men: what can we learn about personality from animal research? *Psychological Bulletin*, 127(1): 45–86.

This review paper provides useful insights into the usefulness of comparative research for understanding human personality.

Lee, K and Ashton, MC (2004) Psychometric properties of the HEXACO Personality Inventory. *Multivariate Behavioural Research*, 39(2): 329–58.

This is a useful outline of an alternative approach to personality and is an important contrast to work on the FFT.

Mischel, W (2004) Toward an integrative science of the person. *Annual Review of Psychology*, 55: 1–22.

A detailed summary of Mischel's situationist approach to personality that provides insights into the subtle nuances of his work.

Mischel, W, Shoda, Y and Mendoza-Denton, R (2002) Situation-behaviour profiles as a locus of consistency in personality. *Current Directions in Psychological Science*, 11(2): 50–4.

This paper offers an alternative approach to describing personality stability and instability using behaviour profiles to capture both aspects of personality.

Nettle, D (2006) The evolution of personality variation in humans and other animals. *American Psychologist*, 61(6): 622–31.

This is an excellent starting point for understanding how evolutionary theory can be used to explain the structure and determinants of personality, and applies evolutionary theory to the FFT.

Saucier, G (1994) Mini-markers: a brief version of Goldberg's unipolar Big Five Markers. *Journal of Personality Assessment*, 63(3): 506–16.

This paper provides a clear and detailed account of the development of the short form of Goldberg's mini-marker and includes the full brief scale, a useful resource.

Saucier, G (2003). Factor structure of English-language personality type-nouns. *Journal of Personality and Social Psychology*, 85(4): 695–708.

This is an important paper that challenges the use of adjectives, rather than nouns, to capture personality characteristics. The research described demonstrates that the FFT are not a fully comprehensive framework for describing the structure of personality, and using nouns produces a different descriptive structure.

Useful websites

www.personality-arp.org/index.htm (Association for Research in Personality)

This site was founded by a group of mainly US- based psychologists interested in personality, and it is an extensive resource of academic papers, with good links to other sites including the Personality Project and Great Ideas in Personality websites.

http://ipip.ori.org/ (International Personality Item Pool)

This is a comprehensive resource of scales for use by students and academics.

www.uoregon.edu/~sanjay/bigfive.html (Measuring the Big Five)

This is a site devoted to the different measures of the five factors, with access to online versions of many of them. The site also contains useful outlines of key concepts and theories of personality.

http://psychoclassics.asu.edu/ (Classics in the History of Psychology)

This site gives you access to many original classic papers in psychology. It is useful for accessing papers by classic researchers on personality, such as Allport and Cattell.

Chapter 3

Personality and physical health

Learning outcomes

By the end of this chapter you should:

- *be able to discuss, critically, conceptual issues surrounding how personality has been linked to physical health and well-being;*

- *understand what is meant by disease prone personality, and be able to critically evaluate what academic research on this demonstrates;*

- *be able to evaluate, critically, contemporary research that links personality, behaviour and emotions to a range of health outcomes;*

- *develop reflection and communication skills when analysing how academic research on personality, physical health and well-being can be applied to yourself and others.*

Introduction

In this chapter you will consider how personality has been linked to physical health and well-being using the following questions.

- Why have we considered the links between these constructs, and what is the broader conceptual context of this research?

- How have researchers used the notion of a *disease prone personality* to study physical health and well-being?

- What is the nature of contemporary research on this topic? Is it very different from the fundamental principles that emerged from the early research dating from the 1950s?

Linking personality, physical health and well-being has been an extensive academic enterprise among psychologists, academics and practitioners in psychology and other disciplines for over half a century. The topic's popularity reflects, to some extent, its potential implications – for improving lives, saving lives and changing the nature of health policies. Your focus in considering these questions is to reflect, critically, on what the research *actually* demonstrates. For example, have we oversimplified the early research? How is contemporary research linked to this? Your critical thinking about these issues will be developed through activities that involve reflection on your assumptions about how emotions and behaviours are linked to well-being in general. You will also consider how you can communicate complex academic information on this topic using different media and reflect on how you can use the research to inform yourself and others about how personality and physical health are linked.

Conceptual issues

Conceptual issues and developments in academic research on health and personality provide an important context for understanding the development of research on the links between these phenomena. Three groups of conceptual issues are important to this research, and these are shown in Figure 3.1. These conceptual issues have to some extent influenced the development of research on personality and physical health: *frameworks* used to organize factors important to *health*, specific *concepts* used currently in *health* and *well-being* research, and *conceptual issues in personality psychology*, many of which we considered in Chapter 2.

Figure 3.1: *Conceptual context of personality, physical health and well-being research*

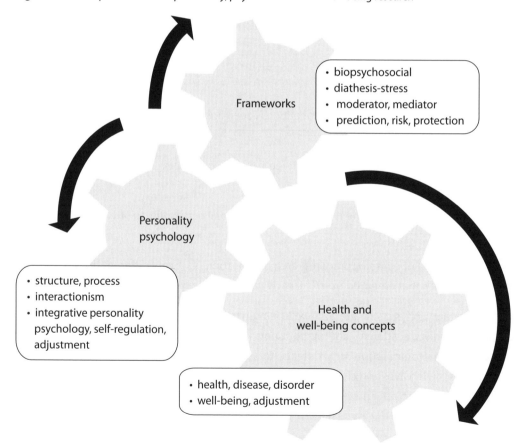

Frameworks
- biopsychosocial
- diathesis-stress
- moderator, mediator
- prediction, risk, protection

Personality psychology
- structure, process
- interactionism
- integrative personality psychology, self-regulation, adjustment

Health and well-being concepts
- health, disease, disorder
- well-being, adjustment

Frameworks

Contemporary approaches to physical as well as psychological health tend to use Engel's (1977) *biopsychosocial model* as a framework for understanding health (Borrell-Carrió et al., 2004). Therefore, we will spend time considering this because it is central to frameworks used to explain physical and psychological health across the behavioural sciences. We will also spend some time considering the biopsychosocial model because it is important not to oversimplify what this model encompasses. The term *biopsychosocial model* was coined by Engel (1977, p129), a professor of psychiatry and medicine. He argued at that:

> all medicine is in crisis and, further, that medicine's crisis derives from the same basic fault as psychiatry . . . namely adherence to a model of disease no longer adequate for the scientific tasks and social responsibilities of either.

Thus his biopsychosocial model developed as a critique of the medical model of disease and health, also referred to as the *biomedical model*. The biomedical model conceptualises health and disease as qualitatively distinct categories that are mutually exclusive. Specifically, the model conceptualises health as the *absence* of disease. Individuals are judged as healthy against some standard criterion or set of criteria, and the presence of disease – or illness – is a category an individual is placed in because they deviate from this *normative standard*. Importantly, this heuristic is used to describe both physical *and* psychological deviations from such standards. Physical and psychological deviations from this standard are therefore diseases per se, which all have a molecular biological or somatic basis. Thus the biomedical model provides a framework based on:

> both reductionism, the philosophical view that complex phenomena are ultimately derived from a single unitary principle, and mind-body dualism, the doctrine that that separates the mental from the somatic.

> (Engel, 1977, p130)

According to Borrell-Carrió et al. (2004), Engel's (1977) critique of the biomedical model has seven key features that form the basis of his biopsychosocial model.

- The presence of biomedical alteration does not mechanistically lead to illness.

- Focusing on biochemical alterations as the causes of diseases or illnesses is both reductionist and mechanistic because this overlooks important psychological and social factors – or psychosocial factors – that are all parts of the diagnostic process, such as the patient's perspective, beliefs and attitudes as well as those of clinicians.

- Psychosocial variables impact on both disease onset and progression.

- The presence of biochemical alterations does not guarantee the presence of sickness in the individual; instead, the effect of the former is *potential*.

- The placebo effect – when a neutral or control substance is administered to an individual but appears to produce the same known effects as an actual substance – also demonstrates that psychosocial variables influence treatment.

- The clinician–patient relationship has an impact on medical encounters.

- Humans are not inanimate objects and the relationship between clinician and patient is reciprocal.

The biopsychosocial model is therefore a framework used by contemporary behavioural scientists to conceptualise both physical and psychological health. It challenges the **mind–body dualism** and reductionism of the biomedical model and the nature of the diagnostic process implicit in the biomedical model, especially the notion of clinicians being *detached observers*. It also challenges the notion of there being a linear causal relationship between biological disturbance and actual disease. Borrell-Carrió et al. (2004, p135) therefore regard the biopsychosocial model as *a blueprint for research . . .. A framework for teaching, and a design for action in the real world of health care.*

However, it is important not to oversimplify what the biopsychosocial model originally encompassed, and a number of caveats can be made about this framework. First, a close reading of Engel's (1977) and other related frameworks that developed as alternatives to the biomedical model, such as the diathesis-stress model, were actually developed as alternative frameworks for understanding either psychiatric disorders in general or specific psychiatric conditions. Second, the biopsychosocial model was developed originally for guiding the clinical relationship between medical doctors or psychiatrists and their patients. It therefore focuses on the therapeutic relationship and the imbalance of power in medical encounters between medical professionals and patients. This has been called biopsychosocially oriented clinical practice (Borrell-Carrió et al., 2004, p579). Finally, the biopsychosocial model has not been embraced universally by clinicians (Pilgrim, 2002).

Nevertheless, the biopsychosocial model provides a framework for conceptualising health per se because of its fundamental tenets. It uses the concept of *circular causality* to explain health and disease. This states that many factors other than the purely biochemical or somatic influence health and disease. It also regards health and disease as processes that are not categorically distinct or demarcated. Instead, degrees of each can be identified using continua that are not mutually exclusive, and health and disease processes can influence each other in a reciprocal and circular fashion. The biopsychosocial model also draws attention to the ways in which the beliefs and attitudes of clinicians and patients influence the disease and health processes.

To some extent the biopsychosocial model as known in psychology is actually referring to applications of the framework to physical and psychological health and disease that are broader than those it originally encompassed. Indeed, subsequent to Engel's (1977) work, researchers revised, modified and generalised the framework to physical and psychological health. For example, Borrell-Carrió et al. (2004) revised the model to produce a framework that not merely focuses on the power differential between medical clinicians and patients but also emphasises the importance of emotions, thoughts and feelings in health contexts, an approach they call a *whole systems approach* (Pilgrim, 2002, p585). Another modification has been developed by Lindau et al. (2003). They modified the biopsychosocial model to produce a framework that focuses on health rather than on disease and illness. Their *interactive biopsychosocial model* (IBM) identifies bio-physical, psychocognitve and social factors as *biopsychosocial capital* (p4), and this clearly requires the inclusion of psychological phenomena. The *diathesis-stress model* is one of the most well known of the biopsychosocial models, and since the late nineteenth century this notion has been discussed (Monroe and Simons, 1991). However, the intellectual ethos of the mid-twentieth century in particular encouraged the development of this approach and its general application beyond the mental disorders it was first developed to account for – the model was originally applied to psychiatric disorder. The diathesis–stress model emphasises the importance of pre-disposing factors or diathesis – premorbid characteristics – that influence how an individual reacts to stressors. The interaction between diathesis and stress can be used to understand the onset of mental disorders such as schizophrenia (Meehl, 1962) and depression (Monroe and Simons, 1991). Related frameworks include vulnerability-stress models (Ingram and Loxton, 2005) of psychopathology and the biobehavioural model of health and illness (Baum and Posluszny, 1999).

Despite the specific differences between the many variants of the biopsychosocial model, they share certain features that have been important to the development of research on the link between personality and physical health.

- Psychological factors influence physical health because they are what Lindau et al. (2003) refer to as biopsychosocial capital.

- The influence of psychological factors on physical health is complex.

- The influence of psychological factors on health is likely to be as *moderators* that shape the influence or impact of disease and stress on the individual, and as *mediators*, or as Baum and Posluszny (1999, p138) say, *thoughts, feelings, and behaviours affect our health and well-being* because these psychological phenomena are the mechanisms that have the potential to explain both health and the onset of disease.

- Psychological variables influence how individuals react to stressors, and as psychological phenomena such as thoughts, feelings and behaviours differ between individuals, these psychological differences will lead to different reactions to stressors (Lazarus, 1993).

The critical issue here is that the ways in which individuals differ psychologically are likely to be related to differences in physical health between individuals. This has encouraged researchers to conceptualise the main ways in which individuals differ psychologically as putting individuals at greater or lesser risk of physical disease. Likewise, these individual differences can also protect individuals from physical disease. In sum, we can use psychological phenomena that differentiate individuals or individual differences, to *predict* and *potentially explain* the onset of physical disease.

Health and well-being concepts

The emergence of the biopsychosocial model framework has also influenced a shift in focus in the research on personality and physical health away from a singular focus on explaining disease. The focus is now on considering the determinants of this as well as the determinants of health and well-being, and these are issues we will return to in Chapter 4 when we consider atypical personality and mental disorder. It suffices to say at this point that part of the biopsychosocial trend in the research includes reconceptualising health as not merely the absence of disease and the development of health-related constructs such as well-being. These reconceptualisations draw attention to the multidimensional nature of health and disease. Changes in health and well-being concepts have encouraged researchers to consider the role of psychological phenomena in disease and health processes. In particular, it has become recognised that psychological differences between individuals can influence how people vary in their risk, **resilience** and experience of disease and health. This has provided fertile ground for research examining the links between individual differences such as personality and physical health. Considering how personality and disease are linked is just one example of this broader trend.

Personality psychology

In Chapters 1 and 2 we considered how the landscape of personality psychology has changed as researchers are returning to the whole person psychology approach. This has meant that researchers are examining personality processes more explicitly, and this includes considering how personality processes function as self-regulation. Thus trends in personality psychology fit those ushered in by framework and concept changes in approaches to health and well-being. Hoyle (2006, pp1507–08) captured this trend in personality psychology when he described the trait approach to self-regulation as involving the study of:

> *processes by which people control their thoughts, feelings, and behaviours. When people succeed at self-regulation they effectively manage their perceptions of themselves and their social surroundings . . . successful self-regulation is essential to adaptive functioning in all life domains.*

The key issue here is that personality traits can tell us about the stable and particular ways that people regulate themselves (Hoyle, 2006). In other words, personality traits indicate more or less successful adaptation, and physical health and disease can be regarded as forms of physical adaptations and maladaptation respectively.

Task ⌐ Select one of the health and well-being concepts in Figure 3.1, and using an
academic search engine such as PsycINFO, search for definitions of this concept.
When doing this, search for definitions from different decades (e.g. 1950s, 1960s, and
so on) and consider how the meaning of your chosen concept has changed in the
academic research.

Comment

This task should demonstrate both the enduring and the more changeable features of definitions.
It should also make it clearer to you that disease, health and well-being are socially constructed.
In other words, how these and related constructs are conceptualised is shaped by the prevailing
social, cultural and intellectual climate. To some extent, the ascendancy of the biopsychosocial
model of disease and health is consistent with the *3-d* approach you were encouraged to take to
individual differences psychology in Chapter 1. You will now need to judge for yourself how *3-d*
research on personality and physical health actually is.

Personality and physical health

The biopsychosocial model highlights the importance of psychological factors for physical health
and disease processes. This leads to the premise that the ways in which individuals differ psychologically is likely to be related to differences in physical health. This premise has underpinned
much of the research on personality and physical health, and in particular the search for the
disease prone personality that we will consider next.

Type A Behaviour Pattern (TABP)

Although the notion of personality being linked to physical health is centuries old (Smith et al.,
2004), the search for the disease prone personality gained pace in the 1950s led by the work of
cardiologists Friedman and Rosenman in the USA (1957, 1959). Their work was based on two
fundamental observations. First, known medical cardiovascular risk factors, such as **hypertension**,
smoking and raised **serum cholesterol** levels, were insufficient to explain the rise in rates of
cardiovascular **morbidity** and **mortality** between 1900 and the 1950s. Second, middle-aged men
presenting with cardiovascular diseases (CVD) display an identifiable set of specific behaviours
that the researchers linked to the **pathophysiological processes** of cardiovascular disease such
as raised serum cholesterol levels and **blood clotting**. They described these specific behaviours
as Type A Behaviour Pattern (TABP) or the *coronary prone personality*. Individuals displaying the
opposite pattern of behaviour were described as having a Type B Behaviour Pattern (TB), also

referred to as the healthy personality. The key features of each are shown in Figure 3.2. According to these researchers, TABP is characterised by the following (Jenkins et al., 1968).

- Extreme competitiveness.

- Achievement striving.

- Aggressiveness that is, at times, *stringently repressed* (p16).

- Frequent and intense expressions of anger.

- Haste, impatience, restlessness and feelings of time pressure.

- Hyper alertness.

- Explosive speech.

- Tense facial musculature.

- Feelings of challenges of responsibility.

An important feature of TABP is that it is an *action-emotion complex*. In other words, it describes how individuals typically react both behaviourally and emotionally to specific situations and circumstances, and these environmental cues trigger these reactions. It is noteworthy that the TABP is consistent with Western cultural values related to work, success and achievement, and sociocultural factors are therefore important to understanding TABP. Finally, TABP consists of subcomponents or different elements. TABP is, therefore, essentially a set of specific *behavioural reaction styles* provoked by environmental cues. These features have implications for how we assess or measure TABP, and two approaches have dominated this research: the *structured interview* (SI) and the *Jenkins Activity Survey* (JAS). The SI was developed by Friedman and

Figure 3.2: *Characteristics of Type A and B Behaviour Patterns*

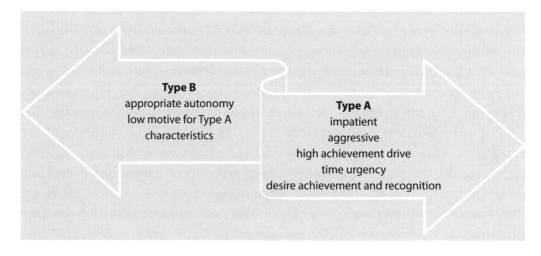

Type B
appropriate autonomy
low motive for Type A
characteristics

Type A
impatient
aggressive
high achievement drive
time urgency
desire achievement and recognition

Rosenman. This involves a trained interviewer observing the behavioural reactions of the individual in response to certain provocative cues from the interviewer. Specifically, the SI involves assessing four aspects of the individual's reactions, that is, characteristic motor signs: drive and ambition; past and present competitiveness; aggression and hostility; and sense of time urgency. For example, a behavioural style characterised by frequent and intense expressions of anger are typical of TABP. Importantly, it is the behaviour style and not the content of the individual's reactions that are assessed. In contrast, the JAS is a self-report inventory (Jenkins et al., 1979) and is the most frequently used self-report measure of TABP, although others exist (e.g. the Framingham Scale and the Bortner Rating Scale).

Methods of assessment are important to understand the research on TABP, and key researchers on the topic have themselves declared the SI as a more valid and therefore more accurate measure of TABP than the JAS (Lachar, 1993). Jenkins et al. (1968) ran a study testing the inter-rater reliability of the SI given the importance of accurately differentiating TABP from TB. They found that the SI and the JAS as measures of TABP and TB differ in important ways.

- The SI assesses aggressiveness and hostility whereas the JAS does not.

- The JAS and similar self-report questionnaires measure stable traits and not observable reactions or behavioural style.

- The SI is resource demanding because it involves training interviewers and because the interview process can be lengthy, involving around 25 questions. In contrast, the JAS is less time consuming to administer and complete.

These assessment issues have raised questions about whether the link between TABP and CVD is measurement dependent. Friedman and Booth-Kewley (1987) compared the effectiveness of the SI and JAS for predicting CVD in men aged between 40 and 69 years of age. They found the SI to be the better predictor because, they claim, it assesses the core feature of TABP. This core feature of TABP is a characteristic style of emotional expression typified by *anger-in* and *hostility*, particularly in the individual's non-verbal speech. The SI therefore appears to be a more valid measure of TABP than the JAS because the latter's self-report inventory focuses on the content rather than the style of an individual's emotional expression. This study is also important because, as the authors state:

> The truly Type A individuals . . . are likely to be rated as Type A in the SI. They may be easily recognized competitive, aggressive strivers. However, our results also indicate that scoring Type B on the JAS is not necessarily healthy.
>
> (Friedman and Booth-Kewley, 1987, p790).

It suggests, therefore, that the subtle complexities of TABP and TB were recognised some time ago in the original research. Friedman and Booth-Kewley (1987) identified that individuals classified as

TB on the JAS could also have high levels of non-verbal emotion expressiveness. They argue that when accompanied by an inability to express their strong emotional reactions and experiences of conflict in their life (e.g. a disparity between what they hoped to achieve and their actual levels of achievement), this variant of TB has potential adverse consequences for the individual's cardiovascular health. This research, along with a close reading of some of the original research, suggests the following.

- TABP as an action-emotion complex was recognised as a complex process in early writing on the construct.

- Early researchers recognised the need to identify *mechanisms* that *mediated* the link between TABP and CVD, including the psychophysiological mechanisms and behavioural patterns that could explain the higher rates of CVD among TABP individuals.

- Concerns about the methods used to measure TABP are far from new.

- Early researchers were aware that the classification of an individual as TABP or TB is complex, and they identified variants of each. For example, Jenkins et al. (1968) developed a subdivision of TABP and TB. The *Type A1 fully developed personality* can be distinguished from *Type A2 partially developed* TABP; and the *Type B3 partially developed* TB can be distinguished from *Type B4 fully developed* TB. They transformed this into a rating scale in their inter-rater reliability test of the SI. Importantly, they regarded this subdivision as a continuum.

Given these methodological complexities, it is unsurprising that evidence supporting TABP as a predictor of CVD has been both supportive and contradictory. Lachar's (1993) review provides a useful rubric for organising the evidence available up to that date, and it remains a useful heuristic for organising more contemporary research on TABP. This is summarised in Figure 3.3. Lachar (1993) identified five groups of research on TABP, each providing support for or against the existence of TABP. Three groups of research provide the most compelling evidence for the existence of TABP: epidemiological research or large typically longitudinal *population* studies of healthy individuals; research on the *subcomponents* of TABP and its psychophysiological mechanisms; and research on *interventions* used to reduce TABP.

Of the *population studies*, the Western Collaborative Group Study (WCGS, Rosenman et al., 1975) is the most often cited longitudinal epidemiological study demonstrating that TABP predicts the onset of CVD. Researchers used the SI to assess TABP among 3,154 men aged 39–59 years who were described as healthy with no history of CVD. After 8.5 years 257 of the original sample had developed a CVD. Importantly, after controlling for medical risk factors, those identified as TABP were twice as likely to have developed CVD, operationalised here as experiencing a **myocardial infarction (MI)** or **angina pectoris**, compared to those described as Type B. This pattern has been repeated in other early population studies of healthy individuals (Brand et al., 1976; Haynes et al., 1980; Rosenman and Friedman, 1961) and outside the USA, for example, in Scandinavia (Bortner Co-operative Study).

Figure 3.3: Lachar's (1993) review of evidence for the existence of TABP

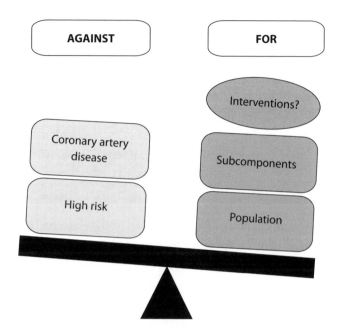

Research on the *subcomponents* of TABP and the psychophysiological mechanisms linked to them, along with *intervention studies*, has also provided some support for the existence of TABP. The TABP subcomponents that appear to be the best predictors of CVD are those indentified in the original research as the defining or core features of TABP. These components are *hostility* – reacting to trigger events with irritation, frustration and disgust – and *anger-in* – a reduced desire or ability to express anger towards the object of one's anger. These subcomponents have come to be regarded as more pathologic or toxic than other subcomponents of TABP (Lachar, 1993). There is considerable evidence that hostility and anger are the best predictors of CVD, ahead of global TABP (Chida and Steptoe, 2009; Edwards and Baglioni, 1992; Hecker et al., 1988; Williams et al., 2000) and across different measures of hostility (Lachar, 1993). There is also evidence that global and subcomponent measures of TABP are related to physiological reactivity that contributes to CVD. However, Myrtek's (1995) meta-analysis of research on the relationship between TABP and neurophysiologic reactivity failed to find evidence of a link. Such a link is important, given the claim by early researchers that TABP is linked to CVD through pathogenic neurophysiologic mechanisms.

Research on individuals at *high risk* of developing CVD has tended to provide support *against* the existence of TABP. For example, the Multiple Risk Factor Intervention Trial (MRFIT; Shekelle et al., 1985) studied 3,000 healthy men for seven years. Those defined as at risk were individuals with two of the following three risk factors for CVD: smoking; hypertension; and raised serum cholesterol levels. Using both the SI and JAS to assess TABP they found no relationship between TABP and the development of CVD in those at risk over a period of seven years. Similarly, research on **coronary artery disease (CAD)** that has examined the relationship between TABP and the presence of coronary artery disease in individuals identified through angiograph has also failed to provide consistent support for the existence of TABP as a predictor of CAD (Booth-Kewley and Friedman, 1987; Friedman and Booth-Kewley, 1987).

This early work has a number of notable features. First, there appears to be an identifiable disposition composed of specific behaviours, emotions and thoughts that increase an individual's risk of CVD. Second, TABP is a coronary heart disease prone personality *action-emotion complex*, and the absence of this, referred to as TB, is regarded as a healthier disposition. Third, this action-emotion complex influences the pathophysiological mechanisms contributing to CVD, although the mechanisms involved are unclear. Finally, the predictive usefulness of TABP appears strongest among healthy adults rather than among those already at risk of CVD.

However, this and subsequent research has raised doubts about the compelling nature of the early research. First, only certain aspects of TABP are consistent predictors of CVD, in particular hostility and anger-in (Miller et al., 1996; Smith and Ruiz, 2002; Smith et al., 2004; Wellisch and Yager, 1983). Hostility and anger-in appear to be the *toxic components* (Smith and Ruiz, 2002, p552) of TABP because they have adverse consequences for the individual's interpersonal relationships (Smith et al., 2004). Smith et al. (2004) have suggested a *psychosomatic hypothesis* (p1219) using an inter-personal approach to personality to explain the link between hostility and TABP. Specifically, personality influences interpersonal relations because it leads to recurring patterns in these phenomena, and individuals covertly (experiences) and overtly (behavioural expressions) generate the same or similar in others. This *social style* (p1222) is one mechanism linking hostility and CVD because of the reactions of others to the social style of individuals with TABP, including social isolation and diminished social support. Second, methods of measurement and administration of assessment tools appear to influence the likelihood of observing a link between TABP and CVD, with the SI being used most frequently in research finding this link. However, it is worth remembering that key early researchers in this field themselves acknowledged the challenges of assessing TABP and classifying individuals as either TABP or TB. For example, Jenkins et al.'s (1968) inter-rater reliability study found that classification of a subgroup from the WCGS of 1,131 men using the SI achieved a test-retest coefficient of +0.82 over a period ranging from 12 to 20 months. They also found high levels of agreement between an original interviewer and an independent judge in subsamples of the SI interviews of around 64 per cent. However, a close reading of this study does suggest that there were disagreements between raters' classifications of participants, and around 20 per cent of the subsample of interviews checked produced different classifications. Notably, less experienced judges tended to classify interviewees more in the direction of TABP than the more experienced interviewer. Finally, research on the pathophysiological mechanisms that should mediate the link between TABP and CVD has produced mixed results. The notion of a disease prone personality as a simple match between a global personality type and a specific disease is therefore likely to be simplistic. However, the link between TABP and CVD was not originally conceptualised as strictly mechanistic or deterministic. It has nevertheless been interpreted as such despite its clear biopsychosocial emphasis – an emphasis that is evident in the original research.

Type C personality

In the search for the disease prone personality the *Type C personality* or the *cancer prone personality* has been identified, which has been described as a *psychosocial risk factor* for the development of cancer – along with the experience of loss and depression. However, early research often considered case studies of cancer sufferers, so this work was actually examining recovery from cancer – or cancer survival – and response to treatment, rather than the onset or risk of developing cancer. The personality characteristics of those diagnosed with cancer were observed to be *highly extraverted* with *low levels of neuroticism* (Amelang, 1997; Kissen and Eysenck, 1962). Originally, the basic premise underpinning the notion of the Type C personality was that a diagnosis of cancer is a stressor that activates the premorbid traits of individuals and the repression of feelings and behaviours associated with high levels of extraversion and low levels of neuroticism. The original premise therefore uses a diathesis-stress framework, with the diagnosis of cancer being the stressor and high levels of extraversion and low levels of neuroticism being the diathesis components. However, research on Type C is not unproblematic. For example, the research does not always distinguish the onset of cancer from recovery. Moreover, the research has focused heavily on specific clinical groups, namely women with a diagnosis of breast cancer, often using small samples or case studies. In addition, in some instances the researcher has been aware of the diagnosis of the individual when assessing personality (Amelang, 1997).

Generally, much of the research published since the early 1980s suggests that the relationship between Type C personality and cancer is complex (Persky et al., 1987; Schapiro et al., 2001. For example, Hansen et al. (2005) conducted a large prospective study of 29,595 twins. They measured participants' anger-in, depression, life events and neuroticism and extraversion using the Eysenck Personality Inventory (EPI). They also examined cancer type, stage of disease, socio-economic status and health behaviour, along with diet, exercise, alcohol consumption and smoking behaviour. This extensive longitudinal study, which ran from 1974 to 1999, found no significant relationship between cancer and neuroticism or extraversion.

Other more recent research using a range of stressors other than the diagnosis of cancer and measures of neuroticism and introversion–extraversion, has also failed to provide convincing evidence of a link between Type C and cancer. For example, Achat et al. (2000) examined the relationship between the onset of cancer and the stressor of **job strain** among a sample of 26,936 post-menopausal women. They used participants' self-reports of breast cancer followed up by a review of medical records to confirm their diagnosis between 1992 and 1994. Among the 219 diagnosed cases there was no significant relationship between job strain and cancer onset. However, there was a negative relationship between breast cancer screening up-take and job strain: they found that job strain predicted a reduced likelihood of having a breast scan. Butow et al. (2000) also found no relationship between the risk of cancer developing, and personality and psychosocial variables. Research that has measured the key personality traits of Type C – neuroticism and extraversion – has also produced inconsistent results. For example, Schapiro et al. (2001) used the EPI among a sample of 1,031 from the Danish Cohort Study. Using a 20-year longitudinal design starting in 1976–77, they found no relationship between the risk of developing cancer and levels of trait neuroticism and trait extraversion. Graham et al. (2002) found no relationship between the recurrence of cancer and the experience of life stressors, and Dalton et al. (2002) found no relationship between depression and the risk of developing cancer. However, Nakaya et al. (2006) found a complex relationship between personality traits and cancer. Neuroticism was found to be a *predictor of cancer survival*, but no relationship between the risk of developing cancer and Eysenck's PEN traits was found. Neuroticism was related to cancer prevalence at baseline and diagnosis in the first three years of the research, but not subsequently. This suggests that increased levels of neuroticism could be a consequence and not a cause of the development of cancer.

Grossarth-Maticek typology

The Grossarth-Maticek typology was developed by Grossarth-Maticek and Eysenck in the 1980s, and was partly an attempt to address some of the limitations of the early approaches to identifying disease prone personalities (Roberts and Duffy, 1995). This typology consists of six behavioural reaction styles that are triggered in response to stressors (see Figure 3.4). The framework uses the notion of *types* of *independent behavioural reaction styles*. Each indicates a proneness to specific collections of physical diseases or mental health problems, and this includes some forms of *social deviance* (Amelang, 1997). The six types are measured using the Short Interpersonal Reactions Inventory (SIPRI) or the Personality Stress Inventory, and classification of individuals into one of the six types uses a diagnostic hit rate approach – the individual must meet certain criteria to be classified.

This typology differs from the previous conceptions of a disease prone personality such as TABP and Type C in important ways. First, it is used to predict physical disease *and* psychological disorders. Second, it is based explicitly on characteristic reactions to stressors, although it is important to remember that TABP is essentially an action–emotion complex. Finally, it captures tendencies in behavioural style, and is linked more explicitly to personality research (Amelang, 1997) than the

Figure 3.4: *Grossarth-Maticek's six typology*

Type I	Type II	Type III	Type IV	Type V	Type VI
• conformist dependency on a withdrawing object	• conformist dependency on a disturbing object	• non-conformist dependency	• appropriate autonomy	• rational anti-emotional	• anti-social

TABP construct. However, research on the six typology has the following in common with that on TABP: evidence supporting the existence of the six behavioural reaction styles is mixed. For example, Schmitz (1992) examined all six types in two samples of 100 and 92 participants. The researchers used the Personality Stress Inventory to measure the six reaction styles, and their main outcome measures were Eysenck's PEN personality traits, participants' behavioural and coping styles, and their self-reported reactions to the stressor. They also assessed participants' psychosomatic complaints, disease, addictions and depression. Their results provided some support for the six typology. For example, Type IV (or the healthy personality) recorded just one diagnosis from across the six groups of physical and psychological disorders over a period of five years, and Type VI reported the highest number of addictions across the six groups as the framework predicts. Furthermore, as the framework predicted, the highest rates of cancer diagnosis were found in those participants classified as Type I (cancer prone), and the majority who reported some form of CVD were classified as Type II (CVD prone), as well as having the highest rates of hypertension and ulcers across the six types. However, although Schmitz (1992) reports some disease mapping, Types I and II also reported the highest number of psychosomatic complaints and behavioural risk factors for both cancer and CVD. Slightly later research by Smedslund (1995) adds to this complex picture. Smedslund (1995) examined Types I, II and IV in samples of 5,014 participants in Norway. Their postal survey, which achieved a response rate of around 50 per cent, used the SIPRI questions transformed into a self-report inventory. Smedslund (1995) measured participants' basic demographic characteristics, lifestyle such as smoking, drinking and exercise behaviour, self-reported health complaints, worry, and incidence of CVD and cancer. The results of this research show a disease mapping pattern in the opposite direction to that predicted by the typology, with the highest rates of cardiovascular disease being found among Type I participants (cancer prone) and the highest rates of cancer among Type II participants (heart disease prone), although Type IV participants (healthy) were more likely to report having no complaints about their health and to be free of any illnesses compared to Types I and II. However, Type I and II participants differed from Type IV in ways that are known to be related to poorer physical health. For example, Types I and II individuals were older, had lower incomes and levels of education, and Type IV individuals were younger and healthier. Furthermore, a greater number of Types I and II participants reported having an unhealthy diet, seldom exercising physically, and having smoked for a greater number of years (although this is unsurprising as they were generally older); they also reported being worried about their jobs and aspects of their leisure activities. What this research suggests is that certain behavioural reactions styles are possibly more generally disease prone because of their behaviour and other psychological characteristics known to predict physical morbidity and mortality.

There are a number of problems with the six typology.

- Classification of individuals into types is difficult.

- Amelang (1997) lists nine flaws from the research and writings on the typology. Most importantly, his research showed that the types are *not* independent.

- Reverse patterns are found in Smedslund (1995).

- Methods of administration can influence classification into types (Grossarth-Maticek et al., 1995).

In summary, the evidence on Grossarth-Maticek's six typology suggests the possible existence of *general disease prone behavioural reaction styles*. In particular, Types I and II appear linked to known major causes of morbidity and mortality, namely CVD and cancer. However, Types I and II also appear to be linked to known behavioural and social risk factors for these conditions. Importantly, the precise nature of how Types I and II, CVD and cancer and these known risk factors are linked is unclear.

Nabi et al. (2008) examined TABP and Grossarth-Maticek's typology, along with aggressiveness, hostility and neurotic hostility as predictors of morbidity and mortality. Their research found only one psychosocial predictor of physical health: neurotic hostility predicted all-cause morbidity and mortality through external causes. They conclude (pp9–10):

> Thus the emphasis in prevention strategies is not on an individual's personality, but on the important processes through which personality is associated with high risk.

This suggests that aspects of *personality processes* might be risk factors for general morbidity and mortality through the mediating mechanisms of emotional and behavioural factors.

Contemporary approaches

The search for disease prone personalities has produced mixed results. The controversies surrounding early research on disease prone personalities has possibly led to a decline in disease-specific research. However, it would be simplistic to dismiss some of the important findings and contributions of this early work. For example, as we saw in the previous section, emotions, cognitions and behavioural reactions were considered in the early research, and this work did draw attention to the impact of psychosocial risk factors on disease and health processes. More contemporary research linking personality and physical health appears to have two features: the emergence of research on personality, physical health and well-being that *explicitly integrates* multiple variables and considers their impact on a range of health outcomes (see Hernandez et al., 2007). Here, you will focus on two issues from this more contemporary research: the growing awareness of the role of behaviours, cognitions and emotions in health and disease processes; and the development of the notion of the Type D personality.

Behaviours and emotions

Contemporary research reflects the recognition that behaviours, thoughts and feelings are important determinants of a range of health outcomes. The research we have considered demonstrates that during the 1990s researchers' doubts grew about the search for a link between specific diseases and specific personality characteristics. Scheier and Bridges (1995) summarise this approach as follows: *the mindset of the field is currently centred around disease foci . . . (and) . . . to be interesting, a particular variable has to be related to one and only one type of illness or disease* (p266). Their analysis of the literature linking *person variables – personality dispositions* that capture more or less stable behaviours, thoughts and feelings and *transient psychological states* or emotions linked to stable dispositions that *come and go* (p255) – found that:

- specific emotions were linked with specific classes of disease (anger and hostility and CVD and emotional suppression with breast cancer);

- a group of emotions they describe as *disengagements* appeared to be linked to a range of disease outcomes – the disengagement emotions included depression, fatalism and pessimism.

These researchers made two other points. First, certain variables *moderate* the link between person variables and health outcomes, namely age, *place in disease course* (p264), and whether the health outcome is acute or chronic. Second, certain changes are needed in the research, including a more coherent and less *disjointed* (p266) theoretical perspective, with prospective research using valid and reliable measures of both person variables and health outcomes, and a recognition that we are unlikely to find a link between specific person variables and specific diseases.

Importantly, the relative failure to support the notion that we can match one personality with one disease has led to a realisation that personality is *part* of a system of reciprocally interacting biopsychosocial factors that influence physical health and not *the* system. Furthermore, what the early research has demonstrated is that personality measures in TABP, Type C personality and the six typology research are actually measures of specific behavioural, cognitive and emotional characteristics that have implications for both health outcomes and behaviours, and this is how personality is most likely to be linked to physical ill health. To some extent, therefore, this field has broadened its focus to a *range of individual differences*.

In particular, individual differences in negative and positive emotions are being used by researchers to explain physical ill health. Gallo and Matthews (2003) consider the role of *negative emotions* in the development of poor physical health. They have developed a *reserve capacity model* that uses socio-economic status (SES), physical health (CVD and all-cause mortality), negative emotions, negative cognitions and health behaviours as important determinants of health outcomes, including general well-being. Their model uses a *meditational hypothesis* that states that *SES is consistently related to cognitive and emotional symptoms, elevations of which do predict worse health outcomes* (p33). Their model has certain key features. First, socio-economic status is linked to diminished psychological resources that protect or buffer the individual against the adverse impact of life stressors on their physical health. This is an individual's *reserve capacity*. Low socio-economic status *shapes interpersonal experiences* (p35) that diminish this reserve capacity, such as negative emotions and thoughts that are known to be linked to worse health outcomes. Second, although Gallo and Matthews (2003) acknowledge that their reserve capacity model does not include all aspects of socio-economic status factors that could adversely affect health (e.g. exposure to environmental hazards such as pollution and crime), their model does at least *incorporate* aspects of individual differences, namely emotionality, which is linked to personality traits in two ways: it acknowledges that personality traits, specifically neuroticism and extraversion, tell us about the characteristic emotions of individuals; and this so-called trait emotionality or affectivity is also assessed using measures of these personality traits – negative trait affectivity is indicated by high levels of trait neuroticism, and high levels of positive trait affectivity are indicated by high levels of trait extraversion (see Chapter 4). The model also considers how social experiences linked to socio-economic status increase the likelihood of the individual experiencing negative emotions, for example given the greater number of life stressors associated with lower socio-economic status.

Lyubomirsky et al. (2005) focus on the role of *positive emotions* in health and disease processes. They argue that positive emotions lead to general success across a range of life domains, and that in turn these positive emotions increase success across life domains, including physical health and well-being. Likewise, they also argue that positive emotions are trait-linked.

Research also demonstrates that personality traits are linked to self-rated health measures such as well-being, happiness and self-rated physical health rather than actual physical health. This suggests that personality might be linked to health cognitions that are important to a range of health outcomes. For example, Korotkov and Hannah (2004) examined the relationship between the FFT and found that these predicted subjective health rather than actual physical health. Hayes and Joseph (2003) found that high levels of neuroticism predicted self-reported subjective well-being, and high levels of extraversion were related to higher levels of self-reported happiness. Williams et al. (2004) examined self-assessed health, including health self-efficacy beliefs and their relationship to personality traits. They found that higher levels of neuroticism were related to poorer health self-efficacy, especially in the presence of low levels of extraversion, and high levels of extraversion were related to engaging in more healthy behaviours and higher health behaviour outcome expectancy scores – such individuals were more likely to expect to be healthy. However, these researchers identified that trait extraversion has a curvilinear relationship with some health cognitions – namely, self-reported symptoms and global health self-ratings. Williams et al. (2004) found that high levels of trait extraversion were related to higher symptom report scores and poorer global health self-ratings.

Type D personality

Type D or distressed personality is characterised by high levels of negative affect (NA) and social inhibition (SI). Denollet (Denollet et al., 1995; 1996) is the researcher most closely associated with the concept, and the key features of Type D are shown in Figure 3.5. Type D personality is characterised by heightened negative emotions but little expression of these (Pelle et al., 2009a). Unlike TABP, the concept of Type D was developed specifically to predict clinical outcomes – such as response to surgery, response to medication and disease progress – and patient-centred outcomes – such as help seeking behaviours. There is evidence that patients with Type D personality are more likely to have between a two- and five-fold increase in poor disease progress, and have poorer quality of life, increased depression and increased anxiety compared to those with non-Type D personalities, *independent* of other medical risk factors and disease severity (Pedersen and Denollet, 2006). Type D personality is also linked to a range of poor health outcomes such as all-cause mortality, cardiac disease, cancer, hypertension, exhaustion, post-traumatic stress disorder, anxiety and depression (Denollet, 2005).

This research has a number of important features. First, the research bridges traditional research on the disease prone personality and more contemporary approaches by focusing on dispositions, especially emotional ones among at-risk individuals. Second, it focuses on the predictive usefulness of personality for not just clinical outcomes but for patient-centred outcomes such as

Figure 3.5: *Type D personality*

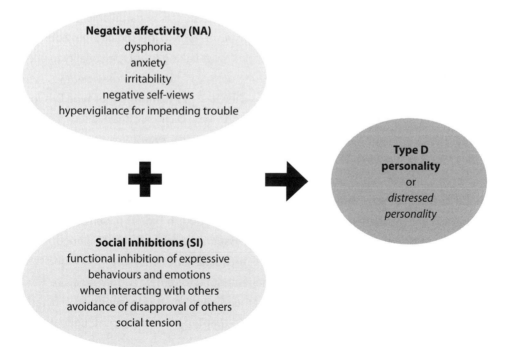

quality of life and emotional well-being. Third, this research acknowledges that global personality traits are important to aspects of CVD and that *It is premature . . . to write off associations between global traits and CHD* (Denollet, 2005, p89). Nevertheless, unlike previous approaches, it includes the adverse consequences of negative emotions and the protective effects of positive emotions.

There is considerable evidence that CVD patients with Type D personality are more likely to experience greater morbidity and mortality than non-Type D patients (Denollet, 2005). Importantly, this impact is shown across CVD patient groups (Pedersen and Denollet, 2006). However, there is disagreement about the extent to which Type D personality is a *new risk factor* among CVD patients (Pedersen and Denollet, 2006). According to Pedersen and Denollet (2006), Type D meets five of the seven criteria that typically constitute a risk factor.

- Its effect is independent of other risk factors.

- It has a prevalence rate among CVD patients of at least 25 per cent and increases risk from poor clinical outcomes by at least two to three times.

- It is dispositional across different patient groups and situations.

- There is a standardised measure for the risk factor known as the Type D Scale-14 or the DS14 (Denollet, 2005).

- We can identify mechanisms that link the risk factor to poor clinical health outcomes.

However, to date Type D personality has not been shown to provide specific diagnostic information about patients, nor is there extensive evidence that it is a modifiable risk factor. Importantly, the high levels of NA and SI characteristic of Type D personality provide two behavioural, cognitive and emotional mechanisms or *pathways* linking Type D personality to poor clinical outcomes among CVD patients: a *psychophysical pathway* and a *behavioural pathway* (see Figure 3.6). This research has two important features. First, the key component of Type D is *low positive affect*. Pelle et al. (2009a) compared Type D and non-Type D chronic heart failure patients and measured positive affect, health status, self-reported cardiac symptoms and feelings of disability. They found that it was low positive affect or anhedonia among Type D and non-Type D patients that predicted poor health status. This suggests that it is positive affect that is protective and NA that is the important component of Type D as a risk factor. Second, the behavioural pathway, in particular consultation behaviour, appears to distinguish Type-D patients. Pelle et al. (2009b) tested a sample of 313 chronic heart failure patients over a six-month period. Their measures focused on consultation behaviour and self-management behaviour. They found that on their 12-item scale a specific consultation management factor emerged that measured the individuals' willingness to contact a doctor because of their symptoms, such as shortness of breath, increased fatigue and weight gain. Their results showed that Type D was the best independent predictor of poorer consultation behaviour over the six months.

Figure 3.6: *Schematic representation of pathways to Type D personality*

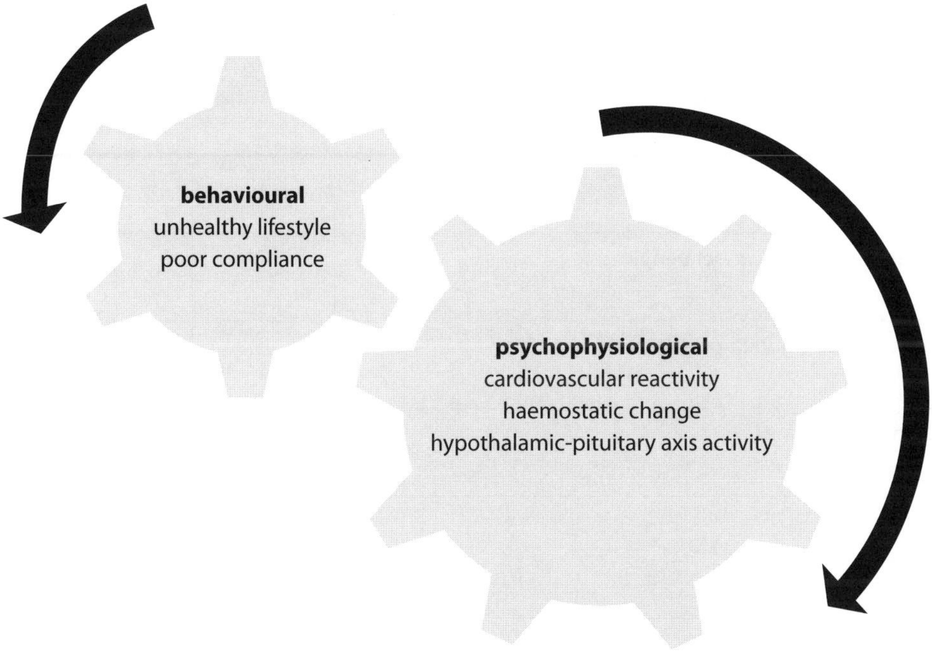

behavioural
unhealthy lifestyle
poor compliance

psychophysiological
cardiovascular reactivity
haemostatic change
hypothalamic-pituitary axis activity

The research on Type D personality raises a number of questions about the existence of the notion of a disease prone personality, and the extent to which this is actually a new approach or merely *old wine in new bottles*. To some extent, the research on Type D personality has some notable features that distinguish it from earlier research on the notion of a disease prone personality. First, it clearly focuses on health outcomes and not merely clinical outcomes, and on the clinical utility of the construct. Second, it focuses on at risk groups and disease progress rather than onset across CVD groups. Third, the focus on negative emotions is reminiscent of the TABP action–emotion complex. However, Type D focuses on SI or how the individual responds to their NA, and researchers are keen to point out that Type D is not merely depression dressed up as a new construct (Pederson and Denollet, 2006). Finally, there is a clear focus in the research on the mechanisms or pathways that link Type D to clinical and health outcomes.

Task ⌐ Denollet (2005) developed the DS14 to measure Type D personality, and this is shown in Figure 3.7. Examine the DS14 items and consider this question: how similar does Type D personality appear to be to both TABP and Type C personality?

Figure 3.7: *The DS14*

Below are a number of statements that people often use to describe themselves. Please read each statement and then write the appropriate number next to that statement to indicate your answer. (0=false, 1=rather false, 2=neutral, 3=rather true, 4=true). There are no right or wrong answers: Your own impression is the only thing that matters.

	0	1	2	3	4
I make contact easily when I meet people					
I often make a fuss about unimportant things					
I often talk to strangers					
I often feel unhappy					
I am often irritated					
I often feel inhibited in social interactions					
I take a gloomy view of things					
I find it hard to start a conversation					
I am often in a bad mood					
I am a closed kind of person					
I would rather keep other people at a distance					
I often find myself worrying about something					
I am often down in the dumps					
When socialising, I don't find the right things to talk about					

Comment

This task should encourage you to think critically about the similarities and differences between Type D personality and earlier conceptions of disease prone personality, such as TABP and Type C personality. In your answers you should ensure you identify the extent to which Type D personality is very reminiscent of TABP, using concepts such as the action–emotion complex.

Critical thinking activity

Personality and psysical health

Critical thinking focus: reflection

Key question: *How can you use academic research on personality, physical health and well-being to understand your own health?*

Research shows that personality is linked both to physical health and to well-being in complex ways. For example, the mechanisms mediating the link between personality and these phenomena are likely to involve behaviours, emotions and thoughts. This research has implications for aspects of the work done by policy makers and health professionals. For example, if evidence suggests that positive emotions can predict physical health and well-being, then this evidence could be used to inform health strategies. This activity involves you reflecting on *your own* behaviours, emotions and thoughts, and how these might be linked to your own physical health and well-being. To do this, please write a brief reflective summary of around 200–400 words in response to the following question.

How have your assumptions about the links between personality, physical health and well-being changed as you have read through this chapter and completed the tasks?

Identify between three to five things you have learnt in this chapter that you could use to make changes to your own physical health and well-being.

Worked example

You might reflect on your assumptions about the existence of a disease prone personality and whether you have actually considered how complex this notion is. You might also reflect on your own psychological phenomena, such as your emotions, and how you respond to these feelings with behaviours and thoughts that have consequences for your physical health and well-being. You might also reflect on how you define your own health and well-being compared to definitions found in the academic literature.

Critical thinking review

This activity involves you reflecting on the content of academic literature, your understanding of this and your own physical health and well-being. This reflection means examining the relevance of academic literature to your own behaviours, emotions and thoughts as well as how you define and make judgements about your physical health and well-being.

Other skills likely to be used in this activity: you will also use written communication skills to express your reflections, and data analysis and evaluation skills to judge the relevance of the academic literature for your own physical health and well-being. You also have to make decisions about how you might like to change your behaviours, emotions and thoughts, and independently judge the potential impact of these changes.

Skill builder activity

Personality and physical health

Transferable skill focus: oral, written and visual communication

Key question: How can you communicate complex information about personality and physical health?

Around the middle of the twentieth century one issue that dominated research on the consequences of personality was the notion of the disease prone personality. However, as we have considered in this chapter, research demonstrates that the link between personality and physical health is complex. Communicating this complex written information to health policy makers is an important task for psychologists. For this activity you should think about how you could develop a poster aimed at health education and promotion policy makers. The poster should be suitable as the focus of a ten-minute oral presentation to this audience. It must summarise the major changes in the research on personality and physical health, and the complex nature of current approaches in the academic literature. The poster must also communicate the implications of this research for health education and promotion policy. Please use the following questions to structure the development of your poster.

- What are the important changes in research on personality and physical health?

- How clear/unclear are the implications of this research for health policy?

- What IT software package(s) could you use to format the poster?

- What visual and other graphic tools could you use in the poster, and what size should the poster be?

- What sections will the poster have?

- How could you structure the ten-minute oral presentation?

- How could you use other written and oral communication to make your poster most effective?

- What are the major challenges when trying to develop such a poster?

Worked example

You could structure your poster around research for and against the existence of a disease prone personality. Alternatively, you could use a chronological approach to structuring your poster that uses the historical development of academic research to communicate how the existence of a disease prone personality has become increasingly challenged.

Skill builder review

This activity helps develop your communication skills and skills of reflection in relation to a specific topic. The activity requires reflection through reviewing the impact of the communication on the audience. This means you are learning to communicate through different media and demonstrate these skills by using them to convey your understanding and use of complex theoretical and empirical data that you have analysed and evaluated. You will also be making decisions about the way this information can be used to solve problems in the real world, and reflecting on your communication skills. The activity requires the development of oral, written and visual communication skills to summarise a large and complex body of work in a brief multimedia presentation. The communication must convey the complexity and practical implications of academic literature in a clear, concise and accessible manner, and this involves making decisions to solve the problems of simplifying complex data. These are important skills that will allow you to become an effective and convincing communicator of complex information to different audiences and different contexts.

Other skills likely to be used in this activity: you will use problem-solving and decision-making skills through the selection of key information and the design of effective communication devices, along with IT skills to construct the poster and a presentation. The activity also involves the use of critical and creative thinking to understand and evaluate the relevant literature, and the development of policy implications requires independent critical and creative thinking, problem solving and decision making.

Assignments

1. Examine critically the view that the disease prone personality is a myth.

2. In what ways are emotions linked to physical health and well-being?

3. Critically consider the extent to which research on personality and physical health can be used to improve the well-being of individuals.

4. Contemporary approaches to personality, physical health and well-being can best be described as merely *old wine in new bottles*. Discuss.

Summary: what you have learned

Research on the disease prone personality, physical health and well-being has developed in the context of a shifting conceptual agenda. Frameworks for understanding health and well-being, concepts used to describe these phenomena and the move towards an integrated psychology of personality have all developed alongside research on this topic. Early research on the disease prone personality, although not faring well in the wake of challenges to its concepts, methods and evidence base, did provide us with some important findings that underpin many contemporary approaches. Importantly, early research has, to some extent, been oversimplified. The current focus on the links between personality, physical health and well-being as circular, reciprocal, complex and existing at multiple levels of analysis is in some respects reminiscent of the early research. What is new is the explicit nature of this focus – on behaviours, emotions and thoughts that mediate the link between personality, physical health and well-being in complex ways. By reflecting on your assumptions about these constructs, your own well-being and by attempting to communicate these complex issues you should have developed a clearer understanding of these issues.

Further reading

Denollet, J (2005) Standard assessment of negative affectivity, social inhibition, and Type D Personality. *Psychosomatic Medicine*: 67: 89–97.

This paper provides a description of how the Type D Scale-14 (DS14) was developed, and some of the individual differences related to Type D personality. It also contains a brief overview of the features of Type D and its known health and well-being correlates.

Friedman, HS and Booth-Kewley, S (1987) Personality, Type A behavior, and coronary heart disease: the role of emotional expression. *Journal of Personality and Social Psychology*, 53(4): 783–92.

This paper summarises the research on TABP and illustrates the complexity contained in early discussions of TABP as an action-emotion complex.

Hansen, PE, Floderus, B, Frederiksen, K and Johansen, C (2005) Personality traits, health behavior, and risk for cancer: a prospective study of a Swedish twin cohort. *Cancer*, 103(5): 1082–91.

This is a report of a large-scale epidemiological study of the link between personality traits and the onset of cancer using longitudinal data across 1974–1999. It is an excellent example of contemporary research on Type C personality in comparison to older research.

Jenkins, CD, Rosenman, RH and Friedman, M (1968) Replicability of rating the coronary-prone behaviour pattern. *British Journal of Preventative and Social Medicine,* 22: 16–22.

This paper from seminal researchers in the field of TABP provides an excellent and readable illustration of the early research and how the original concept of TABP has, to some extent, been oversimplified. It works well if read in conjunction with Friedman and Booth-Kewley (1987).

Ryff, C (1989) Happiness is everything, or is it? Explorations on the meaning of psychological well-being. *Journal of Personality and Social Psychology*, 57(6): 1069–82.

This is an early discussion of the many different ways that psychological well-being can be defined by a key researcher in the area. An outline of Ryff's six dimensions of well-being is given, and these are useful to compare with features of the different types of disease prone personalities and the Grossarth-Maticek typology.

Useful websites

www.bps.org.uk/dhp/ (British Psychological Society Division of Health Psychology)

The site gives you access to information on professional developments in health psychology in the UK. It provides useful insights into the varied ways in which psychological principles are applied to a range of health behaviours. As you work through the resources available here you should consider how this field of the discipline considers individual differences in its research.

www.dh.gov.uk/en/Publicationsandstatistics/index.htm (Department of Health (UK) publications)

You can search this resource for current government health initiatives, and the information here can be examined in contrast to the psychological literature on the links between personality and physical health.

www.apa.org/about/division/div38.aspx (American Psychological Association Health Psychology Division)

The Newsletter of the Division – The Health Psychologist – can be accessed from this link, and this provides information on current research developments. You can use this link in the same manner as the British Psychological Society Division of Health Psychology link, that is, to consider how individual differences are considered in this field of the discipline.

Chapter 4

Atypical personality traits and mental health

Learning outcomes

By the end of this chapter you should:

- understand and be able to discuss, critically, ways in which atypical personality traits, mental disorder and mental health have been defined;

- be able to consider, critically, how mental health and disorder have been linked to the FFT and the dark triad traits;

- understand and be able to evaluate the continuity hypothesis of personality disorders;

- have developed your critical and creative thinking and decision-making skills by completing a literature analysis task, and planning how to communicate this.

Introduction

In this chapter you will consider how personality traits are linked to both mental health and disorder by focusing on five questions.

- What are the different ways in which traits *could* be linked to mental health and disorder?

- How have we defined atypical personality traits, mental disorder and mental health?

- What evidence is there that traits, mental disorder and mental health are linked?

- What are personality disorders, and what do we mean by the continuity hypothesis of these disorders?

- Do psychologists face professional and ethical issues when conducting research in this area?

The overarching goal of this chapter is for you to start thinking critically and creatively about what the research on personality traits, mental health and disorder actually shows about how these constructs are linked. Doing this means analysing what such links mean.

Links between personality traits, mental health and mental disorder

Frequently, personality traits, mental health and disorder are said to be linked because they are related *statistically*. This is usually demonstrated in correlation coefficients between trait scores and scores on some measure of 'mental health'. Research on trait anger illustrates what is meant by this type of statistical relationship. As a construct *anger* is used to refer to a transient emotional state that is associated with specific behaviours, cognitions and other emotions along with autonomic bodily responses (Kassinove and Sukhodolsky, 1995). The emotion of anger is described as a *natural, biologically necessary primary emotion innate to all human beings* (Gardner and Moore, 2008, p897) and can range from mild irritation to fury or even rage (Spielberger, 1988). For some individuals, therefore, their experience of anger can be *problematic* (Deffenbacher, 1993, p49). Gardner and Moore (2008, p898) summarise this difference as follows:

> when generalized to context beyond those in which it is likely to be useful and adaptive, this otherwise normal emotion can lead to chronically heightened arousal and is associated with dysfunctional and problematic behaviour.

Such anger has been described as *generalised* and *chronic* (Deffenbacher, 1993) and *disordered* (Eckhardt and Deffenbacher, 1995); and across a variety of measures (Eckhardt et al., 2004) this type of anger is also referred to as *trait anger* because it typifies an enduring characteristic of some individuals. Anger is a complex construct – it is a transient primary or secondary emotional response, it is a trait, and it has consequences. It is therefore important that we use psychometrically robust tools to measure the construct.

Task

Hawthorne et al. (2006) developed the DAR5, a five-item measure of trait anger towards others. Using a response format ranging from 0 (not at all) to 4 (very much) respondents are asked to rate how well each statement describes how they 'feel'. The maximum score on the DAR5 is 20 – indicating high levels of trait anger – and the minimum score is 0. Individually or in groups, examine each item on DAR5 and consider the following question: what does the item suggest about the characteristics of individuals with high levels of trait anger?

These are the five items.

I often find myself angry at people or situations.

When I get angry, I get really mad.

When I get angry, I stay angry.

When I get angry at someone, I want to hit or clobber the person.

My anger prevents me from getting along with people.

Comment

Each item describes features of anger when it has consequences for how the individual functions. For example, across all five items high levels of trait anger are characterised by intense and sustained feelings of anger at many things in the environment resulting in the urge to commit an act of physical aggression towards the perceived source of the anger. Unsurprisingly, this has adverse consequences for interpersonal relationships, and high levels of trait anger are related to a range of problematic behaviours, such as alcohol misuse, and measures of poor mental health such as depression and anxiety (Deffenbacher, 1993).

Statistical relationships between traits and measures of mental health, such as those shown on the research on trait anger, suggest a number of possible links between these constructs, as shown in Figure 4.1.

The first link is, as already stated, statistical: traits, as continuous variables that describe relatively enduring characteristic patterns of behaviours, feelings and thoughts (see Chapters 1 and 2), can be used to predict differences between individuals, such as who is likely to experience better or worse mental health or a mental disorder. Certainly, some traits do appear to be good predictors or *indicators* of mental health constructs among the non-clinical or general population and among clinical groups. Using traits in this descriptive way is similar to what Cervone (2005) refers to as the *have* approach to personality – traits tell us something about characteristics that different persons or groups of individuals *have*, or inter-individual variation within a population. Evidence shows the predictive power of traits, for these and other psychological and social variables can be the same, if not greater than, socio-economic status or cognitive ability (Roberts et al., 2007).

However, although researchers do acknowledge that traits are useful indicators of psychological phenomena (Caprara and Cervone, 2000; Cervone, 2005) statistical relationships linking traits, mental health and disorder have limitations (Cervone, 2005). For example, traits are surface descriptions of characteristic differences between persons or groups of individuals. These differences are aggregated responses of groups of individuals to items on scales. Therefore, at one level, they are numerical shorthand for inter-individual variation. However, we cannot assume that

Figure 4.1: *Links between traits, mental health and mental disorder*

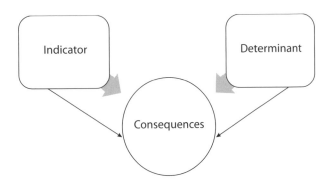

they tell us anything about either the mechanisms underlying these surface descriptions, the processes that link traits and mental health, or about the behaviour, feelings and thoughts of individual cases.

The second link is that traits might indirectly or even directly *determine* mental health and disorder. In this sense, traits might be regarded as *determinants* of mental health and disorder. This might be plausible for the following reasons.

- Research on this topic frequently uses statistical techniques, such as regression and factor analysis, that build on patterns of correlations between trait scores and scores on measures of mental health. These techniques build statistical models of how these constructs are linked. These organised summaries of scores can be used to identify how trait scores *appear to be determinants* of scores on measures of mental health. In terms of validity, such statistical models have a degree of *face validity* – they appear to be plausible explanations of the possible determinants of mental health and disorder.

- Research demonstrates that behaviours, feelings and thoughts that are related to traits might have direct or indirect consequences for mental health and disorder. Again, these are statistical patterns that imply that they might have more than merely face validity. Research on the FFT typifies this work.

This second link is perhaps even more controversial than the first. This is because *statistical* determination does not necessarily tell us about *actual* determination. It is one thing arguing that traits predict statistically mental health and disorder, but it is very different to argue that traits determine causally these complex psychological phenomena. Statistical models built on correlation coefficients cannot be regarded as actual evidence of causation (Boorsboom, 2006; Cervone, 2005). Furthermore, measures of mental health and disorder are themselves surface descriptions just like traits. We must also remember that the links between traits, mental health and disorder are likely to involve complex reciprocal interactions between these and other constructs such as socio-economic status.

The indicator and determinant links are not mutually exclusive. For example, they represent different levels of analysis of the same or similar phenomena. The indicator proposition is, perhaps, a necessary first stage in the development of the determinant proposition. Cervone (2005) argues that research might eventually demonstrate that traits do actually tell us something about the underlying mechanisms of personality. However, we cannot assume this and at present we cannot support this.

However, given the limitations of the first two possible links, a third compromise proposition that more broadly describes the link between personality traits, mental health and disorder is perhaps a better starting point for thinking critically about what such links mean. This compromise proposition states that personality traits appear to have consequences for individuals across a range of life domains because they provide information about how different persons and groups of individuals characteristically *self-regulate* or how *people control their thoughts, feelings, and behaviours* (Hoyle, 2006, p1507). This encompasses the first two links as possible. For example, the consequences of traits for mental health and disorder might be at the level of statistical indicators or they might be at the level of causal determinants through trait-related behaviours, feelings and thoughts. This is consistent with Caprara and Cervone's (2000) integrative perspective to personality and the *3-d* approach you have been encouraged to take to individual differences psychology (see Chapter 1): traits are the surface tendency part, but not the whole, of personality. Nevertheless, traits have consequences for self-regulation. The important point is that we need to interpret with caution data showing links between traits, mental health and disorder. We must avoid over-interpreting what are essentially statistical relationships and models as evidence of the actual mechanisms linking these constructs.

Task

How should we interpret the meaning of trait scores? This is an important question that runs through all three links. This task is designed to help your understanding of why we must interpret trait scores cautiously. It is especially the case when interpreting whether a trait has consequences for complex psychological phenomena such as mental health and disorder. Either individually or in groups, you need to select one of the FFT shown in Figure 4.2. It does not matter which trait you select for this task, but try to choose one that you believe has explicit relevance to how you regulate your own behaviour, such as conscientiousness (Hoyle, 2006).

Now, assume that on each trait you can achieve a maximum score of 60 and a minimum of 12, and that on each of the six facets of each trait you can achieve a maximum score of 10 (indicating the facet is highly typical of you) or a minimum of 2 (indicating the facet is not at all typical of you) – this scaling is hypothetical so you do not need to link it to actual measures of the FFT. Next, imagine you have achieved a score of 40 out of a possible 60 on your chosen trait, suggesting that you have self-reported relatively high levels of this characteristic. Then, look at the six facets for your chosen trait and ask yourself if there are different ways in which you could achieve your score of 40. Try listing some of these.

Comment

You could use a suitcase analogy here – two individuals might have the same sort of suitcases and they might weigh roughly the same, but their contents are not necessarily identical. Likewise, two individuals could achieve the same score of 40 on extraversion, but one's score of 40 could be made up mostly of near maximum scores on gregariousness, positive emotions, and warmth. The

Figure 4.2: *Five Factor traits (FFT)*

openness versus closedness to experience	conscientiousness versus lack of direction	extraversion versus introversion	agreeableness versus antagonism	neuroticism versus emotional stability
Ideas (curious)	Competence (efficient)	Gregariousness (sociable)	Trust (forgiving)	Anxiety (tense)
Fantasy (imaginative)	Order (organised)	Assertiveness (forceful)	Straightforwardness (not demanding)	Angry hostillity (irritable)
Aesthetics (artistic)	Dutifulness (not careless)	Activity (energetic)	Altruism (warmth)	Depression (not contented)
Actions (wide interests)	Achievement striving (thorough)	Excitement-seeking (adventurous)	Compliance (not stubborn)	Self-consciousness (shy)
Feelings (excitable)	Self-discipline (not lazy)	Positive emotions (enthusiastic)	Modesty (not show-off)	Impulsiveness (moody)
Values (unconventional)	Deliberation (not impulsive)	Warmth (outgoing)	Tender-mindedness (sympathetic)	Vulnerability (not self-confident)

other person's score of 40 could be made up of mostly near maximum scores on assertiveness, excitement-seeking, and activity. As facets are typically regarded as lower-level behaviour-like dimensions of traits (see Chapter 2), these two individuals are likely to behave in different ways that might have consequences for how they manage themselves despite achieving the same score on extraversion. Try to identify some of these behaviour differences and their possible consequences for how you might behave in different situations. Remember, different facet profiles can produce the same trait score. This issue applies to self-report scales in general across individual differences psychology. For example, in the previous task on trait anger you considered the DAR5. With this scale, it is also possible to achieve the same trait anger score but by indicating that different features of anger characterise how you feel.

Definitions of atypical personality traits, mental disorder and mental health

Having identified that the links between personality traits and mental health and disorder can take different but equally complex forms, we will now start to tackle how we define the meaning of concepts central to this chapter, and these are *atypical personality traits*, *mental disorder* and *mental health*.

Atypical personality traits

In this chapter we have three ways of defining what is meant by atypical personality traits. First, the *intensity definition* states that typical traits can become atypical because when they reach certain intensities and in certain combinations and conditions, they indicate or even determine mental health and disorder. Second, the *dark triad definition* is based on research that traits originally used to describe the personality characteristics of individuals with certain personality disorders – namely, the traits of psychopathy, narcissism and Machiavellianism – and their consequences can be observed and measured in the general population. Dark triad traits can be described as atypical traits because they are linked to personality disorder characteristics, and they are related statistically with psychological phenomena that might affect adversely the psychological and interpersonal functioning of individuals. Ironically, evidence suggests these atypical traits are perhaps more typical statistically, than first thought. Finally, the *personality disorders definition* states that typical personality traits can be used to describe and diagnose atypical personality in the form of personality disorders. This is the central argument of the *continuity hypothesis*.

These definitions have three features.

- Each specifies a relationship between traits and mental health and disorder.

- Each implies *continuity* between typical and atypical traits.

- Each acknowledges that traits have consequences for how individuals regulate themselves.

Many individuals manage to self-regulate themselves in an adaptive way while some are less successful at this (Caprara and Cervone, 2000). Traits can be described as atypical when they predict less than successful self-regulation and adjustment (Hoyle, 2006). Trait intensity, poorer mental health and mental disorder are evidence of this less than optimal self-regulation and maladjustment (Hoyle, 2006; McCrae et al., 2005a). The research on trait anger illustrates this. Anger as a normal emotional experience is atypical when it becomes a chronic, sustained, intense and characteristic response to events or people in the environment. This general anger (Deffenbacher, 1993) has a range of adverse consequences for individuals and those around them. This general pattern is demonstrated in research that analyses the statistical relationship between scores of trait anger and scores on measures of these consequences.

Mental disorder

As the previous section showed, psychologists can use the same term – atypical – to mean different things when applied to personality traits. Psychologists are also sensitive to the use of terms such as atypical when applied to psychological functioning and mental disorder because of the pejorative overtones of this and related terms such as *abnormal* and *pathological*. This sensitivity has a long history (Smith, 1961), and is a sensitivity shared by other professionals interested in mental health and disorder (Gabbard, 2005). Furthermore, academics and clinicians in different disciplines continue to disagree about how we define mental disorder. A major difficulty here is developing a definition that is both based on 'facts' or evidence about the nature of mental disorder and is value free. Houts (2001) argues that definitions of mental disorder can never actually be value free because *demarcating mental disorders from normal variations in behaviour* (p1100) is difficult, as these constructs are, to some extent, socially constructed. Nevertheless, in this chapter we will use the term *mental disorder* to be consistent with the terminology used in much of the relevant research and the main classification systems. Despite these issues, we still need a working definition of mental disorder that does two things: acknowledges the sensitivities and difficulties of using and defining the construct of mental disorder while at the same time including the more useful features of the main definitions of the construct. The main definitions and some of their key features described by Wakefield (1992) are given in Table 4.1.

The seven definitions shown in Table 4.1 tend to focus on mental disorder as any condition that is unusual, and that has distressing maladaptive consequences for the individual, thus undermining

Table 4.1: *Definitions of mental disorder*

Definition	Features
Statistical deviance	• Any physical or mental diseases that are quantitatively infrequent • Statistical frequency indicates absence of disorder • Health is absence of disorder and qualitatively distinct from disorder • Used in main classification systems (*Diagnostic and Statistical Manual* and *International Classification of Diseases*) and linked to the biomedical or medical model
Social disapproval	• Disorders are any unusual or deviant behaviour • Disorders are devices used to exert and justify medical power (Szas, 1974)
Pure value	• Definitions of disorder are never value free • Reflects social norms, values and ideals
Biological disadvantage	• Disorder is any infrequent condition that has disadvantageous consequences for the reproductive fitness of the individual • Evolutionary theory
Unacceptable distress, disability or dysfunction	• Disorders are conditions that lead to behavioural, psychological or biological dysfunctions that have consequences for the individuals such as poor functioning and the experience of unacceptable distress
Pragmatic	• Disorders are those treated by mental health professionals
Harmful dysfunction	• Wakefield (1992) defines disorders as having: *value dimension* (they deprive or limit the individual's access to social and cultural benefits); *fact dimension* (they are the consequence of flawed or failed); *mental mechanisms* (that have an evolutionary function) (p385)

how they function. For example, the *statistical deviance definition* is evident in the main classificatory systems used to diagnose mental disorders, such as the *Diagnostic and Statistical Manual* (*DSM*) and the *International Classification of Diseases* (*ICD*). However, this definition has limitations. Not all disorders, physical or mental, are statistically infrequent. Also, not all statistically infrequent conditions or behaviours constitute a disorder. This definition also implies that disorder is deviance and that conformity is valued. The *social disapproval definition* also regards unusual behaviours as disorder. However, this definition describes mental disorder as those unusual or deviant conditions and behaviours identified by medicine to exert and justify medical power. Linked to this is the work of Thomas Szas (1974), who argued that mental disorder does not actually exist because it is simply a device used by authorities to control deviant behaviours. However, this definition ignores the actual self-reported distress experienced by individuals with mental disorders, and the ways in which disorders can compromise how individuals function across a range of life domains. This definition is, to some extent, more of a critique of the notion of objective definitions of mental disorder than a clear delineation of what it is.

In this chapter *The International Classification of Diseases* (ICD-10; World Health Organization, 2007, p11) definition is preferred because it meets our two criteria:

> The term 'disorder' is used throughout the classification, so as to avoid even greater problems inherent in the use of terms such as 'disease' and illness'. 'Disorder' is not an exact term, but it is used here to imply the existence of a clinically recognisable set of symptoms or behaviour associated in most cases with distress and with interference with personal functions. Social deviance or conflict alone, without personal dysfunction, should not be included in mental disorder as defined here.

These definition issues are important. An agreed-upon unproblematic definition of mental disorder is elusive. It is therefore important to remember that the main classificatory systems for diagnosing, and therefore *defining*, mental disorders are not value free. Thus the diagnosis of mental disorders is difficult, and this has led to criticisms of the validity and reliability of the main classification systems and how we *differentiate* mental disorder from mental health (May, 2007; Movahedi, 1975).

Task — One way to appreciate how difficult it is to define and therefore diagnose any mental disorder is to examine the classification systems themselves. Such systems also highlight the disagreements about definitions of mental disorder. For this task you should read the introduction to one of the main classification systems – the *ICD-10 Classification of mental and behavioural disorders* (World Health Organization, 2007, pp8–23) available at www.who.int/classifications/icd/en/bluebook.pdf. When reading this, identify any content that you think demonstrates that the authors are aware of the complexities of defining and diagnosing mental disorder, and that this is not value free. You do not need to read all of the introduction – you can stop when you feel you have at least *five* different illustrations of the authors' awareness of the complexities of diagnosis.

Comment

This task should help you develop an evidence-based understanding of some of the current problems surrounding the diagnosis of mental disorder. It should also provide you with specific examples that illustrate that the diagnosis of mental disorder is a complex process that involves clinicians using not only evidence (e.g. signs and symptoms of behaviour) but their *interpretations* of such evidence. For example, in this section of the document clinicians are urged to use *their own judgment* (p8) when considering symptom duration in the diagnostic process because the *ICD-10* criteria regarding this are *general guidelines* and not *strict requirements*. Likewise, clinicians are asked to use their own judgements when deciding if a diagnosis of a specific mental disorder is *confident* rather than *partial* or *provisional*. Finally, the activity should demonstrate that the diagnosis of mental disorder is a decision-making process. For example, clinicians using the system have *flexibility* when deciding which diagnostic category to use because some disorders are *notoriously difficult* (p8) to diagnose and differentiate. All of these examples appear on a single page of the section specified, and suggest that the authors have *some* awareness of the complexities of defining and diagnosing mental disorder.

Mental health

What is missing from many definitions of mental disorder, including the *ICD-10* definition, is a clear definition of *mental health*. The concept is often defined by default using the statistical deviance concept, and the biomedical model of mental and physical disorders expresses this most clearly: health is the absence of disorder, and health and disorder, whether physical or psychological, are qualitatively distinct discontinuous constructs (Kihlstrom, 2004; see Chapter 3). However, in this chapter you are encouraged to use a different approach developed by Keyes (2005; also Keyes et al., 2002). This approach challenges the absence of disorder definition of mental health and is also based on evidence that personality traits indicate mental health.

Keyes's (2005) Complete State Model of Health (CSMH) defines mental health as not merely the absence of mental disorder. It has two assumptions. The first is that health and disorder are separate but correlated dimensions that both contribute to mental health. The second states that mental health is the result of how we function in relation to our social values. Mental health therefore has two components – mental health and mental disorder – that form a continuous dimension with *illness* and *health* at opposite poles on this continuum (see Figure 4.3).

Complete mental health means the individual is free of a diagnosable mental disorder and *flourishing*. This is indicated by hedonia – positive emotions – and positive functioning – the person is functioning well both psychologically and socially. Importantly, even if an individual is without a diagnosis of a mental disorder, they do not always *flourish*. In fact, they could be *languishing* or have low levels of hedonia and positive functioning. Keyes (2002, p607) summarises this definition of mental health as follows:

> *The mental health continuum consists of complete and incomplete mental health. Adults with complete mental health are flourishing in life with high*

Figure 4.3:
Complete State Model of Health

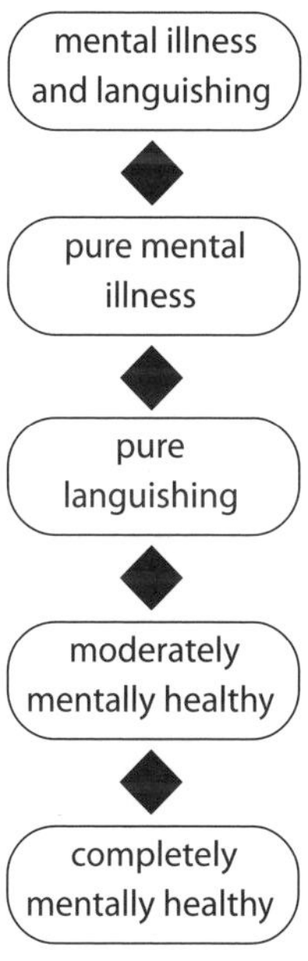

mental illness and languishing

◆

pure mental illness

◆

pure languishing

◆

moderately mentally healthy

◆

completely mentally healthy

levels of well-being. To be flourishing, then, is to be filled with positive emotion and to be functioning well psychologically and socially. Adults with incomplete mental health are languishing in life with low well-being. Thus, languishing may be conceived of as emptiness and stagnation, constituting a life of quiet despair that parallels accounts of individuals who describe themselves and life as 'hollow', 'empty', 'a shell', and 'a void'.

The CSMH makes clear predictions about differences between individuals – in other words, individual differences – in terms of their functioning. This is measured in various ways, for example using scores on scales that assess psychosocial functioning, self-reported mental health, positive and negative emotions, social well-being and mental disorder using *DSM* categories.

Keyes et al. (2002) tested the model with 3,032 participants from the Midlife in the United States Survey (MIDUS), a panel of participants from the United States aged 25–74 years. Using a mixture of telephone interviews and self-completion scales, they assessed the presence of mental disorder in the past 12 months using the *DSM-III* categories of mild depressive episode, general anxiety disorder, panic disorder and **alcohol dependence**. They also assessed participants' general mental health over the previous 30 days, along with their psychological and social well-being and psychosocial functioning – a broad measure of the influence of health on daily life activities, coping and resilience. Importantly, the research also measured the FFT.

The research produced the following key results.

- Participants' mental health and mental disorder were separate but related constructs.

- The majority of the sample, around 60 per cent, were experiencing only moderate mental health, and roughly equal proportions of the sample were languishing (19 per cent) and flourishing (18 per cent).

- Flourishing participants were least likely to have a mental disorder, and those with complete mental health had the best occupational and psychosocial functioning.

- Participants who were classified as having pure mental illness, or the presence of a mental disorder but not languishing, had the poorest overall functioning.

- High levels of neuroticism and, to a lesser extent, low levels of extraversion and conscientiousness predicted poor subjective and psychological well-being ahead of age and education as predictors. Agreeableness was not a clear predictor of mental health in their research.

Using this definition of mental health is important because Keyes et al. (2002) argue that traits *contour* mental health (p1019) along with sociodemographic factors. Traits have consequences for individual's self-regulation and thus have the potential to enhance or compromise well-being and health in general without necessarily resulting in mental disorder. Another important feature of this work is that the researchers found around 19 per cent of their sample were languishing but without a mental disorder. Such a proportion suggests that, while mental disorder is statistically infrequent, we cannot assume mental health is statistically normative. Individuals without a diagnosis of a mental disorder are not necessarily flourishing or experiencing complete mental health, and certain traits can be used to predict this. Keyes et al. (2002) describe this phenomenon as overlooked but *socially important*.

Evidence of the link between personality traits, mental health and mental disorder

The Five Factor Model

Theoretical and empirical evidence from Keyes et al. (2002) suggests that when some of the FFT reach certain intensities, mental health is compromised: flourishing and languishing mental health are predicted by these traits with the exception of agreeableness. Highly neurotic and introverted individuals with low levels of conscientiousness and openness are likely to experience compromised or languishing mental health, and some mental disorders are related to languishing. Importantly, individuals at opposite poles on the FFT experience better or flourishing mental health. The issue here is why the FFT traits are linked to languishing and flourishing mental health as they appear to be.

Revelle and Scherer (2009) argue that emotions mediate the statistical relationship between traits and mental health because traits are, essentially, *emotional dispositions*. This is consistent with Lyubomirsky et al. (2005), who argued that positive emotions lead to success in life, including optimal physical (see Chapter 3) and mental health. These, in turn, enhance positive emotions further. Central to this complex reciprocal interactive process is the assertion that positive emotions increase approach behaviour (Diener et al., 2006) and the likelihood of life successes because they expand the learning opportunities that individuals have to develop successful life skills.

Traits are emotional dispositions, therefore certain emotions are *trait congruent* (Revelle and Scherer, 2009, p1) or typify certain traits. This has led researchers to use neuroticism as a measure of trait emotionality, with high levels indicating trait negative affectivity characteristic of anxiety. High levels of extraversion are used as a measure of trait positive affectivity. Importantly, Revelle and Scherer (2009) argue that individual differences in trait congruent affect processes are the bases for the difference between typical and atypical personality. Reisenzein and Weber (2007) continue this explanation. They argue that the trait taxonomies used to describe typical personality, such as the FFT, are implicitly and explicitly about emotions. Emotional stability is indicated by the intensities and combinations of certain traits. Specifically, high levels of neuroticism and low levels of extraversion, but to some extent all of the FFT, perhaps with the exception of conscientiousness, are linked to positive and negative affect. This point about conscientiousness is interesting, given that Hoyle (2006) identified conscientiousness as an important indicator of self-regulation, and Keyes et al. (2002) found that trait agreeableness rather than conscientiousness was the poorest predictor of mental health. There is also evidence that neuroticism and extraversion predict momentary self-reports of negative and positive emotions respectively, with the FFT being good predictors of variability in such emotions (Yik and Russell, 2001). Overall, this evidence suggests the FFT of introversion–extraversion and neuroticism are *especially* important indicators and therefore predictors of whether an individual is flourishing or languishing in Keyes et al.'s (2002) terms.

Evidence also shows that certain of the FFT predict mental disorder. Kotov (2006) found that neuroticism predicts much mental disorder, although its predictive power is strongest for disorders typified by subjective distress and dysphoria rather than those typified by avoidance behaviours. There is also evidence that the FFT predict the likelihood of developing a mood disorder and the stability of depressive symptoms in the general population. For example, Watson et al. (2005) examined temperament using neuroticism as a measure of negative emotionality and extraversion as a measure of positive emotionality. They found that low levels of extraversion predicted higher levels of anhedonia, symptoms of depression and higher social anxiety. High levels of neuroticism have also been found to predict the maintenance of depressive symptoms over a period of one year, along with low levels of agreeableness, extraversion and conscientiousness (Chien et al., 2007).

McCrae et al. (2005a) provide a framework for explaining *why* the FFT and mental health and disorder are statistically linked in these ways. They argue that when the FFT reach certain intensities they predict *characteristic maladaptations* that have consequences for mental health and possibly the likelihood that a mental disorder will develop. Certain environmental factors can lead typical traits to reach certain intensities and in this sense *become* atypical. When this happens, atypical traits can lead to problems of daily living. They use the concepts of *basic tendencies* and *characteristic adaptations* to explain the link. Basic tendencies are trait- or facet-level characteristics of individuals that are biologically hard-wired aspects of personality, or what could be called typical traits. Characteristic adaptations are psychological phenomena that characterise an individual but have developed as the individual interacts with the environment. It is these characteristic adaptations that influence adjustment. Maladjustment is observed when characteristic adaptations are less than optimal and consist of enduring beliefs, coping skills, social skills and habits – what could be called atypical traits – that have consequences for mental health. Importantly, maladaptive characterisations can lead to *personality-related problems, and, if these are sufficiently severe, a personality disorder* (p272).

This account has a number of important features.

- It defines atypical personality in terms of how traits develop across the lifespan of the individual: typical traits can become atypical because of this process and we identify this when we evaluate both characteristic adaptations and their consequences.

- Characteristic maladaptations are what we frequently measure as the correlates of traits such as specific behaviours, feelings and thoughts, and these are both indicators and potential determinants of mental health problems and even personality disorder. In other words, characteristics adaptations and maladaptations are, essentially, the observable manifestations of hard-wired basic tendencies of personality. This suggests continuity between typical and atypical personality and mental health and disorders. However, the precise mechanisms involved in these links and the process by which personality disorder could develop in this framework are unclear.

- The FFT indicate and therefore can be used to predict personality-related problems of living independent of the clinical status of the individual because traits are not intrinsically problematic for mental health.

McCrae et al.'s (2005a) paper is also interesting because of the research method used. They analysed existing scales of problems of living to test their framework. This approach is based on the rationale that although lists of such problems associated with mental disorders exist, an analysis of the FFT and their facets in relation to these measures has not been completed. By examining the items used to measure the FFT, we can list the daily living problems people *believe* individuals experience at the two poles (high or low) of each trait or trait facet. The daily living problems were identified from a search of the relevant literature on personality trait consequences and using five scales of daily living problems. McCrae et al. (2005a) do acknowledge that traits are surface descriptions and that we can only access these characteristic adaptations or how we engage with and conduct our daily lives. Indeed, the items on the NEO-PI R look like problems of daily living. They therefore conducted an analysis of five measures of problems of living in the domains of physical health, life tasks and social support by asking judges to identify whether the items on these scales were relevant to the high or low poles of the FFT or any of their facets. Using this process they identified items that judges agreed were relevant to the FFT or their facets, checking for inter-rater agreement along the way. Overall, the researchers found that certain poles or intensities of all FFT were linked to daily living problems. They describe these as the *density of problems of living* associated with the FFT. The greatest density was linked to high levels of neuroticism and low levels of all the other traits. This research suggests that the theoretical content of the FFT, and particularly neuroticism and extraversion, are judged to be relevant to what Keyes et al. (2002) would describe as both languishing mental health, flourishing mental health and mental disorder.

The dark triad traits

So far, we have considered how typical traits, such as the FFT, are linked to mental health and disorder. An important issue to emerge from this research is that no trait is intrinsically atypical: traits can become atypical when they reach a certain intensity and when they co-occur with other traits. Another way in which atypical personality traits are linked to mental health can be found in the growing research on traits originally regarded as atypical because they are observed in clinical populations with a diagnosis of a personality disorder. Increasingly, these traits are being measured and their correlates observed, in general populations. The traits in question, often referred to as the *dark triad traits*, are *psychopathy*, *narcissism* and *Machiavellianism*. The dark triad traits appear to be related statistically to the FFT (Paulhus and Williams, 2002; Vernon et al., 2008), with the most consistent finding being that all three are linked to low levels of agreeableness (Jacobwitz and Egan, 2006).

There is evidence that the dark triad traits and the behaviours, feelings and thoughts they are related to can be observed in the general population. For example, Johns and van Os (2001) reviewed the literature on the distribution of the symptoms of hallucinations and delusions associated with schizophrenia using *DSM-IV* (American Psychiatric Association, 1994) and *ICD-10* (World Health Organization, 2007). They claim that evidence suggests these psychotic experiences are on a continuum with *normal* experiences and reported by individuals without a diagnosis of schizophrenia. Research has also shown that the FFT are linked to psychoticism (Ross et al., 2004) and can be used to estimate psychoticism in the general population (Benning et al., 2005).

Other research on the dark triad traits in the general population suggests that these atypical traits are perhaps less statistically atypical than first thought. The research on narcissism illustrates this. According to Emmons (1987) narcissism typified the *me generation* of the 1970s but *showed no signs of abatement in the 1980s*. General measures of narcissism other than those afforded by using diagnostic frameworks such as the *DSMs* and the *ICD* have developed since the late 1970s. For example, the Narcissistic Personality Inventory (NPI) (Raskin and Hall, 1979), a self-report scale developed using *DSM-III* diagnostic criteria for narcissistic personality disorder, captures the main characteristics of narcissism. Individuals showing high levels of this personality trait display:

- inflated beliefs about their leadership ability and authority, and are likely to describe themselves as good leaders and enjoying exercising authority over others;

- self-absorption and self-admiration, and are likely to report enjoyment in displaying their body or looking at themselves in the mirror;

- superiority, arrogance and grandiosity, and report believing they always know what they are doing and that others can learn from them;

- exploitativeness and entitlement, and report ease in manipulating others and envy of the good fortune of others.

Narcissism is now regarded as both a clinical and non-clinical *entity* (Emmons, 1987) that can be both adaptive and maladaptive. For example, Foster and Campbell (2007) described it as a dimensional aspect of typical personality and asserted that individuals without a diagnosis of mental disorder can have similar narcissistic-like illusory self-perceptions and biases. Research on The Narcissistic Personality Inventory (NPI) (Raskin and Terry, 1988) is growing as researchers attempt to test the validity of this tool (del Rosario and White, 2005) and develop short forms of this (Ames et al., 2006). Importantly, narcissism has been linked to the FFT in studies of non-clinical groups. Kubarych et al. (2004) tested the relationship between 338 university students' scores on the Narcissistic Personality Inventory and on the FFT. They found that high levels of narcissism were related to high levels of extraversion and openness, but to low levels of agreeableness and neuroticism. Narcissism is now regarded as having a *bright* and *dark* side (Paunonen et al., 2006), with both maladaptive and adaptive consequences for the individual (Reidy et al., 2008). This reconceptualisation of narcissism as possibly adaptive is further supported by its prevalence both in specific occupational groups and in reports that its prevalence in the general population has grown across the period 1979–2006 (Twenge et al., 2008). Young and Pinsky (2006) examined the scores on the NPI of 200 celebrities and 200 MBA students. They found that the NPI scores of the celebrities were significantly higher than those of the MBA students, with reality television stars, actors and comedians achieving the highest and musicians the lowest NPI scores. Interestingly, they found that, unlike in the general population, females' narcissism scores were higher than males' among the celebrities, especially on the NPI components of exhibitionism, superiority and vanity.

However, Twenge et al. (2008) argue that the increasing mean levels of narcissism observed in USA college students could have general mental health costs. This warning is linked to the known adverse consequences of high levels of narcissism for individuals' overall self-regulation (Morf and Rhodewalt, 2001). It is linked, statistically, to behaviours, feelings and thoughts that might indirectly or even directly compromise mental health such as risk taking, overconfidence and lack of forgiveness of others (Morf and Rhodewalt, 2001). However, this should be seen in the context of research that shows that individuals with high levels of narcissism also report being happier than those with lower levels of the trait (Campbell et al., 2004), although this could be a result of the trait itself.

Research on the dark triad traits has a number of implications for the links between atypical personality and mental health. There is evidence of these atypical personality traits in the general population, and dark triad traits appear to have similar correlates among both clinical and non-clinical groups of individuals. However, these atypical traits are not always problematic for individuals, or at least they do not *perceive* them as such. How researchers handle scales, measures, scores and findings in this area is challenging. For example, it might be important to compare the scores of general population groups with clinical groups to ensure the former are not actually experiencing clinical levels of these traits. This is important because without this we cannot be certain that what we are observing is an actual similarity between these different groups.

Task ⌐ Examine the main characteristics of narcissism that we have considered. Either individually or in groups, identify situations in which such characteristics might have adaptive and maladaptive consequences for individuals.

Comment

This task should help you to consider more critically how we define some personality traits as typical or atypical, and the importance of context for understanding the *dark* and *bright* sides of dark triad traits, such as narcissism.

Personality disorders

Personality disorders (PD) are mental disorders that are currently diagnosed using the closely aligned main classificatory systems of *DSM-IVTR* and the *ICD-10. ICD-10* (World Health Organization, 2007) describes personality disorders as:

> *severe disturbances in the personality and behavioural tendencies of the individual; not directly resulting from disease, damage, or other insult to the brain, or from another psychiatric disorder; usually involving several areas of the personality; nearly always associated with considerable personal distress and social disruption; and usually manifest since childhood or adolescence and continuing throughout adulthood.*

Controversy surrounds the nature and diagnosis of personality disorders. For example, Kendell (2002) discusses the issue of whether it can be considered strictly as a disease or disorder because it is regarded as untreatable. The contemporary hot debate is about how we should *diagnose* personality disorders. The debate is driven by the known difficulties associated with the main classification systems, and the growing evidence base demonstrating that typical traits can be used to describe and diagnose these disorders. A major criticism of current approaches to the diagnosis of PD is that the main classificatory systems are based on discrete clusters of symptoms not linked to the evidence base of research on *typical personality* (Widiger and Trull, 2007). Given the impending publication of *DSM-V*, psychologists are actively debating the benefits of the medical model assumptions in the *DSM* in general (McHugh, 2005; Moffitt et al., 2008). The specific debate about the diagnosis of personality disorders began over 30 years ago (Widiger and Trull, 2007), and is based on the argument that personality disorders are atypical variants of typical personality. If one accepts this argument, then one implication is that typical traits, such as the FFT, can be used to diagnose personality disorders. This is referred to as the *continuity hypothesis of personality disorders*.

There is considerable evidence that supports the continuity hypothesis of personality disorder by demonstrating that typical traits such as the FFT are equally if not more accurate for diagnosing personality disorder than the main classification systems (Axelrod et al., 1997; Evans et al., 2001; Gudonis et al., 2008; Krueger, 2005; Krueger and Tackett , 2003; Lynam and Widiger, 2001; Markon et al., 2005; Tackett et al., 2009; Widiger and Trull, 2007).

However, the continuity hypothesis has been criticised. Some researchers have argued that the use of the FFT to describe and diagnose personality disorders is not straightforward. For example, Shedler and Westen (2004) have shown that trait facets rather than traits might be more diagnostically useful. It is also worth remembering that the continuity hypothesis is not explicitly an explanation or an account of personality disorder – it does not necessarily claim that the aetiology of personality disorders is continuous with typical personality. However, the work of McCrae et al. (2005a) does imply this.

Critical thinking activity

Personality disorders

Critical thinking focus: critical and creative thinking

Key question: *Is the continuity hypothesis of personality disorders evident in the Department of Health document* Recognising complexity: commissioning guidance for personality disorder services *(2009)?*

The continuity hypothesis of personality disorders has encouraged debate about personality and how we conceptualise, diagnose and even treat personality disorders. The Department of Health document *Recognising complexity: commissioning guidance for personality disorder services* (2009; available at www.pdprogramme. org.uk/assets/resources/173.pdf), as its title suggests, claims to acknowledge this complexity. For this activity you must think critically and creatively about whether there is evidence of this in part of the document. The question you are to answer is: does the document acknowledge in any way the continuity hypothesis of personality disorders?

You do not need to read the entire document: simply focus on Part A Setting the Context (pp8–12). You might also like to examine Annexes 2, 3, 4 and 5 on pp50–7 as these describe features of personality disorders. Use the following questions to guide your completion of this task.

- What will you look for in the content as evidence of the continuity hypothesis?

- How will you organise this information once you have identified it?

- What does your analysis tell you about the links between the academic and non-academic literature on personality disorders?

Worked example

The continuity hypothesis argues that there is continuity between typical and atypical personality in the form of personality disorders. Evidence of this might be in references to the behavioural similarities between those with a personality disorder and those without. In Annex 2 of the document descriptions of moderate personality disorders include recognition that individuals with less serious personality disorders are normally able to function; and this Annex also shows that as personality disorders move from less serious through to moderate, severe and complex, functioning becomes increasingly poorer. However, such statements are not explicit statements of the continuity hypothesis. In fact, in Part A of the document the emphasis is upon personality disorders as complex because of the multiple problems experienced by individuals with the diagnosis rather than because of the similarities with typical traits and their related behaviours. However, the document does acknowledge that diagnosis of personality disorders is problematic using current diagnostic guidelines, and this is something argued by those who support the use of other approaches to diagnosis, such as the FFT.

Critical thinking review

This document claims to be based on current academic research on personality disorders, and it does acknowledge that personality disorders are complex in many ways. So your task is to judge whether the document does so in relation to the continuity hypothesis. Psychologists working within the health service and other public sectors often have to work with such documents, and spend time identifying and using their relevant content to inform their work. For this task you have to analyse the document to search for evidence of academic concepts within its content. You might consider if you could use research skills, tools and software to search the document for this information.

Other skills likely to be used in this activity: this activity also requires you to use problem solving, data analysis, and evaluation and decision-making skills when deciding how you will compare the content of the document with your criteria (e.g. what is evidence of the continuity hypothesis?). In doing this you will have to reflect on your knowledge of key concepts, and the skills and tools you could use to search the document efficiently. Finally, you should consider how to record your analyses, thus developing your written communication skills.

Professional and ethical issues

In the introduction the overarching goal of this chapter was described as encouraging you to think critically and creatively about the links between traits, mental health and disorder. An important theme emerging is that the links are complex, due partly to the blurred boundaries between typical and atypical personality, and between mental health and mental disorder. Likewise, boundaries between clinicians and non-clinicians engaged in work on this topic are also becoming blurred. For example, academic psychologists' work is being used to inform the work of clinicians. Furthermore, researchers sometimes use clinical as well as non-clinical scales as research tools, and some research on the FFT and personality disorders suggests that we can use as diagnostic tools concepts and scales originally developed as research tools. Academic researchers need to clarify the clinical relevance of their non-clinical research. While doing this they should also uphold the professional and ethical standards of the discipline. In Great Britain this means adhering to the British Psychological Society *Code of ethics and conduct* (2009). In this code the ethical principle of *competence* or *expertise* of researchers engaged in this work is especially important because of the many different types of experts who work in the field. In particular, the division between practitioners – or clinicians – and researchers is important here.

The division between *expert practitioners* and *expert researchers* is acknowledged in the *ICD-10 Classification of Diseases*. This has separate sets of guidelines for the use of their system – one for clinicians when using the classification for diagnostic purposes and one for researchers when using the classification for research purposes. In Great Britain, the British Psychological Society also recognises the practitioner–researcher division. It offers advice and guidance to practitioners in the form of its *Generic professional practice guidelines* (2008), and for all psychologists generally in terms of ethics and professional conduct (British Psychological Society, 2009, *Code of ethics and conduct*).

However, researchers conducting non-clinical research face difficult and at times professional challenges similar to those of practitioners or clinicians. In the critical thinking activity you considered these issues when you analysed a government document designed to inform how services for individuals diagnosed with a personality disorder are delivered. This activity was designed to encourage you to start thinking about how academic and professional issues are related in the work of psychologists as experts in a field or on a topic. A close reading of the 2009 code highlights the similarities between some of the ethical and professional issues faced by practitioners and researchers. For example, even if a psychologist is not a practitioner, their research participants are regarded as *clients* (p3) and consequently, the psychologist will inevitably have to make decisions about their interaction with them in *difficult, changeable* and *unclear* circumstances (p4). This means reflecting on their technical competence and professional skills and judgements when they make decisions, for example, when briefing participants about the nature of research, the scales they will be asked to complete, the measurement of characteristics that at face value are linked to mental disorder and the meaning of test scores. This is, of course, something all psychologists face when conducting any research, especially with members of the general public. However, research on atypical personality and mental health is likely to be especially challenging because of the very nature of the topic. For example, when measuring the dark triad traits in non-clinical groups, the researcher has to consider how they will debrief participants about the purpose of the research, and whether simply stating that high scores on the measures do not indicate a mental disorder is sufficient to safeguard the welfare of participants once they leave the research context.

Also, non-clinicians should perhaps consider the parameters of their work in terms of clinical relevance. For example, research on the dark triad traits should perhaps consider the actual intensity of these traits among the general population in comparison to clinical populations before making claims about the continuity of these traits across these groups. When using non-clinical scales and then making references to clinical issues, researchers should clarify if, and how, their measures and clinical tools are related.

Skill builder activity

Psychologists as experts

Transferable skill focus: decision making

Key question: *What factors influence your decision making when invited to give a radio interview about the 2009 Department of Health document considered in the critical thinking activity?*

The previous section focused on some of the challenging decisions that psychologists are likely to have to make when doing research on atypical personality and mental health and disorder. Giving expert views to the media is another feature of this work, and one that is recognised in the British Psychological Society (2009) *Code of ethics and conduct*, available at www.bps.org.uk/the-society/code-of-conduct/code-of-conduct_home.cfm.

In this activity you take the role of a psychologist invited to take part in a radio show discussion. You will contribute to a 15-minute slot on a live radio current affairs programme discussing personality disorders in light of a series of high profile local cases involving the release and detention of offenders diagnosed with a personality disorder. You have been invited as the expert on mental health issues to discuss, along with a local mental health charity worker, the 2009 document you considered in the critical thinking activity. The invitation is made to you late in the afternoon of the day before the 7.30 a.m. show airs, and you have to make a decision that afternoon about your involvement. Use the following questions to guide your decision making – you can complete this activity individually or as a group discussion.

- What can you do to ensure you make a professional and ethically sound decision about whether to accept the invitation or not?

- If you accept this invitation, what aspects of the document and academic literature will you need to consider when preparing for the radio show?

- During the radio show, how will you communicate that your comments are based on evidence while remaining clear, concise and accessible?

- What sorts of questions do you think would be inappropriate for you to answer, and how would you respond to such questions?

- What are the main ethical and professional guidelines that you need to consider when preparing for, and taking part in, the interview?

Worked example

You have to understand and analyse the four areas of the Code (respect, competence, responsibility and integrity) to decide which aspects are relevant to the task, along with their implications for your behaviour. For example, first you have to decide whether to accept the invitation by reflecting on your own expertise and professional ethics, and your knowledge of the document. Then, if you decide to accept the invitation, you have to make decisions about which parts of the 2009 document along with other academic information and data are likely to be relevant to the interview.

Skill builder review

Psychologists have to think carefully about their professionalism and ethical responsibilities when invited by the media to comment on any issues, but especially those relating to mental health because frequently they are invited in response to some controversial incident or policy. This means making a number of decisions about whether to accept such invitations and, if they do so, which academic research to refer to in their comments. Commentaries involve communicating information that is often complex to different audiences in a clear and professional manner. This activity helps develop these decision-making skills, which are an important part of the British Psychological Society's (2009) *Code of ethics and conduct*. Importantly, the activity draws your attention to how the Code should be used by practising psychologists and students of psychology, and this, of course, involves making a series of decisions.

Other skills likely to be used in this activity: the activity requires you to understand your professional responsibilities and capabilities as students. The analysis of data and theory, and your understanding of key issues contained in complex data sets are important to this task – the activity involves the fast, efficient and accurate summarising and evaluation of a large and complex document and relevant academic literature. The activity should also develop your oral communication, listening skills and problem solving, and you will have to reflect on the specific characteristics of radio as a medium of communication, along with your own style of oral communication.

Assignments

1. Discuss, critically, how individual differences psychology could contribute to contemporary debates about mental health problems.

2. Critically evaluate how personality traits are linked to mental health and disorder.

3. Critically examine the view that the differences between typical and atypical personality are fundamentally *quantitative*.

Summary: what you have learned

Individual differences psychology has made several important contributions to contemporary debates about mental health. First, it has contributed to discussions about how we define mental health and mental disorder. Second, it has drawn attention to the blurred boundaries between typical and atypical personality, and between mental health and mental disorder. Third, it has provided theoretical and empirical evidence that demonstrates that traits are correlated with mental health and mental disorder. Finally, researchers have used traits to define mental health and diagnose mental disorder. There is considerable evidence that personality traits are mental health indicators – they can be used to predict vulnerabilities to mental health problems. However, no trait is intrinsically atypical, and traits regarded as fundamentally atypical can be both adaptive and maladaptive in certain circumstances. Finally, there is a growing evidence base to support the continuity hypothesis of personality disorders. One implication of this is that typical and atypical personality is quantitatively rather than qualitatively distinct. Understanding how traits, mental health and disorder are linked involves using analytical and decision-making skills to ensure the relationship between these constructs is not oversimplified.

Further reading

Boorsboom, D (2006) The attack of the psychometricians. *Psycometrika*, 71(3): 425–40.

This paper provides a summary of some of the difficulties psychologists encounter when trying to interpret statistical concepts, factors that can lead to these difficulties and what can be done to address these. Boorsboom's publications have stimulated considerable debate about the use of psychometrics in psychology, and this is a useful introduction to this work.

Cervone, D (2005) Personality architecture: within-person structures and processes. *Annual Review of Psychology*, 56: 423–52.

This is an excellent summary of contemporary debates about personality psychology and especially the limitations of the trait approach.

Hoyle, RH (2006) Personality and self-regulation: trait and information-processing perspectives. *Journal of Personality*, 74(6): 1507–26.

This paper provides a clear account of the trait approach to self-regulation and how this differs from the information processing approach. Hoyle also suggests how these competing approaches can be combined to produce a more complete integrated approach to self-regulation.

Keyes, CLM (2007) Promoting and protecting mental health as flourishing: a complementary strategy for improving national mental health. *American Psychologist*, 62(2): 95–108.

This paper is a useful account of the implications of the Complete State Model of Health for mental health interventions.

McCrae, RR, Lockenhoff, CE and Costa, PT (2005a) A step toward *DSM-V*: cataloguing personality-related problems in living. *European Journal of Personality*, 19, 269–86.

This is an important paper because it outlines how the FFT could have consequences for mental health and disorder. It also attempts to address some of the criticisms of the trait approach that you will read about in Cervone (2005).

The Psychologist (2007) Special issue on diagnosing mental disorders, available at www.the psychologist.org.uk/archive/archive_home.cfm?volumeID=20&editionID=147

This issue contains a series of accessible papers written by psychologists and psychiatrists about the difficulties of diagnosing mental disorders, and how psychology can contribute both to the debates about diagnosis and to clinical practice.

Twenge, JM, Konrath, S, Foster, JD, Campbell, WK and Bushman, BJ (2008) Ego inflating over time: a cross-temporal meta-analysis of the Narcissistic Personality Inventory. *Journal of Personality*, 76(4): 875–901.

This research provides evidence that the level of narcissism among American college students has increased between 1979 and 2006. The method used and the researchers' discussion of this increase provides an excellent example of how atypical traits are not necessarily atypical statistically. The research also illustrates how the functions of traits are, to some extent, socially constructed.

Widiger, TA and Trull, TJ (2007) Plate tectonics in the classification of personality disorder. *American Psychologist*, 62(2): 71–83.

This is a definitive and concise summary of the continuity hypothesis, its history and the current 'hot' topic of the viability of the hypothesis.

Useful websites

http://allpsych.com/disorders/dsm.html

This link will take you to descriptions of the main sections and details of DSM-IV or DSM-IVTR.

www.who.int/classifications/icd/en/bluebook.pdf

This link will take you to the International Classification of Diseases 10. Unlike the DSM, ICD-10 is a publically available diagnostic classification system and it is an excellent resource for students wanting free online access to one of the main systems used to classify mental disorders.

www.dsm5.org/Pages/Default.aspx

This link will take you to DSM-5: The future of psychiatric diagnosis – a discussion about the latest version of DSM to be published in 2013.

Chapter 5

Cultural and sex differences in personality

Learning outcomes

By the end of this chapter you should:

- understand and be able to discuss, critically, the issues that shape contemporary research linking personality traits with culture and biological sex;

- be able to describe and consider, critically, theory and empirical evidence on the links between personality traits and culture;

- be able to describe and consider, critically, theory and empirical evidence on the links between personality traits and biological sex;

- understand and be able to examine, critically, sex differences in the nature and prevalence of depression and personality disorders;

- have developed analytical, evaluation and problem solving skills by judging inferences drawn from research on personality and culture, and through designing a study on sex differences in personality.

Introduction

In this chapter you will consider how psychologists are currently examining differences in the personality traits of social groups, specifically research that focuses on groups of individuals that differ in terms of their culture and biological sex. You will examine research on personality, culture and biological sex using the following questions.

- How and why do psychologists examine the links between these constructs?

- What does this research *actually* demonstrate?

- If major social groups, such as those based on culture and biological sex, differ in their personality traits, why might this be the case?

The links between personality traits and social groups is an issue that has experienced a resurgence of interest since the mid-1970s (McCrae, 2001). The social groups considered in this literature have become more diverse. However, most research has tended to focus on personality differences between cultures and between men and women, frequently within the same empirical study. Within this research, psychologists have typically compared the *mean aggregate trait differences* between cultures or between men and women. This approach focuses on measurable differences between social groups and should be distinguished from research on people's perceptions of personality differences between social groups. Currently, research on measurable trait differences in the main focuses on *how personality traits interact with culture in shaping people's lives* (McCrae, 2001, p820). Thus, in addition to identifying mean aggregate trait differences, the research considers *the interaction – intersection – of the individual with society* [that] *has always been a core concern of personality psychologists* (McCrae, 2004, p3). This means using more than causal linear explanations of how traits influence culture and vice versa. These complex questions about how personality, culture and biological sex are linked have given individual differences psychology a number of conceptual, methodological and ethical challenges. To some extent, therefore, the methodologies and concepts used have had to develop considerably to reflect these complexities.

What you will encounter in the contemporary literature are challenging, and possibly speculative (McCrae, 2001, 2004) ideas about the causal relationships between traits and culture. The current agenda is one that regards trait psychology as important and necessary for developing our understanding of how people go about managing themselves and others in diverse socio-cultural contexts. Consequently, the levels of analysis used in this research have diversified as psychologists consider the social, political and ethical implications of this research. As McCrae says (2004, p4):

> the issues it involves are large, and must be approached with intrepid theorising as well as rigorous research . . . it is time to consider culture from the perspective of trait psychology.

To that end, the critical thinking and skill builder activities in this chapter are about developing analytical, evaluation and problem-solving skills that should help you to think critically about this endeavour. You will use analysis and evaluation skills to consider the question *what does the research on traits and culture actually demonstrate?* You will also use problem-solving skills to consider the question *how can we design research that measures differences between men and women's beliefs about personality?*

Personality and culture: contemporary issues

A number of interrelated issues shape contemporary research on personality and culture, and these are summarised in Figure 5.1. Three issues can be identified in the literature: the ways in which researchers have *interpreted* the research, especially in terms of what this tells about the *determinants* of any cultural differences in personality traits; the challenges this research poses for the *research designs* and *methods* used; and the *conceptual assumptions* of this work.

Figure 5.1: *Issues in personality and culture research*

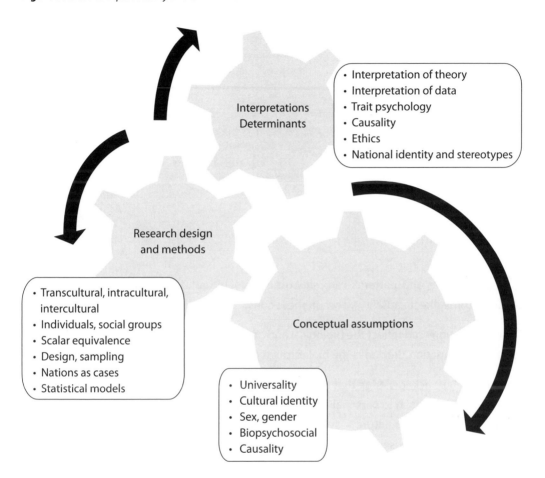

- Interpretation of theory
- Interpretation of data
- Trait psychology
- Causality
- Ethics
- National identity and stereotypes

Interpretations
Determinants

Research design
and methods

- Transcultural, intracultural, intercultural
- Individuals, social groups
- Scalar equivalence
- Design, sampling
- Nations as cases
- Statistical models

Conceptual assumptions

- Universality
- Cultural identity
- Sex, gender
- Biopsychosocial
- Causality

The *interpretations* of research on the universality of personality traits and their *determinants* have developed since the mid-1970s (Hofstede and McCrae, 2004). However, philosophers and behavioural scientists in general have shown an interest in personality and culture for over 200 years (Hofstede and McCrae, 2004). Concepts such as *national character* can be found in the writings of eighteenth-century philosophers such as Hume and Kant, and interest in the topic has waxed and waned in personality psychology. To some extent earlier research on personality and culture focused on the mutual exclusivity of constructs and process – see Figure 5.2. A feature of contemporary research is that it challenges these assumptions by using alternative reinterpretations of theory and data in a number of ways.

- **Pan-cultural** traits and trait patterns do not necessarily reflect the biological and genetic basis of traits, even if we observe the same traits and trait patterns across cultures and nations.

- Cultural variations do not necessarily reflect the sociocultural basis of traits, even if we observe differences between cultures and nations.

Figure 5.2: *Constructs in personality, culture and gender research*

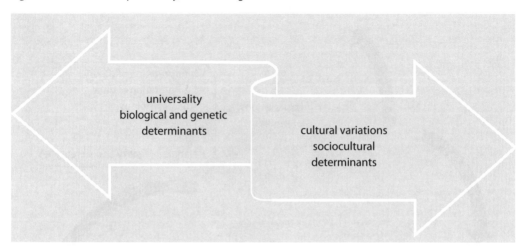

- Pan-cultural traits and patterns can reflect the sociocultural determinants of traits and we cannot assume direct causality between these constructs or the direction of this.

- Cultural variations can reflect the biological and genetic determinants of traits and we cannot assume that variation precludes the biological or genetic basis of personality.

Instead, researchers acknowledge that the links between traits and culture are *complex*. McCrae's (2001, 2004) trait approach to personality and culture illustrates this approach to explain the links between personality and culture – see Figure 5.3. McCrae (2004) identifies two issues from previous attempts to theorise and interpret data on the links between personality and culture. The first is that trait psychology has been treated as *dustbowl empiricism* (p4), but it is no longer regarded as such. In other words, it is no longer purely an atheoretical data-massing enterprise. The second is that past approaches to personality and culture tended to use psychoanalytic concepts that identified childhood experiences as determinants of both cultural universality and variation in personality. McCrae (2004) proposes a personality system that is a biopsychosocial framework for understanding personality and culture. However, this framework is based on a clear causality assumption that *culture does not affect personality* (p5), hence in Figure 5.3 there are no direct links between personality traits and culture indicated. Using evidence that personality traits are both genetically inherited and stable across the lifespan to support this strong causality statement, he does acknowledge that it is a view that others will regard as *extreme, and ultimately will probably be shown to be incorrect* (p5). Nevertheless, McCrae (2004) regards this as a tenable starting point for reinterpreting the nature and determinants of how personality and culture are linked. This framework has a number of key elements.

- The components of the personality system include biology, culture, personality traits and characteristic adaptations; and culture does not affect personality traits.

Figure 5.3: *McCrae's characteristic adaptations framework*

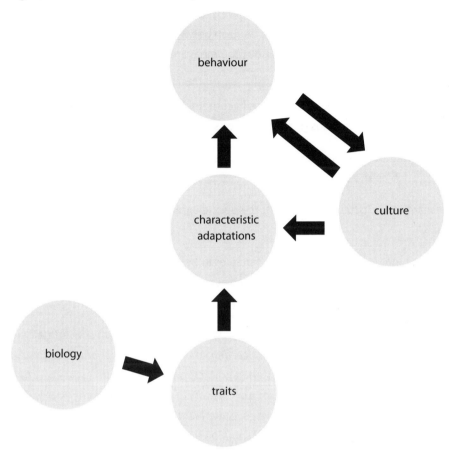

- Personality traits are not characteristic adaptations but the deeper biological basis of personality or *basic tendencies* (p6), an issue we considered in Chapter 4.

- Characteristic adaptations – constructs we discussed in Chapter 4 – are *all the psychological structures that people acquire in the course of life for getting along in the world . . . knowledge, attitudes, goals, roles, relationships, schemas, scripts, habits, even the self-concept . . . the bulk of the phenomena that psychologists are concerned with* (p6).

- Characteristic adaptations result from the interaction of personality traits with the environment – thus the fundamental component of traits *is* universal. However, cultural variations we observe are actually variations in characteristic adaptations or the particular ways that the trait–environment interaction has operated.

This approach is to some extent controversial because of its causality premise that personality traits shape culture. Nevertheless, it draws attention to the centrality of considering the nature of the causality relationship between personality and culture – if one exists at all – and the need to specify clearly the constructs one uses. For example, culture can be defined in different ways, and in some research the terms culture and nationality are used interchangeably when they have distinct meanings. A similar issue is the need to distinguish between research on measured traits as opposed to research on individual's beliefs about the measured traits of their own or other nationalities or cultures.

McCrae (2001) has identified three types of research in contemporary approaches to personality and culture, and each entails specific designs and methods.

- *Transcultural* research that focuses on testing the universality of personality structure and traits and trait patterns, such as age and sex differences.

- *Intracultural* research that focuses on the culture-specific expressions or *operation* (p821) of personality traits.

- *Intercultural research* that focuses on cultural differences in traits and how such differences are linked to cultural characteristics using measures such as aggregate mean trait differences, and mean personality profiles to capture national characteristics.

Hofstede and McCrae (2004) describe the various ways in which culture has been conceptualised and measured in the research, and these all reflect certain *conceptual assumptions* about personality and culture. According to Hofstede (Hofstede and McCrae, 2004) culture is *the collective programming of the mind that distinguishes one group or category of people from another* (p58). This definition has three key features: culture refers to a *collective identity* that is *not directly visible* but latent and measurable in visible behaviour that is *not common to all individuals*. To measure culture, researchers have developed *dimensions* of culture or features that can be used to describe different cultures because they are the important facets along which they vary. Hofstede's global survey study of cultural differences between seven nations used subsidiaries of the company IBM to administer approximately 17,000 surveys. This research made use of the relative homogeneity among IBM staff resulting from IBM's corporate approach to recruitment. This meant that the testing in 1967–1973 produced data that allegedly controlled for variables other than nationality, such as age, education and socio-economic status. The survey collected data on a range of issues related to participants' basic values and situational attitudes. From the IBM data, Hofstede developed his four dimensions of culture.

- *Power distance* refers to the level of acceptance of unequal power distributions or inequality. High levels of power distance are reflected in behaviours that reflect the acceptance of inequality, an acceptance that can be found even among those with little power. Although it is accepted that social inequality is ubiquitous, it is the extent of acceptance of such inequality that is captured by this dimension. Finally, socialisation processes are identified as the main mechanisms for the transmission of power distance values.

- *Uncertainty avoidance* refers to the level of tolerance of ambiguity within a culture, and this is reflected in how comfortable individuals within a given culture feel in unstructured situations. *Uncertainty avoidance cultures* tend to be structured in ways that minimise a lack of structure. For example, this can be reflected in the presence of strict laws and laws relating to safety and security, and in a belief in absolute truths about life and knowledge, for example, as expressed in an organised religion. Individuals in uncertainty avoidance cultures also tend to possess certain typical characteristics, including high levels of inner nervous energy and emotional expressiveness, and overall such cultures are typified by cultural anxiety and neuroticism. Conversely, *uncertainty accepting cultures* are characterised by a tolerance of differing opinions and have relatively fewer rules as is consistent with their relativistic approach to life and knowledge. Finally, individuals in such cultures tend to possess certain typical characteristics, including low levels of emotional expressiveness and a generally contemplative manner.

- *Individualism and collectivism* form opposite poles on a dimension that reflects the extent to which individuals within a given culture are integrated into groups. The individualism polarity is used to describe cultures that are characterised by loose social ties between individuals. In contrast, the collectivism polarity is used to describe cultures that are characterised by individuals that form integrated and cohesive groups, and the protection provided by the group is reciprocated by high levels of loyalty from group members.

- *Masculinity and femininity* form opposite poles on a dimension that reflects the distribution of emotional roles between the sexes. Although Hofstede and McCrae (2004) describe women as typically less variable in their values than men, both men and women within masculine cultures display typically male characteristics, although these are likely to be stronger in men than in women (e.g. assertiveness and competitiveness). The same pattern applies to feminine cultures that are characterised by more caring and modest behaviours and practices.

These dimensions have become widely used in research to operationalise and measure culture. However, Hofstede and McCrae (2004) are quick to point out that despite the development of dimensions of culture, when applying these constructs in research a number of potential confusions or fallacies can take place because of the different levels of analysis that measuring culture involves. For example, the *ecological fallacy* occurs when data are used to compare individuals from different cultures when those data are actually drawn from research that compares societies rather than individuals. In other words, research on the links between culture and personality traits compares aggregate data from different nations or cultures in which each N or case is actually a social group and then uses them to make inferential statements about individuals from those particular nations or cultures. The *reverse ecological fallacy* occurs when the inference making is in the opposite direction – in other words, when we use individual data to make cultural or national level comparisons. Finally, the *uniformity fallacy* occurs when researchers assume that cultural values are shared uniformly across individuals within a nation. We cannot assume that culture is coterminous with nationality. In fact, McCrae (2001, 2004) and Hofstede and McCrae (2004) argue that we have yet to produce research on personality and culture that deals with these definition and terminology issues.

Task — One of the issues that continues to challenge contemporary research on personality and culture is how we define and measure culture. Often, culture is assumed to be coterminous with nationality. An important question about this research is *how can we ensure we do not confound or confuse nationality with culture?* To help you consider this issue, first of all list examples of when individuals with different nationalities might share a cultural identity and examples of when individuals share nationality but have different cultural identities. When you have listed two or three examples of each, consider what methodological challenges these sorts of circumstances pose for researchers conducting transcultural research.

Comment

This task should draw your attention to the challenges of operationalising and therefore measuring the concept of culture. It should also provide you with a starting point for thinking critically about the methods and designs used in research on personality traits and culture.

Universality versus cross-cultural variations in personality

Trait differences between cultures

Before we consider the evidence on how personality and culture are linked, it is worth spending time clarifying what is meant by the *universality* of personality.

Task — In Chapter 2 we examined research evidence demonstrating that the FFT are genetically inherited, and that the basis of traits in a number of models is biological. Stating that traits have a biological basis and are genetically inherited is one way of stating that personality is *universal*. However, this is only one way of making such a statement. In this task, you should start thinking about other ways that we could test whether personality is *universal*. Your task is to try to list some of these other ways. To help you, try to answer the following question: *if the structure and determinants of personality are universal, then what sorts of evidence could we use to support this claim?*

Comment

This task should help develop your awareness of the different ways that the concept of universality as applied to personality traits can be operationalised, and the different ways that the same data can be interpreted.

In the literature on personality and culture, universality has been conceptualised, tested and measured in different ways, including:

- *universal causality* using the biological and genetic bases of personality traits;

- *universal stability* using trait patterns that develop across the lifespan;

- *universal structure* using evidence of the relevance of trait models to describe oneself and others in different sociocultural contexts;

- *universal trait intensity patterns* using evidence of similar patterns of trait strengths or intensity across different cultures.

Research has provided evidence supporting some but not all of these different versions of the universality of personality and this is summarised in Figure 5.4. The right-hand side of this figure shows that certain evidence has provided support for the universal causality, structure and stability of personality.

Figure 5.4: *Evidence for the universality of personality*

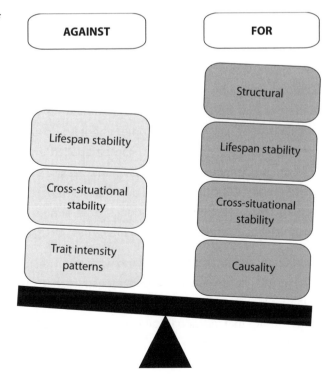

McCrae's (2004) research provides support for the *causal and structural universality of personality*. McCrae (2004) used data from 36 cultures across five continents. The NEO-PI-R was administered to participants, who were classified as either adults or students, with patients and those presenting for employment screening excluded from the data. Using American norms, these data show that around three-quarters of scores fell within the average USA range. Therefore, as we can use the FFT to describe inter-individual variation pan-culturally, McCrae (2004) argues that this supports the universality of personality structure, and that the basis of these traits is likely to be biological, given that McCrae's Five Factor Model of the FFT is based on the premise that personality traits are biologically determined. However, there *was* variation between cultures of at least one standard deviation on the FFT. Hofstede's four dimensions of culture were also measured, and each of the FFT was related to one or more of these dimensions in ways that McCrae (2004) argues supports his personality systems framework. Specifically, he argues that these data support the premise that personality traits affect culture and not the other way around. For example, there was a negative relationship between the personality traits of extraversion and openness and the cultural dimension of power distance, and a positive relationship between the personality traits of conscientiousness and power distance. Power distance is a measure of how accepting the less powerful are of the differential power hierarchy in their culture. McCrae (2004) argues that the most logical explanation of this pattern is that this cultural personality profile of a dutiful and docile population has fostered a culture in which hierarchical leadership is both achievable and acceptable. He argues that the reverse explanation – that a hierarchical culture has been able to subdue a population that is strongly open and extraverted – seems a *less likely* explanation. McCrae (2004) does acknowledge that his data could be interpreted in ways other than those specified by his framework. For example, the data do show that cultures vary in their mean aggregate levels of the FFT, but that this can be accommodated by their framework because although we might expect some cultural variation in mean aggregate trait levels, the *overall* pattern of how personality traits and culture are linked appears universal. Furthermore, the mechanisms by which this link comes about is also claimed to be universal. In other words, the premise that traits shape culture can be applied universally, as traits lead to certain cultural differences that appear relatively systematic. He also suggests that his interpretations assume that the self-report data are **veridical** and that self-report bias could be an alternative explanation. Despite these self-criticisms, evidence does suggest that the FFT can be used to describe personality traits across cultures (McCrae, 2001; McCrae et al., 2010; Terracciano et al., 2005).

However, it is important to distinguish what this research *demonstrates* from how this research is *interpreted*. First, the research does demonstrate that both nations and cultures vary in their mean trait profiles. They vary in the mean aggregate intensity of the FFT. Second, the research demonstrates that individuals' perceptions of the personalities that characterise different nations or cultures vary, but the relationship between actual mean aggregate trait profiles and these perceptions of national character or national identify is low. For example, Terracciano et al. (2005)

examined 49 cultures using a total sample of 3,989 individuals. Using the NEO-PI-R they measured self-reported levels of the FFT, observer reports of others using the FFT, and perceptions of national personality characteristics using the National Character Survey (NCS). The NCS consists of 30 bipolar scales, and each bipolar scale assesses one of the 30 facets of the FFT. Participants were asked to use the NCS to rate the personality traits they believed characterised their own nationality and the typical American. They found that the correlation coefficient between perceptions of personality and actual personality traits was merely 0.04. This suggests that nations and cultures hold inaccurate beliefs about national character, including their own.

Evidence for *lifespan stability* and *cross-situational stability* is mixed, and therefore they appear on both sides of Figure 5.4. For example, Srivastava et al. (2003) tested the plaster hypothesis of personality that states that after around the age of 30 years, personality traits remains stable or *fixed like plaster*. Using participants aged 21–60 years of age they found that on the FFT stability across this range of the lifespan was dependent on both the trait and the sex of the individual. For example, conscientiousness and agreeableness increased across early and middle adulthood generally, but neuroticism declined among women.

The left-hand side of Figure 5.4 lists evidence that has provided less compelling support for the universality of personality. Research on personality trait pattern intensities that has provided support for the structural universality of personality traits has also provided evidence of relatively systematic differences in personality trait intensities between cultures. For example, Mooradian and Swan (2006) found that nations vary in their mean aggregate levels of extraversion and that this is systematically related to the reliance on word of mouth or interpersonal sources of information in that nation. Specifically, they claim that traits *affect* cultural styles of communication, with cultures high on trait extraversion also being more reliant on word of mouth and interpersonal sources of information. However, McCrae (2004) found differences in mean aggregate personality trait intensities and interpreted this as consistent with his premise that personality traits have a structure and causal universality.

Research on the *cross-situational stability* of personality and *implicit theories of personality* have also provided evidence of relatively systematic differences between cultures. Church's research illustrates this. For example, Church et al. (2007, 2008) found that the FFT could be used to describe different cultures, thus to some extent supporting the structural universality of personality traits. However, Church et al. (2008) also found that individuals in collectivist cultures show more cross-situational variability in their behaviour than individualist cultures. Church et al. (2005) have also found that implicit trait theories are stronger than implicit contextual beliefs in individualist cultures compared to collectivist cultures.

Task ⎤ McCrae's (2004) research was described earlier. Table 5.1 shows data from McCrae (2001). They show the mean scores of four nationalities on each of the FFT – that is, these nationalities' mean aggregate personality trait scores. Examine these mean aggregate personality trait data and consider the following question: *what does this data suggest about the universality of the FFT?* Remember that McCrae (2001) did *not* measure cultural identity, for example using Hofstede's cultural dimensions, and he compared mean national trait levels rather than individuals' scores.

Comment

This task should help you understand that data from personality and culture research can be interpreted in often very different ways. McCrae (2001) interpreted these data as consistent with his premise that personality traits affect culture and that the FFT are structurally universal. In fact, they do show cultural variation in mean aggregate trait levels. The important issue here is not whether such differences exist but how we *interpret* these differences.

Determinants of trait differences between cultures

McCrae's (2004) personality systems approach was described earlier. This approach to personality and culture can accommodate much of the transcultural and intercultural research evidence. In other words, both universality and variation can be explained using this framework. The starting point for this view is that the FFT have a genetic basis and are therefore pan-cultural (Yamagata et al., 2006). According to this account, personality traits are universal because they are biological, they can be used to describe the structure or personality across cultures and nations, and the processes that lead personality traits to shape culture are universal. Importantly, traits are regarded as *independent variables* rather than dependent measures. Differences in personality trait intensities between cultures simply reflect the reciprocal influence between the environment and the individual, and cultures differ to some extent because social groups develop cultural-level

Table 5.1: Data from McCrae (2001)

	Neuroticism	Extraversion	Openness	Agreeableness	Conscientiousness
Hong Kong Chinese	53.3	37.4	49.2	54.6	49.2
American	50	50	50	50	50
French	55.4	47.3	54.1	52.1	47.4
Norwegian	47.4	53.6	51.5	49.9	45.7

practices that are coherent with aggregate trait levels. For example, collectivist cultures develop in response to relatively low aggregate means of trait extraversion. However, as even McCrae admits (2004), the precise direction of causality here is speculative.

However, some researchers argue that there is evidence that sociocultural and other environmental conditions can actually lead to changes in mean aggregate personality trait levels between cultures. In other words, traits are *dependent* rather than independent measures. Research on personality and infectious diseases illustrates this approach, and you will consider this in more detail in the critical thinking activity at the end of this chapter.

Task — Research on personality traits and culture raises ethical issues. McCrae (2001, 2004; McCrae et al., 2010) is clear in stating that traits are biological dispositions that are genetically inherited. Behaviours we observe reflect the interaction of biological and environmental factors that result in characteristic adaptations. These principles can be applied to explain both the universality of trait structures and differences between aggregate trait intensities of different cultures. Such knowledge has potential implications – for example, for how we conduct ourselves when interacting with others, international politics and diplomacy, the global community, behaviour change and acceptance. The British Psychological Society's *Code of ethics and conduct* (2009) states that we must know the limits of our knowledge and ensure we do not misrepresent what we know. For this task, you should attempt to speculate on the potential implications of this research for education, health or work by re-examining the table in the previous task. For example, some cultures have higher aggregate mean levels of trait neuroticism; could this have implications for that culture's health and well-being? (see Chapters 3 and 4).

Comment

This task should help your awareness of the social implications of psychological research, and the ethical responsibilities of those conducting personality and culture research. It should also highlight the complexity involved in interpreting research findings in this research.

Universality versus cross-cultural variation: sex differences

Research of the nature and extent of psychological differences between the sexes was to some extent reinvigorated by Sandra Bem's (1974, 1975, 1977) gender schema theory. In essence, Bem challenged existing notions of the nature of sex differences by introducing the concept of *gender identity* that is measurable using the Bem Sex Role Inventory (BSRI). This scale uses contrasting pairs of adjectives to measure the social meanings that individuals attach to biological sex. Importantly, this conceptualisation includes the premise that biologically male and female individuals can display both masculine and feminine characteristics. Consequently, an individual's gender identity reflects the strength of both the feminine and masculine characteristics of the individual. Individuals scoring higher on masculinity on the BSRI are classified as having a masculine gender identity, and those scoring higher on femininity are classified as having a feminine gender identity. Individuals can score highly on both femininity and masculinity and are described as *androgynous*, while individuals scoring low on both are described as *undifferentiated*. There are a number of important issues to be drawn from this work. First, in psychological research the term 'gender' is frequently used interchangeably with biological *sex*, but technically these terms have distinct meanings. Gender refers to the social meanings attached to biological sex, and such meanings include characteristics of masculinity and femininity (Bem, 1974, 1975). In much of the research on personality traits, the phrase *gender differences* is often used to refer to what are actually differences between individuals who regard themselves as *biologically* female or male. Second, although masculine and feminine characteristics are attached to biological sex, they are not exclusively displayed by males or females (Bem, 1974, 1975). These issues are important to bear in mind when considering the research that has examined how an individual's biological sex and personality traits are linked, and we will consider this literature next.

Trait differences between the sexes

Much of the transcultural research considered in the first part of this chapter also considered aggregate differences in traits between men and women as another way of testing for the universality of personality. Unlike research on personality and culture, there is compelling evidence that males and females differ *systematically* in their aggregate mean personality trait scores. This has provided strong support for the universality or pan-cultural nature of sex differences in personality traits. Much research has examined the FFT, and the pattern found typically is shown in Figure 5.5.

Figure 5.5: Trait intensity differences between men and women

MALES
low C, E, A, N

FEMALES
high C, E, A, N

There is compelling evidence of sex differences in mean personality trait scores. Schmitt et al. (2008) conducted a study with 17, 637 participants across 55 nations. Using the Big Five Inventory they found that personality traits of neuroticism, extraversion, agreeableness and conscientiousness were higher among women than men. A similar pattern of sex differences in aggregate mean personality trait scores was found in a large study conducted by Lippa (2010). This study of 200,000 participants over 55 nations used the BBC Internet survey to assess the personality traits of extraversion, neuroticism and agreeableness as well as *gender-related occupational preferences*. Personality traits were measured using items drawn from the International Personality Item Pool (IPIP), and the ten-item measure of occupational preferences consisted of five occupations identified as preferred by men (e.g. car mechanic, electrical engineer and inventor) and five identified as preferred by women (e.g. costume designer, school teacher, social worker). Lippa (2010) reports that across the nations sampled an individual's sex best predicted the intensity of their personality traits. Again, women reported higher levels of extraversion, agreeableness and neuroticism than men. However, Lippa (2010) found that women's trait extraversion scores were more variable than men's, and that men's trait agreeableness scores were more varied than women's. Lippa (2010) also found that lower mean aggregate trait neuroticism scores were related to higher levels of economic development and greater equality between the sexes. Such research does suggest some pan-cultural trends in personality traits between the sexes, a pattern of differences that is to some extent stable across the lifespan (Chapman et al., 2007). However, there is evidence that suggests the link between personality traits and biological sex are moderated by socio-economic status and age (Al-Halabi et al., 2010), and by the method used to assess personality traits (Wood et al., 2010).

Task — In this task you are to consider the potential implications of sex differences in personality traits. In Chapter 4 we examined McCrae's characteristic adaptations approach to personality traits as well as the importance of trait neuroticism and trait extraversion – the big two – as predictors of mental disorder and poor mental health. One implication of this is that if social groups have known differences in their personality traits, and especially extraversion and neuroticism, we might expect them to experience different levels of mental health. Specifically, we might expect there to be sex differences in mental health and mental disorder because of the personality trait differences between these groups. This inference is consistent with the known higher prevalence of both depression (Kornstein et al., 2000; Matud, 2004) and borderline personality disorder (Beauchaine et al., 2009; Boggs et al., 2000; De Moor et al., 2009) in women. However, the extent of sex differences in the prevalence rates of these disorders is controversial. Your task here is to conduct a brief search of the literature using an electronic search engine, such as PsycINFO, on the links between biological sex and either depression or borderline personality disorder. When conducting this search, make sure you identify around five key papers, and make sure these are papers that you believe capture the conflicting perspectives on sex differences in these disorders.

Comment

This task should enable you to start developing an evidence-based response to the question of whether sex differences in personality traits or temperament can help us explain the apparent differences in prevalence rates of depression or borderline personality disorder among men compared to women.

Universality versus cross-cultural variation in personality perception

The majority of research we have considered examines how personality, culture and biological sex are linked by comparing the self-reported personality traits of different social groups. There is also evidence that people *believe* that the personality traits of different cultural groups, nations, and men compared to women, differ. Such research is typically qualified as demonstrating stereotypes about social groups that have low levels of validity. Irrespective of whether such beliefs are false or are not veridical, they provide information that could impact on how individuals manage their interactions with others. In a similar way that knowledge about memory or metamemory can influence how you manage or self-regulate your memory, this sort of knowledge about personality and beliefs about how certain dispositions are linked to certain social indicators is a type of metaknowledge about personality. In other words, these personality perceptions are potentially an important source of knowledge individuals draw on when making judgements about the dispositions of others (see Chapter 2). This broad notion has been described using various terms such as *implicit personality theories* and is linked to work on person perception. However, we will use the term *personality metaknowledge* because these other terms have distinct theoretical qualities. Here, we simply want to emphasise that such beliefs are a form of knowledge that consists of beliefs about the links between social groups and dispositions, and that such beliefs have a range of potential self-regulatory functions.

Research has considered beliefs about the personality characteristics of specific social groups other than those based on culture and biological sex. For example, there is evidence that features of individuals themselves, such as their speech style (Dixon and Mahoney, 2003; Dixon et al., 2002), and their material possessions (Christopher and Jones, 2004; Christopher and Schlenker, 2000; Christopher et al., 2005) are believed to be linked to specific personality traits. Christopher's research on wealth cues is particularly interesting because it illustrates how cultural values, in this case the positive regard for symbols of affluence and wealth, are linked to beliefs about the personality characteristics of the materially wealthy.

Christopher's research (Christopher and Jones, 2004; Christopher and Schlenker, 2000; Christopher et al., 2005) demonstrates how culture appears to be linked to perceptions of how an individual's personality is linked to their affluence. This research also raises a number of issues about the universality and cross-cultural variation of personality perception.

Christopher and Schlenker (2000) position their research in the context of both the limitations of economic psychological research on personality perceptions and research showing how individual differences correlate with personality perceptions.

- **Economic psychology** has shown that individuals believe people with high socio-economic status have more *favourable* (p2) personality traits when socio-economic status is symbolically represented by *affluence cues* (Christopher and Jones, 2004) such as material possessions. However, this research has tended to assume such perceptions are held universally.

- Research has shown that the perceiver's socio-economic status and affluence have inconsistent effects on these perceptions. However, there is evidence that individual differences in dispositional materialism do predict perceptions. Specifically, if a perceiver has high levels of dispositional materialism they are more likely to perceive the personality of an affluent target individual as favourable – judging them to have greater personal attributes and resources than a less affluent target.

The same methodological paradigm was used across three studies using samples of university students (Christopher and Schlenker, 2000; Christopher et al., 2005) and the general population (Christopher and Jones, 2004). Participants read a vignette of a target individual whose affluence was manipulated by varying the *affluence cues* of the characters such as the consumer goods they possessed. In some cases, the sex of the target was manipulated to compare perceptions of both male and female more or less affluent targets. Having read the vignette, participants then completed a range of scales, including their judgement of the personality traits or dispositions of the target and the extent to which the perceiver found the target's lifestyle to be desirable. Below is a typical scenario from this research, with the target person here being referred to as Mark, and with the less affluent cues being shown in parentheses (taken from Christopher and Jones, 2004, pp290–1).

Mark works for a large technology company. He is quite tall with short black hair and blue eyes. He is 28 years old, although he looks slightly younger than that. He now owns a condominium (rents an apartment) in Dallas, which is well furnished with comfortable furniture (furnished with second-hand furniture). Mark is particularly proud of his new dining room set that he bought at Ethan Allen Furniture Galleries (of a set of chairs that he bought at an unfinished furniture store and finished himself). He also has an avid interest in cars, and he currently drives a 2000 Ford Mustang (a 1990 Ford Escort).

Typically, Mark returns home from work, feeds his Afghan Hound (Beagle), and prepares a steak (some chicken) for himself. He may also select a vintage wine to enjoy with his meal (he may occasionally, on the way home, pick up a bottle of wine from the grocery store). Before eating, Mark selects several compact disks from his extensive collection (a cassette) to enjoy with dinner. After eating, he puts the dishes in the dishwasher (washes up the dishes), and then relaxes in his Jacuzzi (takes a long hot bath). Later, he often goes out with friends or watches a video on his widescreen TV set (or watches TV on his 14-in colour set) for the rest of the evening.

Across these studies a number of key findings emerged. First, personality perceptions were linked to affluence cues but in ways that are complex. For example, in comparison to the less affluent target, the more affluent target person was perceived to have stronger *personal abilities*, such as intelligence and self-discipline, more sophisticated personal characteristics, such as being cultured and successful, and their lifestyle was perceived as more desirable. However, affluent targets were perceived to be low on considerateness – as less kind, honest and likeable than the less affluent target person. The means by which affluence is acquired also influences perceptions of the target person. For example, Christopher et al. (2005) manipulated whether the target person's affluence was acquired through internal means, such as promotion at work, or through external means, such as inheritance. Affluence acquired by internal means led participants to rate the affluent target person as high on the FFT of conscientiousness and openness in comparison to the low affluence target. However, affluence gained by external means led participants to rate the affluent target person as low on trait agreeableness compared to the target person whose affluence was gained by internal means. Finally, the only individual differences variable that appeared to be linked to perceivers' perceptions was their Protestant work ethic – the belief that work is a central part of life, a dedication to hard work and avoidance of idleness, deferred gratification, and a belief in conserving rather than spending one's financial resources. Participants with a strong Protestant work ethic perceived the affluent target as more considerate than participants with weaker Protestant work ethic beliefs. However, the latter participants had a stronger preference for the affluent lifestyle depicted in the vignette. The researchers suggest that perceivers' characteristics – or stable individual differences – have little systematic impact on their perceptions of the personality characteristics of affluent targets because *affluence is seen as so inherently tied to personal ability, sophistication, and considerateness that there is little room for dramatic modification of the relation to personality* (Christopher and Schlenker, 2000, p16).

This research raises a number of interesting issues about how personality and culture are linked. In Western cultural contexts it is possible that people believe that affluent individuals have a trait intensity pattern that is distinct from that linked to less affluent individuals when affluence is indicated by affluence cues, such as consumer goods. This pattern is modified to some extent if the means by which affluence is acquired can be linked to their own endeavours rather than luck or other individuals' efforts. There is also evidence of a stereotype of affluent individuals as being capable but less considerate than the less affluent, and this is consistent with research that has used other indicators of affluence, such as speech style. Finally, there is little compelling evidence that perceptions of the personality traits of the affluent and less affluent are related to the perceivers' personality traits or dispositions.

Critical thinking activity

Infectious diseases and personality

Critical thinking focus: analysis and evaluation

Key question: *Can cross-cultural differences in aggregate personality trait scores be determined by the prevalence of infectious diseases?*

Earlier we referred to theory and empirical evidence suggesting that cross-cultural variations on aggregate mean personality trait levels are related to the prevalence of infectious diseases. This work suggests that certain traits are linked to psycho-social conditions that increase the risk of infections spreading. Specifically, traits are linked to risk behaviours such as increased social or sexual interaction that appear to relate to high levels of extraversion and openness. This premise leads to the prediction that the pattern of traits observed in cultures where infectious disease prevalence is high will differ from patterns observed in cultures with lower prevalence rates. Interest in this approach to the relationship between personality traits and culture has grown in the twenty-first century. The work of Schaller, Murray, Mortensen and Fincher has provided compelling evidence that the intensity of certain personality traits – low levels of trait extraversion, trait openness, and a more restricted sociosexual style – has been found in regions with high levels of infectious diseases (Schaller and Murray, 2008), a pattern repeated in other research (Duncan et al., 2009; Fincher et al., 2008; Mortensen et al., 2010; Murray and Schaller, 2010). This research suggests that in cultural contexts where infectious diseases are highly prevalent, the mean aggregate trait levels observed suggest psychosocial conditions – behaviours – that should reduce or restrict the spread of infectious diseases. What is unclear is whether cross-cultural differences in aggregate trait levels are a *cause* or *consequence* of the prevalence of infectious diseases (Schaller and Murray, 2008), or some combination of both. In addition, given the issues involved in this research – race, culture, disease and sexual behaviour – the work touches on a number of sensitive social and political issues.

For this activity you are required to use some of this academic literature to analyse and evaluate fictional newspaper headlines. You have to imagine that this research has caught the attention of the tabloid press, leading to a flurry of articles with the following headlines.

> *Extraverts spread disease*

> *Infections make you introverted*

> *The spread of diseases in the developing world – are psychological differences the cause?*

Either individually or in groups, your task is to think critically about these headlines by analysing and evaluating the academic literature of this topic. You should then, either in a group discussion or individually, produce an evidence-based response to these three headlines in the form of a brief list of qualifications you believe should be made to these headlines. Please use the following questions to structure your discussions/responses.

What are the three headlines *implying*?

Is there any *actual academic evidence* to support these headlines?

How could the academic literature have been analysed and evaluated by the press to produce such headlines?

Is there anything psychologists can do to improve the accuracy with which the press analyse and evaluate academic research findings?

To help you, it would be useful to examine some of the primary literature on this topic and two such papers and hyperlinks are given below.

Fincher, C.L. Thornhill, R., Murray, D.R. and Schaller, M. (2008) Pathogen prevalence predicts human cross-cultural variation in individualism/collectivism. *Proceedings of the Royal Society Bio*, 275: 1279–85. Available at http://rspb.royalsocietypublishing.org/content/275/1640/1279.full.pdf+html

Mortensen, C.R., Vaughn Becker, D., Ackerman, J.M., Neuberg, S.L. and Kenrick, D.T. (2010). Infection breeds reticence: the effects of disease salience on self-perceptions of personality and behavioral avoidance tendencies. *Psychological Science*, 21(3): 440–7. Available at http://web.mit.edu/joshack/www/Mortensen_Infectionreticence2010.pdf

Worked example

There is some academic evidence that could be used to support all three headlines. For example, Schaller and Murray (2008, p213) state that:

> *disease prevalence may also help account for crosscultural differences in personality. Within regions in which disease prevalence is relatively high, the costs of an incautious disposition may outweigh*

its benefits. This may result in a general tendency for individuals to be interpersonally cautious and conservative in their responses to unfamiliar things. In contrast, within regions in which disease prevalence is relatively low, the costs of an incautious disposition are likely to be lower and possibly outweighed by the potential benefits. As a consequence, individuals living within these regions may be more outgoing and open to unfamiliar things.

However, what these headlines suggest is a simplistic analysis of the research – in the research it is made clear that the causal direction of the relation between traits such as extraversion and openness and infectious disease prevalence is unclear (Schaller and Murray, 2008). Furthermore, the literature does not state that *traits cause disease.* Furthermore, the academic literature does not make definitive statements about individuals. Instead, this research tends to be based on group aggregate means and on trait intensities over relatively lengthy historical periods.

Critical thinking review

This task involves the analysis and evaluation of both non-academic information and academic literature. You have to analyse – or deconstruct – fictional newspaper headlines and then analyse the academic literature for evidence of these headlines. This also involves the analysis and evaluation of what the newspaper headlines *imply* and what the academic literature of personality and culture actually *demonstrates.* You also need to reflect on the processes involved in the analysis and evaluation of academic literature. How is psychological research interpreted? How accurate are such interpretations? Do the media analyse academic literature simplistically and miss important details?

Other skills likely to be used in this activity: this activity also involves the use of problem-solving skills to find and search relevant academic literature, along with decision making when deciding which aspects of the academic literature are being referred to in the headlines. If the activity is completed as a group discussion, it involves the development of oral communication and teamwork skills to co-ordinate individuals' responses. If completed individually, the activity involves the development of independence and written communication skills to produce a brief set of evidence-based responses to the headlines.

Skill builder activity

Sex differences in personality

Transferable skill focus: problem solving

Key question: *Do men and women agree that personality traits differ between the sexes?*

Earlier in this chapter we examined evidence that shows that the FFT scores of men and women differ. This is usually found in research based on self-reports of individuals' own personality traits. For this activity you have to solve a problem related to this finding: *how can we find out if men and women agree with this pattern?* This involves designing, but not running, a research study that tests the question *do men and women believe that, typically, women are more open, conscientious, agreeable and neurotic than men?*

There are no restrictions on the study you choose to design or the nature of the data you can collect (e.g. quantitative or qualitative). However, you *must* develop a study:

- that will enable you to produce evidence of whether men and women agree/disagree on this issue;

- in which the sample is restricted to 20 male and 20 female first-year psychology undergraduates;

- in which the data can be collected in a single group session lasting no longer than 15 minutes.

This can be completed as either a group or individual activity.

Worked example

You have to solve the problem of what sort of data to collect given the time and test condition constraints you face. The research question is essentially about individuals' perceptions of personality or what we can describe as their implicit personality theories, so you might want to base your study on this literature. You might also tackle whether you have the time, resources and conditions within which to collect qualitative data or whether you could collect quantitative and qualitative data. Will you use a paper and pencil test with forced-choice responses? What limitations do the sample size and composition pose for you as researcher and can you overcome these constraints?

Skill builder review

This activity involves problem-solving skills as you have a research question (a problem) that you must test through developing a proposal for a small research study (a solution). The activity has some restrictions that influence how you can develop the study, and these could pose additional problems in your search for a solution. Given the research question, what sort of data can be collected during a single group session with the whole sample present? How can you ensure that the data are valid and reliable measures?

Other skills likely to be used in this activity: this activity also involves reflection, analysis and evaluation skills to make sure you understand what the current literature actually shows on this topic, IT and searching skills to provide an evidence-based rationale for your study, and decision making when deciding which options to use in your actual study.

Assignments

1. To what extent does psychological evidence suggest that personality is universal?

2. Traits determine culture and not the other way around. Discuss.

3. Critically evaluate whether differences between the personality traits of men and women have been exaggerated.

4. How important are personality traits and temperament to explanations of sex differences in the prevalence of *either* depression *or* personality disorders?

5. Critically examine the extent to which we believe the personality traits of affluent individuals differ from those of the less affluent.

Summary: what you have learned

Research on personality, culture and biological sex has demonstrated that the links between these constructs are complex, and these constructs themselves are not straightforward to define and measure. Moreover, the evidence from much of this research demonstrates that some aspects of personality appear relatively universal, while other aspects do not. However, this is dependent upon how researchers choose to interpret this sometimes ambiguous and complex data. Nevertheless, differences between the personality traits of some social groups appear to exist, and these differences have potential implications beyond those usually considered in psychology. By completing a close reading of a specific aspect of this research and attempting to design a research study, you should have developed analytical, evaluation and problem-solving skills that help you think critically about these important but controversial issues.

Further reading

Hankin, BL and Abramson, LY (2001) Development of gender differences in depression: an elaborated cognitive vulnerability-transactional stress theory. *Psychological Bulletin*, 127(6): 773–96.

This paper provides a comprehensive outline of an important model of sex differences in depression. It includes personality traits as pre-existing vulnerabilities contributing to the gendered nature of depression.

Hofstede, G and McCrae, RR (2004) Personality and culture revisited: Linking traits and dimensions of culture. *Cross-Cultural Research,* 38(1): 52–88.

This is an excellent summary of the key issues surrounding the conceptual, methodological, theoretical and social challenges of trait approaches to personality and culture – a good starter paper.

McCrae, RR, Terracciano, A and 78 members of the Personality Profiles of Cultures project (2005) Universal features of personality traits from the observer's perspective: data from 50 cultures. *Journal of Personality and Social Psychology*, 88(3): 547–61.

This paper demonstrates clearly the predominant methods used in trait approaches to personality and culture. The complex results also illustrate the multiple interpretations that can be applied to this type of research data.

Putnam, KM and Silk, KR (2005) Emotion dysregulation and the development of borderline personality disorder. *Development and Psychopathology*, 17: 899–925.

This is a useful outline of the importance of emotional dysregulation to borderline personality disorder and how this might help explain the gendered nature of the prevalence of borderline personality disorder.

Schmitt, DP, Realo, A, Voracek, M and Allik, J (2008). Why can't a man be more like a woman? Sex differences in big five personality traits across 55 cultures. *Journal of Personality and Social Psychology*, 94(1): 168–82.

This has become an important paper in discussions about the pan-cultural nature of sex differences in traits, and it also contains important evidence about cultural differences.

Useful websites

www.internationalpsychology.net/home/ (International Psychology)

This is the website of the American Psychological Society's Division 52. Its mission statement asserts that it seeks to develop a psychological science and practice that is contextually informed, culturally inclusive, serves the public interest, and promotes global perspectives within and outside APA. *This is a useful site for familiarising yourself with the current issues in international psychology, and the ways in which both individual differences psychology and the discipline generally is engaging with cultural, social and political issues.*

www.ejop.org/presentation.html (*Europe's Journal of Psychology*)

This is an online free peer-reviewed journal that is aimed at psychology students and academics, and using a more generalist and eclectic approach on psychology issues given the current tendency to produce rather highly specialised works. Although the journal is described as 'European' its purpose is also to consider the global relevance of psychology using an eclectic and multidisciplinary approach. It is a useful resource for research papers and academic debates about psychology and culture, including a broad range of issues relevant to individual differences psychology.

Chapter 6

The structure and determinants of intelligence

Learning outcomes

By the end of this chapter you should:

- be able to define intelligence and discuss, critically, how psychological research on intelligence has developed historically;

- be able to outline and evaluate, critically, theories of intelligence;

- understand and be able to discuss, critically, whether individual differences psychology has changed its conceptual approach to intelligence;

- be able to examine, critically, evidence on the determinants of intelligence;

- be able to discuss, critically, the importance of factors other than cognitive ability for intelligence;

- develop critical and creative thinking skills by completing an activity that involves reflecting on your beliefs about your own intellectual achievements, and by organising information about a fictional character's beliefs about their own intellectual abilities and achievements.

Introduction

This chapter will examine how psychologists have attempted to describe, measure and explain an important aspect of individual differences – intelligence – by focusing on four questions.

- How have psychologists attempted to define intelligence, and how has their research and theory developed?

- What are the main philosophical and conceptual debates in individual differences research on intelligence?

- What are the main theories of intelligence, and how convincing are they as explanations of both inter-individual variation in intelligence and the processes underlying such variation?

- How new are the allegedly new approaches to intelligence?

In Chapter 2 we considered one of the big two topics in individual differences psychology – personality. Intelligence can be regarded as the second of the big two topics in the field. Intelligence research has been central to individual differences psychology for over a century (Ackerman and Heggestad, 1997; Gardner and Hatch, 1989; Garrett, 1946; Perkins et al., 2000; Weinberg, 1989). In fact, *few topics have sparked such heated debate within the academic community and society at large as that of intelligence and intelligence testing* (Schlinger, 2003, p15). Given the importance and controversy of this topic, extensive coverage of the full history of individual differences research on intelligence is beyond the scope of this single chapter. Papers listed in the Further reading section by Lubinski (2004), Plomin and Spinath (2004) and Schlinger (2003) provide useful summaries of the history of intelligence research. These papers, along with Sternberg, Grigorenko and Kidd (2005) also cover the issues of sex and race differences in intelligence. Instead, we will focus on some of the main conceptual and content areas of this work. You will consider to what extent the salient conceptual, theoretical and methodological issues in intelligence research have changed in the past 100 years or so. A notable feature of this change is that the predominance of the psychometric approach to understanding and measuring intelligence as a context-independent construct has been challenged. Some researchers argue that despite such challenges to intelligence research the fundamental nature of much of this work remains unchanged (Schlinger, 2003). Central to this debate is the role of individual differences psychology in the changing agenda; for example, some researchers argue that many accounts of intellectual performance remain *abilities-centric* (Perkins et al., 2000, p270). Despite the pessimism about the extent of change in individual difference research on intelligence, these challenges have led to certain developments. Especially since the 1980s, a number of theories of intelligence have been developed that focus on the multidimensional and context-dependent nature of intelligent behaviour, and how this ability enables success across a range of life domains. Clearly, there has been a shift from measuring the intelligence that individuals *have*, to examining intelligent behaviour as those phenomena that *work* for the individual when faced with a complex diversity of tasks.

There has also been a resurgence of research on the links between personality and intelligence – links discussed by classic early researchers such as Thorndike (Ackerman and Heggestad, 1997). To some extent, the increased use of terms such as intellect, intellectual processes, intelligences and intelligent behaviour is indicative of this conceptual change. The change has also involved challenges to the ontological status of intelligence as a psychological construct. Furthermore, as a student, any matters related to *intelligence, intellect, ability, achievement* and *performance* and their measurement will obviously be important to you. Many of the theories of intelligence that post-date the period in which intelligence was conceptualised as either a *unitary lump* of cognitive ability or *split* into specific types of intellectual ability (Mayr, 1982) have captured the interest of educators. These theories focus more explicitly on the nature of *intellectual processes* and learning, and how we can use theories and empirical research on intellectual ability to design learning environments and foster learning experiences that will enhance intellectual development, performance and achievement. The overall approach of this book (see Chapter 1) is consistent with such ideas and how you can become an expert student (Sternberg, 2003) through thinking critically about psychology. An important goal of this chapter is to encourage you to develop your critical thinking about individual differences research on intelligence by reflecting on *your own* intellect and your beliefs about this, both in general and personally. In the critical thinking activity you will therefore reflect on your beliefs about your intellect, and in the skill builder activity you will attempt to organise information in a fictional case study by considering beliefs about intellectual ability and their consequences for the fictional character. Finally, the overall goal of this chapter is for you to develop knowledge of the mainstream approaches to intelligence and to challenge these by developing critical thinking skills of reflection and organisation.

Definitions of intelligence

It is conventional to define key terms at the outset of any consideration of a psychological construct, and this chapter is no exception. In Chapter 1 we defined individual differences and identified personality as one aspect of this field studied by psychologists. We also stated that universal agreement about what precisely constitutes the field of individual differences is relatively elusive. In Chapter 2 we acknowledged that this pattern is repeated when considering definitions of personality – psychologists again disagree on what the term means. However, we identified that to some extent there is broad agreement in the literature about some of the key features that define personality. The same can be said about intelligence, but with slightly less confidence. Just as personality was described as a latent construct that is operationalised through the measurements we take and the data we produce, intelligence has similar qualities as an aspect of individual differences. However, what distinguishes intelligence from personality in this respect is the *centrality of definitions* to past, present and – no doubt – future debates about the construct. What is meant by the term intelligence is central both to academic and to popular debates and controversies on the topic. These controversies make it difficult to identify a clear and universally accepted definition. Nevertheless, as with personality in Chapter 2, we will attempt to define intelligence by searching for key features of the construct in both explicit academic definitions and in your own ideas about the construct.

To start, let us return to our definition of individual differences described in Chapter 1. The study of the *structure and determinants of enduring psychological characteristics as perceived by the individual and those around them*. These enduring characteristics are *collections of behaviours, feelings and thoughts* that *systematically typify how individuals and groups of individuals appear to be similar or different*. These psychological phenomena also have *consequences for how individuals react and therefore regulate themselves across a range of life domains*, and the relationship between these person and situation variables is *complex and reciprocal*.

We would expect any definition of intelligence to at least contain these features. As with personality, we will examine a number of explicit academic definitions of intelligence, starting with a definition from Binet (1905), a name synonymous with the notion of intelligence testing.

> *But here we must come to an understanding of what meaning to give to that word so vague and so comprehensive, 'the intelligence.' Nearly all the phenomena with which psychology concerns itself are phenomena of intelligence; sensation, perception, are intellectual mani-festations as much as reasoning. Should we therefore bring into our examination the measure of sensation after the manner of the psycho-physicists? Should we put to the test all of his psychological processes? A slight reflection has shown us that this would indeed be wasted time.*

> *It seems to us that in intelligence there is a fundamental faculty, the alteration or the lack of which, is of the utmost importance for practical life. This faculty is judgment, otherwise called good sense, practical sense, initiative, the faculty of adapting one's self to circumstances. To judge well, to comprehend well, to reason well, these are the essential activities of intelligence.*

Binet's (1905) definition has a number of notable features.

- It is what has been described as an *omnibus* (Garrett, 1946) definition of intelligence – it is broad and underpins all psychological phenomena.

- Intelligence is described as essentially *practical ability*.

- It is a fundamental ability.

- Despite being closely associated with the psychometric and testing approach to intelligence, Binet's definition is not especially reductionist simply because it encompasses so many psychological phenomena.

- It regards intelligence as essential for adapting to the challenges of life and in this sense is consistent with our definition of individual differences, which focuses on self-regulation.

Garrett (1946) took a different approach to defining intelligence. He argued that *omnibus* definitions such as that of Binet (1905) are unhelpful because they are:

> *in general too broad to be wrong and too vague to be useful . . . we must avoid obvious and circular definitions. It is undoubtedly true that intelligence involves the ability to learn but our understanding is not greatly helped by saying so . . . (however, intelligence is) at least the abilities demanded in the solution of problems which require the comprehension and use of symbols . . . words, numbers,*

diagrams, equations, formulas, which represent ideas and relationships ranging from the fairly simple to the very complex . . ..

However, Garrett (1946) goes on to acknowledge that Thorndike's (1920) definition of three levels of intelligence – abstract, social and mechanical – is a compromise between omnibus definitions and ones that are so narrow that they overlook individual differences in *behaviour . . . within fairly defined areas. Books, people and machines.* Although this definition states that intelligence is *multidimensional* and *practical*, it does clearly focus on what can be described as *cognitive abilities*. Cooper's (2002, p17) definition captures this cognitive focus when describing intellectual ability as *performance on some task that has a substantial information processing component.*

Such a cognitive definition can be contrasted with the following two definitions of intelligence. Gardner and Hatch (1989, p5) state that:

Human intellect is . . . capacious . . . a wide variety of human cognitive capacities . . . [these are] skills valued in a variety of cultural and historical settings . . . autonomous human intelligences . . . [including] the capacity to solve problems or to fashion products that are valued in one or more cultural settings.

Sternberg (2005) also defines intelligence as those talents needed to succeed in life.

- To achieve one's life goals in a given sociocultural context.

- Capitalising on one's strengths and correcting or compensating for weaknesses.

- Adapting to, shaping and selecting environments.

- Using a combination of analytical, creative and practical abilities.

Consequently, for Sternberg (2005) *intelligence means a somewhat different thing to each individual.*

Task — Compare and contrast the definitions of intelligence we have considered, and ask yourself whether there are any features of intelligence that appear common across them.

Comment

Analysing definitions is one way of thinking critically because it encourages you to focus on the conceptual and technical details of the constructs being considered. Some of the similarities between these definitions include the conceptualisation of intelligence as both context independent and context dependent, and as manifest and deeper or intrapsychic. You should also have noted that older definitions of intelligence share some features in common with more contemporary ones. For example, they conceptualise intelligence as essential for self-regulation and adjustment. Surprisingly, differences between these definitions are at times subtle.

Considering these definitions suggests important differences exist between researchers' conceptualisation of what intelligence is. Nevertheless, some general points of agreement about key features of intelligence can be identified. First, it is primarily cognitive ability, although some researchers also include non-ability phenomena. Second, intelligence has the *potential* to influence how an individual functions and can determine adjustment and self-regulation. Third, it is typically conceptualised from the observer's perspective – in other words, it is operationalised through observable performance, typically captured by performance on a test or series of tests. Intelligence varies between individuals – in other words, it is characterised by *inter-individual variation*. However, researchers disagree about the nature of this variation. Finally, researchers have not always been explicit about the processes underlying intelligence – in other words, the *intra-individual processes of intelligence* have tended not to be the focus of much intelligence research. This means that the search for the determinants of intelligence has not always been at the forefront of individual differences research.

History, concepts and methods

History of research on intelligence

An important feature of the definitions we considered in the previous section is the distinction researchers do, or do not, make between intelligence as cognitive ability, that is, the abilities individuals have, and *intelligent behaviour*, that is, behaviour that *works* for individuals because it enables them to adapt to life's challenges. The distinction can be situated within the context of the history of research on intelligence. For example, the late nineteenth century and early twentieth century saw the rise of the use of intelligence tests as ways of quantifiably measuring maximal performance or ability independent of context (Ackerman and Heggestad, 1997) – what has been called the *testing movement*. Some of the critical features of this history are shown in Figure 6.1.

Streams of research tended to develop as interest in theoretical explanations of intelligence waned. In particular, researchers began to focus on intelligence testing in children and adults. The work of Binet (1905) is synonymous with the early testing movement of intelligence, and the *IQ controversy* linked to his notion of the intelligence quotient is part of Americana, as is the nature–nurture debate also linked to this early work (Weinberg, 1989). Binet's (1905) focus was clearly on the *identification* of individuals with, to use his terminology, *inferior intellect*.

Figure 6.1: *The development of research on intelligence and intelligence testing*

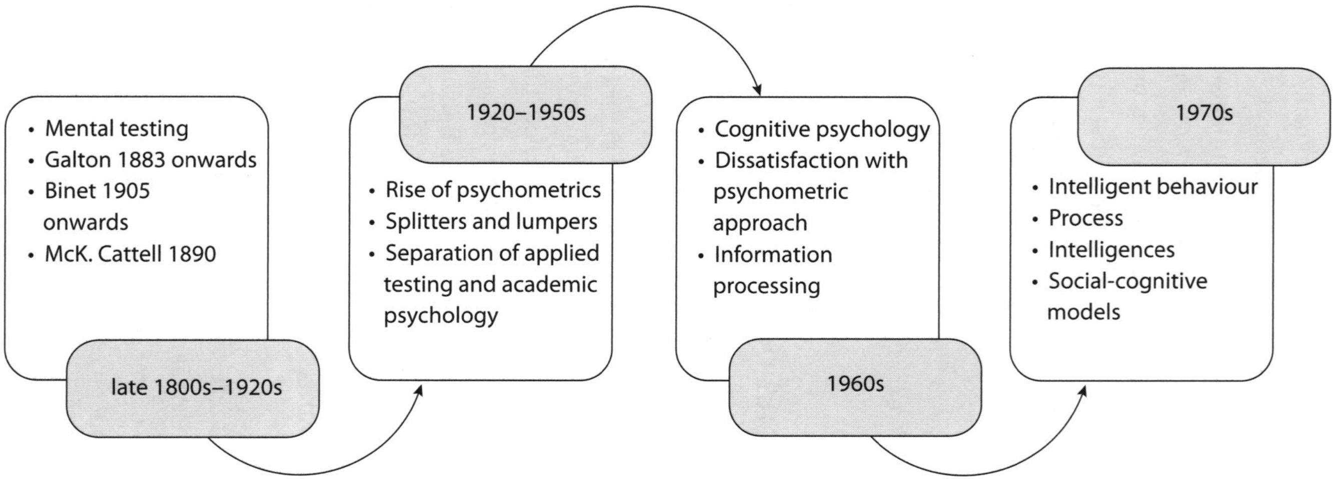

late 1800s–1920s
- Mental testing
- Galton 1883 onwards
- Binet 1905 onwards
- McK. Cattell 1890

1920–1950s
- Rise of psychometrics
- Splitters and lumpers
- Separation of applied testing and academic psychology

1960s
- Cognitive psychology
- Dissatisfaction with psychometric approach
- Information processing

1970s
- Intelligent behaviour
- Process
- Intelligences
- Social-cognitive models

From this early research on the measurement of intelligence a number of important principles about the how intelligence can be conceptualised can be drawn.

- Definitions of intelligence have been both implicit and explicit (Weinberg, 1989).

- Early research focused on the testing, measuring, operationally defining, diagnosing and comparing individuals achieving different test scores.

- The correlational research paradigm dominated this work (Spearman, 1904).

- Intelligence is a context-independent fundamental ability that underpins a range of behaviours.

- Intelligence is, essentially, intellectual ability that reflects cognitive information processing.

However, even in early classic writings on intelligence, debates that have also appeared more recently can be found, especially those relating to the importance of the *applications* of intelligence tests. Binet's work (1905) has to some extent been misrepresented (Schlinger, 2003). Binet (1905) was explicitly unconcerned with the determinants or remediation of intellectual deficits – a position fairly typical of the testing movement:

> *Our purpose is to be able to measure the intellectual capacity of a child who is brought to us in order to know whether he is normal or retarded. We should therefore, study his condition at the time and that only. We have nothing to do either with his past history or with his future; consequently we shall neglect his etiology, and we shall make no attempt to distinguish between acquired and congenital idiocy; for a stronger reason we shall set aside all consideration of pathological anatomy which might explain his intellectual deficiency. So much for his past. As to that which concerns his future, we shall exercise the same abstinence; we do not attempt to establish or prepare a prognosis and we leave unanswered the question of whether this retardation is curable, or even improvable. We shall limit ourselves to ascertaining the truth in regard to his present mental state.*

Binet's (1905) purpose contains a number of key points. **Semantics** and language use are important features of research on intelligence. For example, some of the language used by Binet (1905) is now regarded as somewhat pejorative. Furthermore, the history of research on intelligence and intelligence testing is to some extent characterised by semantic confusions, myths and the misreading of evidence. Indeed, some of the early research has been oversimplified, thus making the reading of primary sources an important part of developing your critical thinking about this aspect of individual differences.

Task ⌐ Given the importance of reading primary sources, this task requires you to examine critically excerpts from Binet's (1905) work, and to reflect on what the content actually states about his conceptualisation of intelligence. The quotation from Binet (1905) we considered earlier suggests that despite the IQ controversy being synonymous with nature–nurture issues, Binet's focus was actually on the *measurement* of intellect. In this task you will examine his 1905 paper, in which he identifies three methods for assessing intellect – medical, pedagogical and psychological. It is his psychological method – which involves directly observing different degrees of intelligence – that you should focus on. Please access his paper – available at http://psychclassics. asu.edu/Binet/binet1.htm – and examine his psychological method – it contains 30 different tests. Your task is to critically evaluate these tests in terms of whether they *look like* measures of intelligence. In other words, you should examine their face validity. Are you surprised by the inclusion of any of these tests?

Comment

This task should draw your attention to how an early classic researcher on intelligence operationalised the construct. Binet's (1905) series of tests were designed to measure the observable psychological aspects of intelligence, and to enable those with better or poorer intellect to be differentiated. By examining the specific tests you should notice that many of these appear to assess broad skills and capacities that appear to be more physical than explicitly psychological. Nevertheless, Binet argued that such tests measure fundamental aspects of intelligence and that those appearing later in the series were better approximations of real-life intelligent behaviours.

From 1900 to the 1950s there was a growing *separation* of intelligence research from general psychology as interest in the psychometrics or measurement of intelligence became the predominant issue (Gardner and Hatch, 1989). In particular, the work of Spearman (1904) and his correlational paradigm had a substantial impact on both the research paradigms and structural theories of intelligence developed across that period. The period saw the rise of factor analysis for both intelligence theory building, and the development of tests of intelligence. This period also saw the debate about the existence of *g* – a *general intelligence* factor that could explain and predict performance on different subtests of intelligence tests – as opposed to the existence of *intelligences* – the *componential approach* (Sternberg, 2005). The testing movement in intelligence research also provided an impetus for researchers to consider the existence and nature of measurable differences in intelligence between social groups. The perennial nature–nurture debate about the determinants of intelligence differences between racial groups and between the sexes preoccupied researchers during the first half of the twentieth century. To some extent, such debates encouraged researchers to challenge mainstream approaches and the nature–nurture debate as applied to intelligence. From the 1960s onwards, challenges from educators, social and political scientists and behavioural science, and the changing nature of research in cognitive psychology all fostered an intellectual climate receptive to new approaches to intelligence. However, despite these challenges, intelligence research remained relatively separate from general psychology until the mid-1970s when mainstream psychology saw a *rediscovery of the centrality of intelligence* to the discipline (Gardner and Hatch, 1989, p4).

This brief consideration of the history of mental testing suggests that challenges to the psychometric approach can be found in the early intelligence research. For example, early research shows that even researchers synonymous with the IQ testing approach acknowledged that intelligence is a broad *ability* with consequences for *life skills*. In fact, approaches to intelligence in individual differences psychology encompass both the psychometric – the testing movement – and the more cognitive – a focus on the intellectual processes of intelligence. However, the testing movement has been increasingly challenged, and dissatisfaction with the predominance of factor analysis as a method for developing models and tests of intelligence has been part of this challenge. Finally, to some extent there remains a separation between applied, academic research, and educational and school research on intelligence.

Key concepts

Despite a lack of consensus on the meaning of intelligence, some concepts have remained synonymous with individual differences research on intelligence.

Mental testing and *measurement* remain central to individual differences research on intelligence. The research in the late nineteenth century and early twentieth century saw the emergence of both psychometrics and the use of psychophysical tests to measure and thus operationally define intelligence (Galton, 1865, 1883). Spearman (1904) discussed the use of experimental methods and simple physical measures of intelligence and his work contains a number of fundamental premises about the nature of intelligence. First, we can use the correlational method and mathematics or statistical methods to identify the structure of intelligence. Second, general intelligence or *g* is a fundamental characteristic of intellect. He argued that the *experimental methods* associated with European psychological research at that time provided suitable methods for identifying the nature of intelligence, along with the statistical analysis of the relationship or correlation between scores on such tests, or *how far the observed ranks in the several abilities tend to correspond with one another*. Importantly, he also argued that the use of statistical tests of correlation would replace the existing methods that he regarded as relying on *psychological ingenuity . . . complex arbitrary tables and plausible but more or less fanciful exploratory stories*. Instead, Spearman (1904) claimed that the scientific study of intelligence required:

- relationships between measures and intelligence operationalised through measures;

- impartiality in the methods used;

- full use of all the information or data collected;

- quantitative values, in other words, that researchers needed to *give way to mathematics*.

Intelligence – or *intellect* – as the *optimal performance* that can be *achieved* – remains at the core of the research. We have outlined some of the historical developments in intelligence research and alluded to the issue of definitions. How we define intelligence is at the heart of individual differences research on the construct (Garrett, 1946). Some argue that researchers are preoccupied with the wrong questions (Schlinger, 2003). Your challenge as a student of psychology is to understand these questions, why they concern psychologists, and to consider critically whether these are the key questions we should be asking about intelligence.

Nevertheless, we can identify a number of central concepts in intelligence research.

- Intellect is reflected in intelligent behaviour.

- Intellectual ability is the *optimal* performance an individual can *achieve* rather than their typical performance or what they can attain having completed a course of instruction.

- Intellect is a trait or a relatively stable fundamental dispositional quality of individuals that we can measure using motivated cognitive performance.

- Intelligent behaviour is distinct from *attainment*, which is performance following instructional learning. In other words, intelligent behaviour is about *thinking* as opposed to knowing or remembering. Intellect is actually a form of information processing that is context independent, hence the focus on basic or fundamental intellectual ability such a *g*.

Methods

In Chapter 1 we stated that psychometric methods dominate individual differences research, and this includes research on intelligence. The psychometric approach entails operationally defining intelligence using *domain sampling* (see Chapter 1). In other words, the *domain of intelligent behaviour* is sampled, and these sampled intelligent behaviours or *intellectual abilities* are operationalised in test subscales. Importantly, unlike measures of personality traits, tests of intelligence, and thus how we conceptualise intelligence, is based on correlations between test scores and *not* correlations between responses to individual items. Another difference between intelligence tests and tests used to assess personality is that responses to intelligence tests are either correct or incorrect, and essentially these responses are added to produce raw test scores. Finally, norms and percentiles are used to help us interpret an individual's intellectual achievement.

Factor analysis and related statistical methods for summarising the relationship between sets of scores are central methods in the psychometric approach to intelligence. Importantly, factor analysis is used on tests and subtest scores to *develop models of intelligence*. This is what Facione (2000) describes as an *a posteriori* approach to validating the construct of intelligence because it *begins with an overall idea, and goes to constituent elements a posteriori. Given a valid and reliable test of a given construct, one can statistically explore that construct to see if there are different variables or factors working within it* (p69). This is an important characteristic of much of individual differences research on intelligence because to some extent this method means that intelligence is a *statistical entity*. Put another way, when researchers make inferences about the structure of intelligence or intellectual ability based on statistical patterns observed in test and subtest scores, such inferences emerge from the tests we select. The *a posteriori* approach to validating the construct of intelligence involves developing a theory or model that emerges from the statistical analyses, and this is distinct from what Cronbach and Meehl (1955) describe as a *highly theoretical approach* to testing the validity of a construct. The *a posteriori* approach means that a hypothesised entity – by which we mean *intelligence* here – is tested, and we select our tests because they *reflect* our conceptualisation of the construct. Unfortunately, individual differences research on intelligence often confuses *a posteriori* with the *highly theoretical approach* to testing the validity of the construct of intelligence. Consequently, there has been some over-interpretation of some of the psychometric research on intelligence because much research on intelligence is actually concerned with assessing the validity of intelligence tests rather than testing the validity of the theoretical construct of intelligence.

Theories of intelligence

Over 20 years ago Mayr (1982) used the terms *lumpers*, *splitters* and *intermediary*, or *hierarchical, models* to describe the different theoretical approaches to intelligence. This still has relevance today. Mainstream textbooks on individual differences and intelligence tend to focus on these three types of theoretical approaches. They also tend to focus on how researchers have challenged the notion that intelligence is essentially a single or unitary lump of intellectual or cognitive ability, a notion most closely associated with Spearman's (1904) theory of intelligence as *g* or general. Given the importance of these issues to individual differences research on intelligence we will consider them here. However, in considering this work you will be encouraged to focus on how *new* these allegedly new approaches to intelligence are.

Before considering these different theories of intelligence, it is worth bearing in mind a number of complexities in the research.

- Theories of intelligence can be grouped in different ways, and using the structure of intelligence as unitary or componential (Sternberg, 2005) is merely one such approach.

- Theories of intelligence also vary in their focus on the structure, determinants or consequences of intelligence.

- The term *intelligences* is sometimes used to refer to theoretical approaches that have challenged the strictly cognitive approach to intelligence. However, this term can be used to describe the componential cognitive approach to intelligence, and thus can have different meanings.

We will consider *lumpers* and *splitters* first, and then consider challenges to these along with other approaches that have called for the reconceptualisation of intelligence as more than simply cognitive intellectual ability.

Lumpers or splitters?

Spearman (1904) is often cited as the first researcher to formally conceptualise intelligence as a lump, which he referred to as *general intelligence* or *g*. His approach was based on his observation of the weaknesses of current approaches to measuring intelligence, which he regarded as lacking objectivity. In his 1904 paper, Spearman claimed that experimental methods can be used to administer tests of intellectual ability, and that such tests were more or less direct measures of fundamental intellectual processes. Importantly, he argued that by using *correlational psychology* we can *connect together the so-called mental tests* that measure general intelligence, the cardinal function of intellect. Having examined a diversity of previous research from across the behavioural sciences, including the work of Galton (1883), Binet and Henri, Titchener, Ebbinghaus and Cattell, he concluded that the administration of simple psychophysical tests using experimentation offered the best method for identifying the fundamental function underlying intelligence. Spearman conceptualised intelligence as hierarchical, a conception he developed using test performances of school children in the UK. He constructed six tests he believed assessed different types of thinking ability, namely *knowledge of vocabulary, mathematical ability, visualisation, colour matching, musical pitch matching*, and *following complex instructions*. He developed the statistical technique of factor analysis to summarise the large amount of statistical data his research produced. Using factor analysis he found that children's intellectual performance *across* tests appeared to be determined by a general intelligence factor or *g*. Importantly, his statistical analyses used a form of correlation that used the *ranks* of scores rather than the actual test scores, and by correlating test score *ranks* rather than actual test scores, he identified *g* or *general intelligence* or *basic thinking ability*. Spearman's theory can be described as the classic example of a *lumping theory of intelligence* (Mayr, 1982) because it conceptualises intelligence as fundamentally a single or general factor that underpins all other types of thinking ability. The essence of Spearman's theory is that intelligence is *abstract ability* that underpins the *formation of concepts, language* and *comprehension*. Furthermore, Spearman's (1904) conceptualisation of intelligence appears to have been developed using the *highly theoretical approach* to testing the validity of a construct (Cronbach and Meehl, 1955).

However, there are a number of problems with Spearman's (1904) concept of *g*. It seems doubtful that we can reduce intelligence to a single *lump* or *essence*, and doubts have been raised about the statistical process used by Spearman, with subsequent researchers identifying a *greater* number of factors and thus an *independence* of intellectual abilities. Nevertheless, we should not oversimplify the nature of Spearman's work or dismiss his approach to the development of *g* as fundamentally flawed. The title of his 1904 paper *General intelligence objectively determined and measured* indicates the impetus behind his research, namely, to use a more objective quantitative approach to exploring intellectual abilities – or, as he referred to them, *quintessences* – than previous researchers. His review of the research on intelligence from the late nineteenth century is a useful resource for those interested in the history of scientific research on intelligence testing; and the research Spearman (1904) describes does show that early researchers such as Thorndike and Woodworth (1901), Galton (1883), Oerhrn (1889 in Spearman, 1904) and Cattell and Farrand (1896 in Spearman, 1904) did use methods that appear broadly scientific. Spearman's (1904) analysis of this work acknowledges this, but he concludes that overall this research, collectively, has four flaws or *fallacies*.

- Few researchers used *precise quantifiable expressions* or numerical data, with many using what we could describe as O-DATA – the observations of researchers or individuals known to participants such as their school teacher or instructor.

- Early research did not identify the *probable error* – what Spearman describes as *accidental coincidence*. By this Spearman meant that many of the measures used and the ways in which they were administered to participants are not always clear, and thus we cannot identify the reliability of the methods used.

- Much of the research lacks *any clear explicit definition of the problem to be resolved*, with researchers frequently not setting limits on the nature of the participants and the numbers tested. This diversity often appears to have been haphazard, making the specific parameters of the research difficult to ascertain. This approach also introduced variables that cannot be easily defined and measured by researchers.

- Much of the early research also appeared to make *errors of observation. For having executed our experiment and calculated the correlation, we must then remember that the latter does not represent the mathematical relation between the two sets of real objects compared, but only between the two sets of measurements which we have derived from the former by more or less fallible processes.*

We have spent some time considering the details of Spearman's (1904) paper for a number of reasons. First, his work does appear to have a theoretical basis and thus is more than simply an exercise in test construction and test validation. Second, his four flaws or fallacies do suggest an awareness of the limits of the psychometric measurement of intelligence. Importantly, his comments about the errors of observation show that he recognised that we should not over-interpret the results of our statistical analyses of intelligence test scores because, ultimately, these tell us about *relationships between test scores*. This comment is reminiscent of arguments used by researchers who challenge the cognitive ability approach to intelligence.

Thurstone's (1934, 1935, 1938) work on *primary mental abilities* (PMAs) is often cited as an antidote to Spearman's (1904) *g*. Thurstone's approach was based on scepticism about the notion of *g*.

Although he conceptualised intelligence as *hierarchical* he argued that it was *not as a unitary lump*. His work – conducted in the USA – involved the testing of university students using 60 subscales. These subscale scores were factor analysed to produce 12 primary mental abilities (PMAs). Thus Thurstone conceptualised intelligence as *split* or made up of *components* – what has been described as the *componential approach*. The approach has also been regarded as a theory of multiple intelligences, and tests of these PMAs formed the PMA Test. The test was subsequently developed into the Well Replicated Common Factor (WERCOF) test of PMAs. The WERCOF is composed of tests of primary abilities and when scores on its subtests are correlated, they produce seven WERCOF PMAs.

- *Short-term memory apprehension and retrieval abilities*, e.g. recall of items that are related meaningfully.

- *Long-term memory storage and retrieval abilities*, e.g. ability to produce words that have a similar meaning to a given word.

- *Visualisation and spatial abilities*, e.g. ability to find an embedded figure within a display of distracting figures.

- *Listening and hearing abilities*, e.g. immediate recall of a set of notes that have been played once.

- *Acculturation knowledge abilities*, e.g. completion of basic arithmetic.

- *Reasoning under novel conditions,* e.g. identification of new instances of a concept having been presented with several examples of the concept.

- *Thinking speed*, e.g. copying of printed letters or words as quickly as possible.

However, to some extent some PMAs appeared similar to the individual intelligence tests used by Spearman. Furthermore, the method of factor analysis used by Thurstone – orthogonal factor analysis – treats factors as *statistically independent*, making it impossible to identify correlations between PMAs. In fact, subsequent research has found PMAs to be related.

Spearman (1904) and Thurstone's (1938) work raises a number of important issues about the nature of early research on intelligence. Although early theory development appeared to be based on a priori theoretical notions about the nature of intelligence, to some extent it does also *appear* at times to be using what Facione (2000) describes as an a posteriori approach to validating the construct of intelligence. Much of the early debate about whether intelligence is a single lump or split into intelligences or intellectual abilities was shaped by the decisions made by researchers when analysing test scores statistically. For example, factor analysis involves summarising the relationship between scores or data, and researchers decide when to stop this analysis. The first order factors produced represent the outputs of the first stage in analysing the relationship between sets of scores. Researchers can then decide to continue analysing their first order factors into second order factors that represent the relationship between the first order factors, and so on.

In other words, differences between theories and the debate about the existence of *g* are actually *debates about the statistical decision making of researchers*. Another important feature of this early work is that researchers often used other researchers' data either by using the data as a starting point for their own work or by reanalysing the data. (This recursive approach is similar to that used in the development of the FFT – see Chapter 2). The work of Thurstone (1938) formed the basis of later attempts to develop theories and tests of intelligence and in particular the conceptualisation of intelligence as *crystallised* and *fluid* intelligence by Horn and Cattell (1966) and Hakstian and Cattell (1978). Cattell (1971) added to Thurstone's 60 tests and found 17 PMAs rather than 12. Subsequently, Hakstian and Cattell (1978) found 20 PMAs and, when these first order factors were analysed they identified six second order broad intellectual ability factors. This became known as the *Gf-Gc theory of intelligence*. Despite identifying six second order factors – see Figure 6.2 – two have received most attention in the research because Cattell (1943) regarded *general ability* as

Figure 6.2: *Cattell and Horn's second order ability factors*

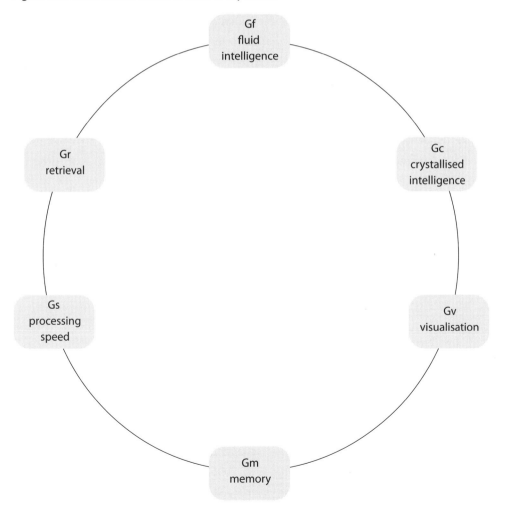

essentially composed of these two types of ability. Generalised fluid reasoning or *Gf* is essentially *reasoning ability*, including the ability to reason inductively and deductively, to understand relations between stimuli, and to identify inferences and implications from essentially abstract stimuli. Cristallised intelligence or *Gc* is essentially the individual's knowledge – also called *comprehension knowledge* or *acculturation knowledge* – and is essentially the breadth and depth of culturally relevant knowledge the individual has. Importantly, this knowledge is relative or *culturally relevant knowledge*.

A number of key issues can be drawn from this work.

- Many approaches to intelligence have described its structure as essentially hierarchical in nature but to varying extents.

- Across different theoretical approaches researchers have acknowledged that the notion of *intelligences* is central to describing the nature of intelligence. However, the overarching conceptualisation of intelligence in the research and theory we have considered has been cognitive. Importantly, intelligence is cognitive information processing underpinning academic performance. There is evidence of some variation in the extent and nature of the view that intelligence and intellectual ability can actually be conceptualised as different cognitive abilities.

- Irrespective of the way in which intelligence is conceptualised, many of the approaches we have considered acknowledge that these different abilities are related in some way or other.

- Researchers have tended to use batteries of tests and, in some instances, a cross-battery approach to assessment in which tests are taken from different test batteries, to produce another battery.

- Intelligence is regarded as essentially context independent. For example, Cattell (1943) argued that all individuals possess the ability to perceive and analyse stimuli and their complex relationships, and this ability is an abstract ability. In fact, he argued that in *this* sense his conceptualisation of intelligence was culture-fair.

Challenges to cognitive ability approaches to intelligence

Conventionally, the cognitive ability approach to human intelligences is contrasted with research dating from the 1960s that challenged many of the concepts and methods of what can be called the testing movement. In keeping with convention, we will consider some of these challenges next.

The three researchers most closely associated with challenging the cognitive ability approach to intelligence are Guilford (1967), Sternberg (1985, 1986, 2005), and Gardner (1993). Although their work is distinct in terms of their specific theoretical details, they share a common view, namely, that the methods and concepts used to theorise about the structure and functions of human intelligence are fundamentally flawed. We will focus on the work of Sternberg.

Sternberg's (1985, 1986, 2005) *triarchic theory of intelligence* conceptualises intelligence as *successful intelligence* or the abilities and skills that enable individuals to be successful in twentieth-century American society. Sternberg therefore focuses on *intelligent behaviour* that is not exclusively intellectual or academic. Three important *subtheories* form his triarchic theory, and each subtheory is underpinned by a corresponding *type of intelligence*. According to Sternberg (2005) intelligence is:

> *the ability to achieve one's goals in life, given one's sociocultural context . . . by capitalising on strengths and correcting or compensating for weaknesses . . . in order to adapt to, shape, and select environments; and . . . through a combination of analytical, creative, and practical abilities. p189*

Importantly, Sternberg (2005) argues quite simply that intelligence cannot be defined generally or absolutely because its meaning is different from each individual. Moreover, traditional cognitive approaches to intelligence, and especially the notion of *g*, imply that there is a general type of intelligence that underpins all achievements; he challenges this because *really, virtually no one is good at everything or bad at everything* (Sternberg, 2005). Sternberg's three *subtheories* of intelligence are *independent*:

> *the contextual subtheory encompasses practical intelligence that involves individuals applying their abilities to the kinds of problems that confront them in daily life, such as on the job or in the home. Practical intelligence . . . involves adaptation . . . when one changes oneself to suit the environment and this is also described as tacit knowledge or what one needs to know in order to work effectively in an environment that one is not explicitly taught and that often is not even verbalized; the experiential subtheory encompasses creative intelligence which is essentially how well an individual can cope with relative novelty; the componential subtheory encompasses analytical intelligence that is involved when the information processing components of intelligence are applied to analyze, evaluate, judge, or compare and contrast. (p189)*

The triarchic theory emphasises that intelligent individuals shape their environment in order to adapt to life's challenges. In this sense, intelligence *emerges* from individuals' behaviours in their environment. This conceptualisation of intelligence can be compared with the conceptualisation that typifies the cognitive approach to intelligence. The latter focuses on cognitive abilities or even *g* as underpinning – determining – intellectual achievement. Furthermore, the triarchic theory does not focus exclusively on academic achievement as the main expression of intelligence. Another important feature of Sternberg and other challengers to the cognitive ability approach to intelligence is their focus on intelligence as a *process*. For example, Sternberg (2005) argues that intelligence involves making decisions. This includes *selecting* certain environments and strategies, and *shaping* these environments through our behaviours. Intelligence is therefore a process that influences how we adapt to or function in our social and cultural context. It would be simplistic to dismiss cognitive ability research on intelligence as ignoring these process issues. Indeed, earlier in this chapter when we considered the work of Binet (1905), we identified some general references in his writings to the *adaptive functions* of intelligence that *imply* that intelligence involves a range of *psychological processes*. The issue here is that the historical development of the cognitive ability approach to intelligence, and especially the ascendancy of the testing movement, suggest a rather different approach to intelligence than that proposed by researchers such as Sternberg. The triarchic theory also has implications for how we measure intelligence because it is unlikely that successful intelligence as Sternberg conceptualises it can be measured using solely the sorts of abstract tests developed by researchers such as Spearman, Thurstone and Cattell. For example, Sternberg (2005) describes how practical intelligence is measured using tests of tacit knowledge comprised of *work-related problems*, often with paper and pencil tests such as the following:

> *in a paper-and-pencil measure of tacit knowledge for sales, one of the problems deals with sales of photocopy machines. A relatively inexpensive machine is not moving out of the show room and has become overstocked. The examinee is asked to rate the quality of various solutions for moving the particular model out of the show room. In a performance-based measure for sales people, the test-taker makes a phone call to a supposed customer, who is actually the examiner. The test-taker tries to sell advertising space over the phone. The examiner raises various objections to buying the advertising space. The test-taker is evaluated for the quality, rapidity, and fluency of the responses on the telephone.*

Kline (1991) regards this approach as problematic because its concepts are broad and inclusive, making it unclear whether, for example, Sternberg's practical intelligence is an ability, a behavioural style or a personality trait.

Task ⎯ Sternberg argues that, given the structure of intelligence and the independence of these intelligences (2005), *people can be intelligent but foolish* (p199). The characteristics of such individuals are that they are *unrealistically optimistic, egocentric, believe they have omniscience or all knowledgeable, they are omnipotent or all powerful, and believe they are invulnerable*. In this task you should speculate about the *potential consequences* of such characteristics for the individual's overall adaptation or how they are likely to cope with life's challenges. You could also want to refer back to Chapter 4 when we considered the links between personality and mental health and disorder as, to some extent, some of these characteristics appear reminiscent of the characteristics of the personality of trait narcissism.

Comment

This task should draw your attention to the issues of how we define intelligent behaviour, Sternberg's notion of successful intelligence and intelligence as a process. For example, using Sternberg's theory, successful intelligence involves adapting to life's challenges. However, it is possible for an individual to appear intelligent in terms of their cognitive ability, or *wise*, but to possess rather less *practical intelligence*. The research on narcissism that we considered in Chapter 4 suggests that a number of the characteristics of the foolish (Sternberg, 2005) are also possessed by those who have high levels of trait narcissism. By thinking about the potential consequences of these characteristics you should start to appreciate the complexity of these issues and begin synthesising across different literatures from individual differences psychology. This should also draw your attention to the common phenomena considered across the field even though researchers often use very different terminology to describe the same or similar constructs.

The work of Sternberg has also drawn attention to the role of individuals' beliefs about intelligence to understand intelligent behaviour. For example, Sternberg et al. (1981) argued that people have *conceptions of intelligence* and use these beliefs to judge themselves and others. Such implicit theories of intelligence (Sternberg, 1986) can influence how we see ourselves and others, thus giving individuals' beliefs about intelligence *functional power* (Weinberg, 1989). To some extent we started to consider the impact of beliefs about individual differences in Chapter 2 when you identified what sort of person theorist you were, and some researchers argue that such beliefs about intelligence and intellectual ability can influence the trajectory of intellectual performance (Dweck and Leggett, 1988). Such beliefs are a type of tacit metacognitive theory (Schraw and Moshman, 1995), and these are *acquired or constructed without any explicit awareness that one possesses a theory*. Importantly, such knowledge can influence actual behaviour or performance, and this knowledge is quite robust because it is tacit – not easily expressed. This can be the case even when this knowledge about oneself, others or a construct, including beliefs about these phenomena, are *false and maladaptive*. Although there is debate over the changeability of such beliefs over the life course (see Kuhn, 2000), evidence suggests that beliefs about one's intellectual ability can influence performance. For example, Blackwell et al. (2007) found that school children's beliefs that intelligence is *malleable* predicted longitudinally an *upward trajectory* in school performance. An intervention used to promote incremental thinking about intelligence also had similar consequences for school performance, including the reversal of a previous downward trajectory to one that was upwards. This sort of research has led some researchers to propose that we should distinguish *intellectual ability* from actual *test performance* and *beliefs about one's own intelligence* (Chamorro-Premuzic and Furnham, 2004). Importantly, it has been argued that beliefs about one's intelligence, in the form of *subjectively assessed intelligence* (SAI), constitute the mechanism that mediates how intellectual ability and test performance are linked. In other words, your beliefs about your intellectual ability can have consequences for your performance on tests of intellectual ability.

Determinants of individual differences in intelligence

The theories of intelligence we have considered vary in how explicitly they consider the determinants of intelligence. To some extent, the focus on testing intelligence in much of the research has led to the relative neglect of the determinants of intelligence.

We have already described the theories of intelligence we considered that emerged from the testing movement as essentially *cognitive*. These theories tend to focus on cognitive information processes as the determinants of intelligence. Many of the subtests on tests of intellectual ability appear similar to those used to assess basic cognitive abilities, and working memory (WM) and processing speed have been identified as key cognitive processes that appear to underpin *measured cognitive intelligence*. However, the issue of whether intelligence and such information processing abilities are identical is a matter of debate. For example, Conway et al. (2003) reviewed the published research up to that date on intelligence and WM. They found that although intelligence and WM are related, they are *not* the same constructs. In particular, they argue that although both *g* and WM are essentially information processing abilities, WM is distinct because it involves an *executive attention-control mechanism* to limit WM interference. Overall, it is important to remember that to some extent the cognitive determinants of intelligence are *implicitly assumed* in some cognitive theories of intellectual ability. Furthermore, as stated at the outset there has been a degree of separatism between researchers considering the cognitive processes that could determine intelligence and those focusing on the construction of intelligence tests that in terms of face validity appear to measure cognitive processes.

Approaches that claim intelligence is determined by biological factors are diverse. For example, early researchers such as Galton (1883) and Hebb (1949) proposed that intelligence was determined by the speed of neural processing an individual is capable of. This was typically measured using reaction times (RTs) to various stimuli to operationalise speed of neural processing. Given the widespread use of RTs in experimental and early cognitive psychology, there is some conceptual overlap here between this type of biological account and some cognitive approaches. Other variants of research have focused on the genetic inheritance of intelligence (e.g. Galton, 1876). Increasingly, research are integrating genetic and neuroscientific research paradigms to identify not merely the extent to which intelligence, and in particular *g*, is inherited but to identify the genetic markers of intelligence (Chorney et al., 1998; and see Chapter 2 for a similar approach to the determinants of personality). The work of Deary (Deary et al., 2009; Deary et al., 2010) suggests that we can integrate techniques from behaviour genetics, neuroscience and molecular genetic studies to identify these broad biological determinants of intelligence. To date the evidence suggests that substantially intelligence has heritability of around 30 per cent in childhood, rising to around 50 per cent in adulthood. Moreover, this research shows that differences in measured intelligence can be related to structural differences in specific brain pathways such as the parieto-frontal pathway. In particular, the ratio of **grey matter** to **white**

matter in this area is related to differences in measured cognitive intellectual ability, with higher levels of intelligence being related to a greater ratio of grey to white matter. However, as we discussed in Chapter 2, the relationship between genotype and phenotype – in this case, measured intelligence – is complex, and it would be unwise to simplify their relationship (Noble, 2008; Plomin and Spinath, 2004).

Approaches that claim intelligence is determined by social factors are possibly even more diverse than those that appear biological in their focus. Generally, these approaches focus on the role that social factors play in the development of intelligence through processes such as socialisation. This collection of approaches also includes those that regard intelligence as a social construction or as the result of social and cognitive processes (Dweck and Leggett, 1988) that develop across the lifespan. However, many of these approaches are not exclusively social. In other words, they often use a biopsychosocial framework (see Chapter 3) that identifies the determinants of intellect as including social as well as biological maturation and cultural factors (e.g. Li et al., 2004).

Task —— In this task you will consider how *evolutionary theory* can be used to explain the determinants of human intelligence. Goetz and Shackleford (2006) argue that the application of evolutionary principles to explain intelligence has at times been oversimplified, but that modern or neo–Darwinian theory can provide useful insights into the determinants of complex psychological phenomena such as intelligence. For example, some researchers have used Darwinian principles to explain both cognitive and social intelligence (Byrne, 1996). Herrmann et al. (2007) use evolutionary principles to explain the different levels and types of skill sophistication observable in humans in comparison primates. Specifically, humans have evolved sophisticated cognitive abilities and skills for dealing with the demands of our most salient domain, namely our social world. However, primates have evolved far more sophisticated skills for dealing with the demands of their most salient domain, namely the physical domain. Using your knowledge of evolutionary theory, try to develop a list of reasons why human intelligence has evolved into the psychological construct it appears to be. You can complete this task individually or in a group.

Comment

This task presents you with a number of challenges. First, you have to decide how to define intelligence as well as ensure you understand the basic principles of Darwinian theory. This task should also help develop your knowledge of theoretical explanations of intelligence. Darwinian theory is challenging but important to understand because there is a tendency to oversimplify its premises. For example, in some ways this theory uses a biopsychosocial framework, and it focuses on behaviour processes albeit at a macro level.

Critical thinking activity

The Imposter Phenomenon

Critical thinking focus: reflection

Key question: *What are your beliefs about your intellectual achievements?*

In this activity you will consider the Imposter Phenomenon (IP). Please examine the individual items of the Harvey Imposter Phenomenon Scale (Hellman and Caselman, 2004) that is given in Figure 6.3. Read each item, and ask yourself the following questions.

- To what extent is the item true of you?

- What evidence do you have to support your judgement?

- What are the actual or potential consequences of holding this belief about yourself for your academic performance?

Figure 6.3: *The Harvey Imposter Phenomenon (Hellman and Caselman, 2004)*

1	Others believe I'm more competent
2	Achievement reflects ability
3	Fear discovery of who I really am
4	Can accept compliments of my intelligence
5	Deserve honours I receive
6	Present position due to mistake
7	Confident I will succeed
8	Feel like a phony
9	Personality impresses persons in authority
10	Accomplishments adequate for my experiences
11	I let persons in authority know if I disagree
12	Sometimes succeed when I thought I failed
13	Feel as though I hide things from others
14	I am the same person in public as in private

Worked example

Item 12 is *sometimes succeed when I thought I failed*. You might judge that on more than 50 per cent of occasions when you make such a judgement you hold this belief. You might also reflect on how general or specific this belief is. You might judge that it is relatively true of you when considering your academic performance. You might have subjective evidence of this – before you submitted the work you experienced a lack of confidence and discussed this with your friends. However, you felt unpleasant emotions such as embarrassment about this and did not ask for help from your lecturers with the work because you believed that you could not make any useful changes to the work. You therefore gave up working on this quite quickly. Your actual mark was better than you thought it would be, so you felt surprised when you received a relatively good mark and feedback because your expectations were relatively low. The actual consequences of this belief appear to be that you gave up working on the assignment quite quickly, did not ask for help that was available, and you experienced a number of negative emotions such as anxiety about the work. The potential consequences of this belief could be that you will avoid challenges in the future and be drawn towards activities and intellectual challenges that you feel you can cope with easily because you believe that you are likely to fail and that any success is just a lucky mistake (item 6).

Critical thinking review

This activity requires you to reflect on your beliefs about your intellectual abilities and performance. It also requires you to reflect on the sources of information you use to support such beliefs and the consequences (actual or potential) for your academic experiences.

Other skills likely to be used in this activity: this activity also requires you to use evaluation and analysis of yourself and the literature on IP, and to understand and use this literature and the scale items to evaluate your beliefs and intellectual performance.

Skill builder activity

Beliefs about intellectual ability

Transferable skill focus: organisational skills

Key question: *What are the consequences of beliefs about academic ability?*

In this activity you will reorganise the information in a fictional case study using your knowledge of beliefs and expectations about intellectual ability. Read the case study and identify examples of such beliefs. Then try to reorganise the case study text into a diagram showing the actual and/or potential consequences of Sally's beliefs, and/or others about her academic abilities. You can select one belief or more but you must make sure your diagram shows their actual or potential consequences for Sally.

Sally, 30, is a mature student living at home with her father and in her second year at the North Merseyside University (NMU) studying for a degree in English. She is currently performing around the 2.2 level though her tutors think she is more than capable of getting a 2.1 if she would put in the effort, instead of the minimum that she has been doing so far. Sally has come to the NMU Student Counselling Service because she has a dilemma, which she feels she cannot solve on her own. She has been offered an exciting job, but her father is adamant that she continues with her studies. Sally is clearly distressed and presents her story in rather a disjointed way, skipping from one problem area to another. She looks like a person who is nearing the end of her tether.

Sally has been offered a good job as a helper to her very rich disabled aunt (her father's sister). Aunt Jane has difficulty in walking following a stroke, but wants to travel the world and is prepared to pay handsomely for her own personal caregiver. She would like Sally to leave college and accompany her. Aunt Jane does not get on with Sally's father, as she did not approve of the way he left her niece to look after her mother, who suffered from multiple sclerosis and was confined to a wheelchair. Sally was the eldest child of three and the only girl. She was expected from an early age to be a second mother to her brothers as well as look after her own mother during her long illness. Both her brothers went to university and are now doing well for themselves. Sally was kept at home to be the carer and to look after the house. Her father, who is a staunch Catholic and a Professor of Sociology at a neighbouring university, told Sally that the main way he could contribute to the family was by working harder to support them, so he was rarely at home. He also told her that since she was not as clever as her brothers, it was important for them to be given the chance to make good careers for themselves and it was her duty to help them. He would regularly enforce his will by making her attend church, confess her sins and pray to God to be given the humility to serve by looking after the family and not to pursue her own selfish goals. When her mother died two years ago, her brothers both moved out of the family home and took jobs down in the south of England. It was at this time that Sally's father insisted that she should apply to NMU to do a degree. Sally was a little reluctant, believing herself to be rather 'thick'. In spite of what her tutors say, she does not think she is capable of getting a degree or of ever really living an independent life. She describes herself as 'a carer' for others. Her aunt's offer appeals to her, partly so she can escape from doing academic work and partly so she can get away from looking after her father who is adamant that she stays at home and continues her degree studies at college. She says she has tried talking to him, but every time she does, he flies into a rage or sinks into a depression, emotionally blackmailing her and reminding her of her duty to God. 'Honour thy father and thy mother' is one of his favourite phrases. Sally says that she is worried that if she does go, he will sink into a decline and it will be her fault. She has a strong religious faith herself and feels she may be eternally damned if she does not comply with her father's wishes.

Sally does not look well. She is pale and unattractive looking with no care paid to personal hygiene or her clothes. She looks more like a woman in her early forties. She admits that she drinks heavily but denies that this is a problem. She clearly has little self-esteem. The NMU Student Counselling Service offers the best provision in the whole of the north of England. It is served by counsellors who adopt a wide range of theoretical approaches, including specialists in person-centred, cognitive-behavioural, existential, psychodynamic, individual psychology, and transactional analysis, as well as those who take a more eclectic approach.

Sally clearly has little self-esteem and she is consumed with feelings of guilt, is sleeping badly and feels she is a wicked and worthless person for wanting to do something for herself. She feels trapped because she knows her aunt is very similar in temperament to her father so she may well be exchanging one dominated lifestyle for another. She also has been very encouraged by what some of her English tutors have told her about her abilities and wonders if she really is capable of getting a good degree and making her own way in the world. Everyone seems to be putting her under pressure and she cannot see her way out of the dilemma . . .

Worked example

Towards the end of the case study, Sally is described as *wondering if she is really capable of getting a degree and making her own way in the world*. This textual information suggests that Sally doubts her intellectual abilities despite feedback from her tutors that *she is more than capable of getting a 2.1 if she would put in the effort*. This could be diagrammatically displayed as shown in Figure 6.4.

Figure 6.4: *Consequences of Sally's beliefs*

Skill builder review

This activity requires you to organise the textual information of the case study in diagrammatic form. This involves organising the textual information into beliefs and consequences, and then representing this information using a diagram. The diagram should organise textual information into a process of actual and potential consequences for the fictional character Sally. Thus the task involves both reorganising the structure and the presentation format of the case study.

Other skills likely to be used in this activity: the activity also requires you to use problem-solving and decision-making skills to identify the research relevant to the scenario and to reflect on the ethical dilemmas such an approach raises. The activity involves understanding and using data as well as evaluating and analysing data. You should also engage in reflective thinking about the beliefs you identify in the case study along with the consequences of such beliefs.

Assignments

1. Critically evaluate the view that the notion of intelligence as a measure of optimal intellectual abilities organised hierarchically is redundant.

2. To what extent has individual differences research on intelligence changed from a focus on measurement to one that focuses on *intellectual processes*?

3. Critically discuss the importance of beliefs about intellectual ability for understanding intellectual performance.

4. The history of research on intelligence is a catalogue of conceptual and methodological errors. Critically examine this statement.

Summary: what you have learned

Individual differences research on human intelligence has been shaped by a number of conceptual and methodological debates. Conceptualising intelligence as measurable cognitive intellectual abilities or related intelligences has to some extent been challenged since the 1960s by researchers questioning the fundamental cognitive and psychometric assumptions of the testing movement. However, although these challenges have to some extent shifted the focus of intelligence research from the development of tests of cognitive ability to considering intelligence as processes that have different forms, much of the research remains focused on issues that are synonymous with the testing movement. This is despite a growing body of research that demonstrates that non-ability factors, such as beliefs about the nature of intelligence and one's own intellectual ability, can influence intellectual performance and achievement. The tasks and activities in this chapter should have encouraged you to think about the more challenging aspects of this area of research, and focus specifically on the consequences of beliefs about intellectual ability for yourself and a fictional character.

Further reading

Conway, ARA, Kane, MJ and Engle, RW (2003) Working memory capacity and its relation to general intelligence. *Trend in Cognitive Sciences*, 7(12): 547–52.

This paper provides a clear explanation of the relatively complex statistical methods used to test the relationship between g and WM. It is a generally useful paper for clarifying some of the fundamental conceptual issues in individual differences psychology we examined in Chapter 1, especially the notion of latent variables.

Deary, IJ, Penke, L and Johnson, W (2010) The neuroscience of human intelligence differences. *Nature Reviews Neuroscience*, 11: 201–11.

This is a useful summary of evidence on the genetic and neurophysiological determinants of individual differences in intelligence. The paper takes a clear cognitive approach to intelligence, and a stance in favour of differences in such abilities having both genetic and brain wave determinants. The paper offers an approach that is in sharp contrast to the notion of intelligences and dispositional thinking that can be found in the papers by Schlinger (2003), and Sternberg et al. (2005) described below.

Facione, PA (2000) The disposition toward critical thinking: its character, measurement, and relationship to critical thinking skill. *Informal Logic*, 20(1): 61–84.

Facione argues that we should separate cognitive skills from the act of critical thinking. This paper offers a readable account of conceptual distinctions between the component skills that constitute cognitive intelligence and the motivation to apply these. Facione's account is clearly related to the notion of intelligences and is a useful critique of strictly cognitive approaches to intellectual ability, performance and achievement.

Lubinski, D (2004) Introduction to the special section on cognitive abilities: 100 years after Spearman's (1904) 'General intelligence, objectively determined and measured'. *Journal of Personality and Social Psychology*, 86(1): 96–111.

This paper attempts to make a case for the importance of g across different life domains. This paper works well as justification for focusing on g and is best read after Schlinger (2003).

Plomin, R and Spinath, FM (2004) Intelligence: genetics, genes, and genomics. *Journal of Personality and Social Psychology*, 86(1): 112–29.

This paper provides an overview of the genetics of intelligence, with a particular focus on the contribution of genetics to variance in human intelligence across the lifespan, and cutting edge approaches being applied to the intelligence-genetics controversy.

Schlinger, HD (2003) The myth of intelligence. *The Psychological Record*, 53: 15–32.

This is an excellent discussion of the fundamental flaws in conceptualisations of intelligence. Schlinger's analysis of conceptualisation as either essentialist or functionalist is particularly useful for developing a more critical perspective on individual differences research on intelligence.

Sternberg, RJ, Grigorenko, EL and Kidd, KK (2005) Intelligence, race, and genetics. *American Psychologist*, 60(1): 46–95.

This paper is a readable overview of the controversies and fundamental conceptual challenges of research, linking race and intelligence. The paper provides a useful deconstruction of the problems of interpreting race and genetics.

Useful websites

http://psychclassics.asu.edu/ (Classics in the History of Psychology)

This website is a collection of classic primary resources across psychology. The site contains original papers on intelligence from seminal researchers including Binet (1905), Galton (1865, 1875) and Spearman (1904). Reading primary resources is essential to effective critical thinking because they give you access to details often lost in secondary sources. This site is invaluable for students examining the history of psychological approaches to intelligence and intellect.

www.pz.harvard.edu/index.cfm (Project Zero)

Project Zero is based at Harvard University's Graduate School of Education. It started in 1967, and its mission is to understand and enhance learning, thinking, and creativity in the arts, as well as humanistic and scientific disciplines, at the individual and institutional levels. *This is the Project's main website and it contains a range of resources including research, reports and papers. The website is an invaluable collection of academic and applied research focusing on thinking styles.*

Chapter 7
The use of intellectual ability tests

Learning outcomes

By the end of this chapter you should:

- *be able to outline the main types and uses of psychological tests;*

- *understand and be able to discuss, critically, what is meant when using psychological tests in high-stakes decision-making;*

- *be able to examine, critically, how intellectual ability tests are used in high-stakes decision making in educational contexts;*

- *be able to analyse, critically, the sociopolitical implications of the use of intellectual ability tests in educational contexts;*

- *develop data analysis, evaluation and IT skills when constructing resources that can be used to facilitate classroom learning.*

Introduction

In this chapter you will consider the following questions.

- What do we mean by the terms psychological tests 'and standardised psychological tests'?

- How are such tests used by psychologists and non-psychologists?

- How are standardised tests of intellectual ability used by psychologists and non-psychologists?

- Of what value are standardised intellectual ability tests when making high-stakes decisions about individuals in educational contexts?

- Should psychologists consider the sociopolitical consequences of using tests of intellectual ability?

The overarching goal of this chapter is for you to develop a critical understanding of the main issues surrounding the use of standardised intellectual ability tests. In particular, we will examine how scores on such tests are used as *evidentiary* when making *high-stakes decisions* about the test taker. The academic literature in psychology and other behavioural sciences on the use of tests of both intellectual ability and other psychological phenomena is extensive (Sackett and Lievens,

2008; Sackett et al., 2008, 2009). This is unsurprising given the socio-economic and political importance of the topic. Indeed, it has been commented that across the social and behavioural sciences there is a *shared goal . . . to use the most powerful measurement and analysis tools to understand and improve the human condition* (Duckworth, 2009, p280). Thus the stakes are high for both *test takers* and those administering tests or *test users*. However, at the heart of debates surrounding the use of standardised psychological tests of intellectual ability across different life domains – from occupational and work contexts to a range of educational and health contexts – is the generic question: *are such tests good predictors of achievement . . .?* (Sackett et al., 2008). It is the conflicting responses to this question that underpin the controversy surrounding this use of tests of intellectual ability; and in this chapter you will focus on their use in one particular domain – education. The issues covered will be those surrounding testing in educational contexts in general rather than the minute details of specific tests, although some tasks will involve examining such tests. It is also worth remembering that many of the issues we will consider are not exclusive to tests of intellectual ability in an educational context. They also apply to standardised tests of other psychological phenomena, and to the use of standardised tests of other psychological phenomena in other real-life domains. Further reading on the use of psychological tests in other domains can be found at the end of this chapter. Finally, the activities in this chapter are designed to encourage you to think critically about the use of intellectual ability tests by considering how academic research on this topic can be used to inform teachers' practice.

Psychological tests

Types and uses of psychological tests

What are *psychological tests*? The meaning of the term *test* used here is that given by the British Psychological Society's Psychological Testing Centre in their work (Bartram and Lindley, 2005). It encompasses all types of psychological tests and not merely those of intellectual ability that we focus on in this chapter. Psychological tests are: assessment procedure(s) designed to provide objective measures of one or more psychological characteristics. These include ABILITIES, APTITUDES, ATTAINMENT, INTERESTS, beliefs, personality, and so on. The important feature of psychological TESTS is that they produce measures obtained under standardised assessment conditions which have known RELIABILITY and VALIDITY. They find a way of comparing a person's performance against that of others . . . The term, test, is used as shortened for psychological test or psychometric test, which includes various inventories and questionnaires.

This definition appears to encompass the majority of measures used in psychology. However, we need to clarify more precisely what sorts of tests we are referring to here.

• *Explicit high-stakes tests*: these are tools used for the expressed purpose of assessing psycho-logical characteristics of individuals. The use of these sorts of tests has also been called *in vivo testing* (Bartram and Lindley, 2005) in which the outcomes of the test – the individual's score and its interpretation – are used to make decisions about the test taker across different domains. This is also called *high-stakes testing* (e.g. Sackett et al., 2008) because it involves using test scores to make potentially life-altering decisions about individuals. Other features of these tests are the use of *standardisation, norms* and *percentiles*. In Chapter 1 we introduced the notion of standardisation in measures of individual differences. More specifically, psychological tests tend to be standardised in two ways – their *format* and *administration* are reproducible, and a test taker's score can be interpreted by *comparison* with the scores of others who have taken the test previously – or *norms*. The most usual comparison made is the *percentile* – the individual's raw score on a test is transformed into a percentile that informs us about the percentage of individuals likely to achieve that score or one lower. Tests meeting all these criteria can therefore be described as *explicit standardised tests*.

- *Explicit research tests*: explicit testing can also mean using high-stakes tests but as part of a programme of research. The important distinction here is that the outcomes are not used to make high-stakes decisions about the test taker. Instead, they are used as research data.

- *Standardised ability* and *standardised non-ability tests*: these are sometimes referred to as cognitive and non-cognitive tests. The latter distinction has been described as a misnomer because all tests involve some form of cognitive processing. Instead, some prefer to distinguish tests by whether they assess capacity or the optimal performance of what the individual can do. This can be compared with measures of the individual's typical (or usual) performance (Duckworth, 2009). This distinction in reality is between tests of cognitive ability and personality, respectively.

- *Psychological tests*: this is an omnibus term because according to Bartram and Lindley's (2005) definition, it includes the majority of psychological tests whether they are psychometric, psychophysiological, observational or interview based.

- *Evidentiary* tests: this refers to test scores and their interpretation being used as *evidence* about an individual or as a measure of some psychological characteristic of the individual.

In this chapter we will focus on the use of *high-stakes standardised tests of intellectual ability in educational contexts*. Education is one of a number of real-life domains in which these types of psychological tests are used. The Psychological Testing Centre identifies four real-life domains in which standardised explicit tests of intellectual ability are used for high-stakes purposes, and they are listed in Figure 7.1. It is important to note that although we can identify distinct domains in which such tests are used, often specific types of tests, specific tests and their uses are *not* mutually exclusive. In other words, the same tests are often used for different purposes and across different real-life domains, and this complexity is important to understand. These overlaps are illustrated in the use of psychological tests in clinical assessments.

Figure 7.1 Domains of use

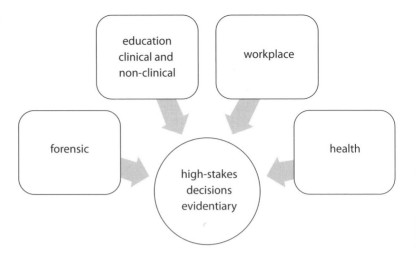

Clinical assessments are used in clinical psychology, forensic psychology and health domains. In these domains a range of explicit standardised psychological tests, including tests of intellectual ability, are used to assist the diagnostic process. Clinical assessment typically uses the assessment interview in which such tests are part of a package of psychological assessments. The clinical assessment itself provides evidence that is then documented in a psychological report, and Groth-Marnat (2003) identifies three broad uses of these reports: *screening*; *assessment*; and the *planning and monitoring of treatment*.

Importantly, clinical assessment uses explicit standardised tests of intellectual ability that were not originally developed for clinical uses. Groth-Marnat's (2003) *Handbook of Psychological Assessment* identifies a number of explicit standardised psychological tests as among the main ones used in clinical assessments; these are shown in Figure 7.2. Tests of intellectual ability are used across different assessment domains and for different purposes. In clinical assessments, tests such as the *Wechsler Intelligence Scales* and the *Wechsler Memory Scales* are used to identify the individual's cognitive strengths and weaknesses, given that memory complaints are observed in clinical populations. They are also used to identify a baseline against which to compare change within the individual over time, and in comparison to others. However, although tests such as the Wechsler Scales *can provide useful information about cultural, biological, maturational, or treatment-related differences among individuals* (Groth-Marnat, 2003, p130), the use of such tests can be problematic.

- Tests of intellectual ability when used in clinical assessments are subject to the same *conceptual biases* as when used in any setting; we discussed some of these in Chapter 6.

- The type of intellectual ability tests typically used in clinical assessments are not process-oriented; they assess what the individual has achieved rather than how they have achieved it.

- The *interpretation* of scores on any test, and the integration of a range of scores from diverse tests into a coherent interpretation or clinical assessment can be difficult.

Figure 7.2: *Standardised tests used in clinical assessments*

In particular, Groth-Marnat (2003) is cautious about using test scores to organise clinical psychological reports because focusing on tests scores in this context can depersonalise the client to *a series of numbers* (p625), leading to a fragmented assessment using test norms to describe the client. Psychological reports are usually domain oriented – being organised around specific capacities and topics – or, most typically, hypothesis-oriented – being organised around specific clinical questions about the client. Nevertheless, the limitations of test-oriented psychological reports draw attention to the question of the clinical usefulness of certain test scores, especially when used as part of a clinical assessment battery and when not designed specifically for that purpose. For example, D'Amato and Denney (2008) examined the use of the Wechsler Memory Scale–III Rarely Missed Index (RMI) subscale for detecting malingering in forensic populations. Malingering is the exaggeration or faking of cognitive deficits, with the intention of being diagnosed with some form of specific deficit or clinical disorder. The RMI is frequently used in forensic settings to detect malingering, and a cut-off score is used to differentiate individuals with genuine deficits from those whose RMI score is sufficiently high to raise suspicion about the validity of their score. The RMI is often cited as a good detector of malingering. However, D'Amato and Denney's (2008) analysis of archival data found that the recommended cut-off point was a poor discriminator. This sort of finding raises important points about the types and uses of explicit standardised psychological tests. First, test purposes can be transparent to test takers, and this can undermine the test's usefulness given the high-stakes evidentiary nature of test scores. Second, interpreting test scores is challenging and requires the test user to have appropriate expertise and competence. Third, standardised explicit tests of intellectual ability have their own limitations as measures of cognitive intellectual ability, and whether they actually assess other abilities that have clinical relevance and utility is controversial.

Neisworth and Bagnato (2004) identified more specific evidentiary uses of explicit standardised psychological tests when making decisions about individuals. They focus on the testing of preschool children in what they describe as *early care* and *education* domains, but their doubts about the uses of standardised psychological tests with young children can be applied to testing in general. Specifically, they argue that:

> *Measurement has been conducted more often for the benefit of the assessor; certainly the history of racial and ethnic devaluation and relegation illustrates the complicity of (mis)measurement in justifying and validating social biases. We refer primarily to the attempts to assess personal qualities, often vaguely defined, such as character, morality, criminality, talent, and, of course, intelligence . . . Misrepresenting children through mismeasuring them denies children their rights to beneficial expectations and opportunities. (p198)*

They argue that psychological tests with young children are used for four purposes.

- *Screening* – to detect developmental disorders efficiently. However, given the known biases of some standardised psychological tests, there is a likelihood of false negatives or false positives.

- *Eligibility determination* – to assess if the individual deviates sufficiently from known test norms and, if so, this renders them eligible for intervention. Relying on deviation from test norms to judge an individual's eligibility for intervention assumes that standardised psychological tests provide a complete and therapeutically relevant assessment. Specifically, they argue that currently assessment should be *authentic assessment* or *the systematic collection of information about the naturally occurring behaviours of young children and families in their daily routines (p204)*. Clearly, reliance on standardised decontextual psychological tests is inconsistent with this therapeutic trend.

- *Planning interventions and progress monitoring* – to inform the planning of the individual's intervention package and to detect change as the intervention progresses. This use assumes that standardised psychological tests are valid measures of the content of the intervention, and thus of any outcomes that the individual could achieve.

- *Intervention evaluation* – to provide evidence of the effectiveness of a programme of intervention. As with the previous use, this assumes that the psychological test and the outcomes achievable from the intervention are linked.

Neisworth and Bagnato (2004) identify five problems with the use of standardised psychological tests, including tests of intellectual ability among preschool children, and these are summarised in Figure 7.3. These problems have resulted in what they refer to as the *mismeasure of children*. Rather than rely on standardised psychological tests, they suggest an alternative approach that they describe as *authentic assessment*, and this has four features. It is contextual and involves assessing the child in their natural environment rather than the decontexualised environment of standardised psychological testing contexts. It focuses on how the child functions rather than the form of the capabilities being assessed, thus identifying the processes and potentials of the child. It uses natural observation to assess the child. Finally, the authentic assessment process involves those familiar with the child working with the interdisciplinary team. This is based on the premise that assessment is not merely the exclusive province of those professionals deemed competent to administer standardised psychological tests.

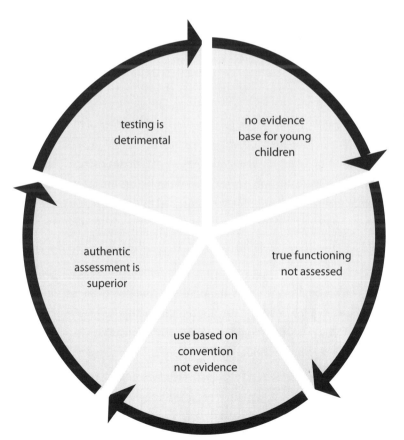

Figure 7.3: *Problems with using standardised psychological tests with young children*

Task — This task involves comparing different standardised psychological tests that you have already encountered in previous chapters and judging what type of tests each appear to be and how they are generally used in individual differences psychology. In Chapter 2 we considered the FFT the most widely used measure of these, the NEO-PI-R. In Chapter 3 we considered the Jenkins Activity Survey (JAS), a measure of Type A personality. Finally, in Chapter 6 we considered the Harvey Imposter Phenomenon Scale, a measure of the Imposter Phenomenon (IP). Use the different ways we have distinguished types of tests so far in this chapter to describe these three explicit standardised psychological tests. To help you complete this task, ask yourself the following questions about each.

- Is the test a standardised psychological test?

- Is it an explicit test?

- Is the test norm-referenced?

- Is the test a high-stakes test?

- Is the test used in a specific real-life domain?

- Is the test a measure of cognitive ability or not?

Comment

The purpose of this task is to draw your attention to the flexible nature of the uses of many explicit standardised psychological tests. Many of the measures used in individual differences psychology fit Bartram and Lindley's (2005) definition of an explicit standardised psychological test. However, tests vary considerably in the way they are used and how scores on such tests are interpreted. The same test can be used for different purposes in different domains, and this raises questions about the suitability of some explicit standardised psychological tests for the purposes they are often used for. This is the sort of potential misuse identified by Groth-Marnat (2003) and Neisworth and Bagnato (2004).

Sackett et al. (2008) argue the case *for* the use of explicit standardised psychological tests in high-stakes decision making because *there is much myth and hearsay regarding standardized tests* (p215). They argue that academic evidence supports the *criterion-related validity* of such tests – and thus the use of test scores for *criterion referencing* – when *a person's score on a test is used to predict or anticipate how they will perform on types of task not directly sampled by the test but which have been shown to be correlated with test performance* (Bartram and Lindley, 2005), in the domains of education and work. However, the very nature of high-stakes decision making raises questions about the suitability of using psychological tests in general as *evidentiary*. In particular, the use of standardised explicit tests of intellectual ability in the domain of education is surrounded by controversy. It is this issue that we will focus on for the remainder of this chapter.

Intellectual ability tests

In Chapter 6 we examined individual differences research on intelligence. Importantly, psychometrics and criterion-related validity have been central to the development of theories of intelligence and the construction and use of intelligence tests. It is these tests that we refer to when using the phrase *explicit standardised intellectual ability tests*. Explicit standardised tests of intellectual ability have a number of general uses in high-stakes decision making about individuals (Lynn et al. (2007).

- As part of clinical diagnosis.

- To screen for eligibility for entry to an institution, course of study or training or an occupation.

- In system processes, to evaluate how effective the education system is, and to identify what can be done to improve its effectiveness.

However, these uses are controversial because of what some researchers describe as the over-interpretation of correlations, particularly as evidence of the determinants of achievement (see Chapter 6). The correlation controversy is far from new, but despite the known dangers of such over-interpretation, it is a mistake that continues to be made (McClelland, 1973, p7).

> *Criticisms of the testing movement are not new . . . (yet) . . . The testing movement continues to grow and extend into every corner of society . . . What hopefully can happen is that testers will recognise what is going on and attempt to redirect their energies in a sounder direction.*

The psychometric assumptions that underpin the use of explicit standardised tests of intellectual ability are central to these criticisms. For example, Nunnally's (1975) discussion of the testing movement between 1950 and the mid-1970s identified three psychometric assumptions of the testing movement.

- *Deductive reasoning* is used to justify the use of standardised tests of intellectual ability. As discussed in Chapter 6, this type of reasoning has been criticised because of its circularity.

- Empirical research on *individual differences in intellectual ability* demonstrates that individuals vary in intellectual ability, with the bell-shaped curve being often used to describe the shape of the distribution of variance in intelligence. This research has also demonstrated that standardised tests of intelligence or intellectual ability have criterion validity.

- We can *measure differences* in intellectual ability and thus need to develop psychometric measures of such differences.

Despite the expansion of research on the complexity of using explicit standardised tests of intellectual ability in an educational context to make high-stakes decisions about individuals, McClelland's (1973) hope for the future of such testing has not necessarily been realised. According to some contemporary researchers the outlook is pessimistic. The recognition of flaws in the assumptions underlying high-stakes decision making using such tests has not led to substantial changes in how these tests are *actually used*. As White (2008, p15) has commented:

> The traditional notion of intelligence associated with IQ is an oddity. Why the heavy emphasis on abstract, logical ability, when in everyday life your intelligence can be displayed as much by how well you sort out a delicate problem of personal relationships as by how well you solve a suduko puzzle? Why take for granted that we all have our own differing ceilings of ability, when this looks for all the world like an untestable assumption?

Nevertheless, as commented in Chapter 6, the past 100 years has seen the rise and rise of the development of standardised tests of intellectual ability. Sparrow and Davis (2000) identified 15 such tests used when completing neuropsychological assessments of children and adolescents, and these are shown in Figure 7.4. Sparrow and Davis (2000) emphasise that these tests are used to assess independently six aspects or *domains* of cognition. These are *attention*; *auditory, visual and tactile perception*; *verbal and language abilities*; *spatial* or *construction processing abilities*; *memory* and *learning*; and *executive functions* such as problem solving and reasoning abilities, planning and the extent to which the individual is capable of using cognitive strategies flexibly. Importantly, the use of these tests as part of the neuropsychological assessment of individuals *differs* from what we might encounter in academic or research contexts. For example, they are not used to assess intelligence per se. Instead, performance on such tests is interpreted in terms of the strengths and weaknesses in the individual's cognitive abilities, and as Sparrow and Davis (2000)

Figure 7.4: *Standardised tests of intellectual ability*

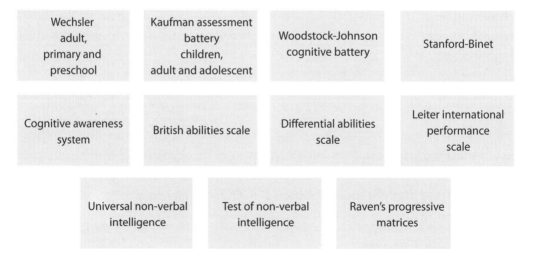

Further reading

Barrington, E (2004). Teaching to student diversity in higher education: how multiple intelligence theory can help. *Teaching in Higher Education*, 9(4): 421–34.

Barrington's paper is a readable discussion of the potential consequences of using a predominantly cognitive approach to intellectual ability, and its assessment, for higher education. The paper considers how we can apply the notion of intelligences to the tertiary education sector and provides a useful critical overview of this contentious issue.

Brown, JS, Collins, A and Duguid, P (1989) Situated cognition and the culture of learning. *Educational Researcher*, 18(1): 32–42.

This early paper summarises Brown and Collins's situated learning approach to academic achievement. The paper is important because it outlines the fundamental principles of an approach that challenges many of the psychometric assumptions underlying the use of tests of intellectual ability. In particular, it presents a context-dependent approach to measuring and predicting academic achievement.

Crosby, FJ, Iyer, A and Sincharoen, S (2006) Understanding affirmative action. *Annual Review of Psychology*, 57: 585–611.

This paper provides a helpful introduction to the issue of whether it is ethical for psychologists to be political. It focuses on affirmative action and thus is directly relevant to the use of intellectual ability tests for high-stakes decision making.

Deary. I. and Batty, GD (2007) Cognitive epidemiology. *Journal of Epidemiological Community Health*, 61: 378–84.

This is a brief glossary of key concepts and methods used in research on the links between measured intellectual ability and morbidity and mortality. Cognitive epidemiological research is typically used to support the case for the criterion-related validity of scores on tests of intellectual ability. This paper illustrates the interdisciplinary nature of the research on this topic, and helps demystify much of the technical jargon you will encounter in the literature.

Groth-Marnat, G (2003) *The handbook of psychological assessment* (4th edn). New York: Wiley.

This is a specialist resource for clinicians conducting psychological assessments. However, the book is a comprehensive and readable overview of ways in which intellectual ability tests are used as part of assessment packages. This is an excellent resource for illustrating the many uses of intellectual ability tests, along with other standardised psychological tests. In places, it also provides a critical view of the difficulties of administering and interpreting standardised test scores.

Sackett, PR, Borneman, MJ and Connelly, BS (2008) High-stakes testing in higher education and employment. *American Psychologist*, 63(4): 215–27.

This is an important paper that summarises both the case for, and the case against, the use of intellectual ability tests for high-stakes decision making. It provides a useful framework for organising this complex and substantial literature. It is therefore advisable to read this paper before considering the others listed.

White, J (2008). Intelligence testing in education. *Education Journal,* 97: 15.

White's single page article is a condensed account of his views on the flawed use of intelligence tests in education. This article offers a hard-line perspective against test use, and a consideration of some of the reasons why test use remains robust in the face of counter-evidence. This is a useful and concise summary of key issues.

Useful websites

www3.imperial.ac.uk/business-school/currentstudents/careers/career_process/accessing opportunities/psychometric/onlinetests (Imperial College Business School)

This site gives access to online practice tests of intellectual ability for graduates, and is a useful resource for accessing the sorts of tests used for graduate selection.

http://html-pdf-convert.com/cari/watson-glaser-critical-thinking-practice-test.html (Watson-Glaser Critical Thinking)

This site will give you free access to manuals and articles on the Watson-Glaser Critical Appraisal test. This is a useful site for accessing an explicit standardised test of intellectual ability that does attempt to address some of the criticisms of the more abstract and context-free tests.

Chapter 8

Motivation

Learning outcomes

By the end of this chapter you should:

- *be able to discuss how psychologists have attempted to define and conceptualise what is meant by motivation and self-regulation;*

- *understand and be able to examine, critically, conceptual shifts in the history of motivation research;*

- *be able to outline and discuss, critically, examples of top-down and bottom-up approaches to human motivation;*

- *be able to consider, critically, ways in which personality has been linked to human motivation;*

- *have a critical understanding of current conceptual and methodological challenges faced by individual differences research on motivation;*

- *develop skills of reflection and knowledge of teamwork by considering your motivation when working individually and when working as part of a team.*

Introduction

In this chapter you will consider the following questions.

- Why do people behave as they do?

- How have psychologists attempted to explain this?

- How are individual differences psychology and motivation research linked?

The first two questions have a familiar generic quality to them – they appear to capture the very essence of psychology. Moreover, in Chapters 1 and 2 you were encouraged to consider the extent to which individual differences research on personality, and especially the trait approach, helps us predict behaviour. We also identified that, for some researchers, a fundamental issue remains unresolved in the literature on personality – whether trait psychology provides more than statistical explanations that merely describe relationships between test scores. In other words, the question of *why we behave as we do* is at the heart of individual differences and trait psychology. One consequence of this is that the topic of human motivation is traditionally considered in undergraduate courses on individual differences, and rightly so. However, this can entail dealing with the topic towards the end of the text and implicitly rather than explicitly linking it to individual differences psychology. In these circumstances the student can be left to work out for themselves where motivation research fits into the complex landscape of individual differences. Given the sheer breadth and depth of research on both motivation and individual differences in general, this can be unhelpful and leave the student with a daunting analytical task. Here, we also cover the topic of human motivation towards the end of the book. However, an attempt will be made to explain this placing, and we will also attempt to consider the links between personality and motivation research.

To try to achieve these challenging goals, we will consider the three questions listed above. Motivation research has tended to take a particular approach to the first two generic questions. To consider this particular approach, you will – as we have done with other topics – first examine definitions and conceptualisations of the term motivation. What is meant by the term? How have different fields within psychology approached this construct? The broader context of motivation research is important here. Conceptual shifts have taken place in this research over the past 100 years. Importantly, there has been a conceptual shift as *top-down approaches* have been supplanted by more *bottom-up approaches* to motivation; in this chapter you will be encouraged to consider the *extent* of this shift (Caprara and Cervone, 2000). Another feature of this shift is that currently there appears to be a degree of consensus among psychologists about the nature of human motivation; in this chapter you will be encouraged to think critically about the extent of this theoretical consensus. Towards the end of the chapter we will consider how motivation research and individual differences psychology are linked. This is not a straightforward issue despite the fact that some researchers state that motivation and personality processes are the same or at least closely linked (Caprara and Cervone, 2000). In some instances this statement is not explained. Sometimes it is assumed that students can work out the links for themselves, or that stating that *individuals differ in their motivation* suffices as coverage of this issue. In this chapter, you will be encouraged to take a slightly more direct approach to this question, and towards the end of the chapter we will suggest four possible links between trait psychology and motivation. The overall goal of this chapter is for you to develop a critical understanding of the complexity of motivation research, and to understand that individual differences research on motivation faces a number of conceptual and methodological challenges. The tasks and activities here are designed to develop your critical thinking skills about motivation by getting you to reflect on a specific aspect of your own motivation and to then reconsider it when working as part of a group of individuals or team.

Definitions and concepts of motivation

Definitions

What do we mean when we use the term *motivation*? One way to start considering this question is to reflect on your everyday use of this and related terms, and this is what you are asked to do in the following task.

Task — In this task you will consider what you believe is meant by the term *motivation*. Please identify as many ways as possible that you use the term motivation and related terms such as *motive* or *motivated* in your everyday talk. Simply write down your personal views. Do not ask friends or colleagues for their opinion to assist you in deciding on your answers, and do not use any form of reference text (e.g. dictionaries, textbooks and internet) to help you answer the question. Feel free to use examples or experiences you may have to illustrate your answer. Make your answer as short or as long as you like. Finally, the task asks you to identify the different uses of the term motivation; if you have only one use of the term, please simply state that.

Comment

In Chapter 2 we considered your lay theory of personality, and used the distinction between entity and incremental theories to categorise these. The purpose of that task was to encourage you to reflect on the implicit theoretical assumptions you hold about people and their dispositions, and how your assumptions might influence your critical thinking about personality. That task also drew attention to conceptual differences that underlie the use of the same or similar terms, such as personality and dispositions. Conceptual differences also exist about the term motivation, and the task here uses an approach based on the work of Beedie et al. (2005). They elicited people's implicit theoretical assumptions – which they refer to as lay theories – to examine the differences between academic theories and what they call people's *common sense theories* of the meaning of *emotion* and *mood*. They argue that *conceptual clarity is the bedrock of science* (p848). By this they mean that the many different ways that both academics and non-academics use the terms emotion and mood make it difficult to identify what some research is actually about and the psychological phenomena that have actually been studied in such work. Although these researchers did not examine common-sense definitions of motivation, their research has relevance here.

- Common sense definitions or theories are worth considering when there has been a pro-liferation of academic research on a topic; this has been the case with research on motivation as well as emotion and mood. The issue here is that as research proliferates on a topic so does the terminology, and this can lead to the inconsistent use of terminology, a pattern Beedie et al. (2005) found in research on emotion and mood.

- As with the terms emotion and mood, motivation is a term used in everyday language. Our folk theories of such terms are therefore worth examining because they are central to our everyday experiences of these constructs.

- We use motivation and related terms in conjunction with emotion and mood – we refer to *feeling motivated* or *being in the mood* (or not) to engage in behaviours, feelings and thoughts that look like they have motivational relevance.

Beedie et al. (2005) asked 106 participants, who were not academics, what they believed the difference to be between an emotion and a mood. They found some agreements between their participants' common sense theories about these differences, and also between the distinctions made in the academic literature. For example, their participants defined emotion but not mood as being typified by *lack of control* and that emotion is a feeling whereas mood is about *thoughts*. They also found that participants disagreed about the relative stability of emotion compared to mood. This research suggests that to some extent definitions of motivation and related terms found in the academic literature and more common sense definitions are not always identical.

There is also evidence that academic definitions of motivation are inconsistent. Murphy and Alexander (2000) conducted a review of motivational terms used in academic and achievement research, and found 20 terms used in this research. Although they state that the use of *fuzzy concepts* (p4) is not specific to motivation research, their point about the confusion over motivation terminology in research on academic motivation can be applied to motivation research in general. They draw attention to the particular problems posed for motivation research by the use of fuzzy concepts, problems aggravated by the very nature of the topic. Namely, when considering human motivation they argue that researchers *are endeavouring to overlay diverse traditions, each with its own phraseology and its own cadre of troublesome, but potent, constructs* (p5). The diverse range of terms they found in the research on academic motivation is summarised in Figure 8.1.

These researchers found that 20 different terms were used in the literature. They also found that motivation and related terms were used frequently to describe domain-specific motivation – in other words, to describe specific aspects of motivation in certain contexts – or motivation more generally. In the literature they examined they found that on 38 per cent of occasions the motivation-related terms used were defined *explicitly*. However, on 31 per cent of occasions, such definitions were implicit – their meaning had to be inferred from surrounding text – and on the remaining 31 per cent of instances terms were left undefined. They state that their results show that frequently definitions of motivation and related constructs are *absent* in the academic literature. Consequently, when clarifying what these terms actually mean in academic literature

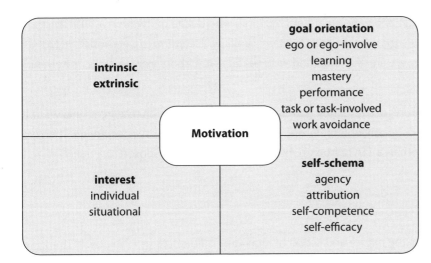

Figure 8.1: *Murphy and Alexander's (2000) summary of academic motivation terminology*

the *onus . . . falls heavily on the reader* (p32). This lack of conceptual clarity over the meaning of motivation and related terms appeared to be worsened in the literature they examined by the fact that researchers were increasingly using subcomponent terms – or splitting motivation into more specific concepts. The result of this is that:

> *The burgeoning of motivation terminology has contributed to potential confusion in understanding the subtleties and distinctions that may or may not exist between and among families of terms (e.g., goal orientations). This potential for confusion is greater for those who do not belong to the community of motivation researchers or who do not understand the traditions from which these families of terms arose.*
>
> (Murphy and Alexander, 2000, p36)

We have spent some time considering how motivation and related terms are defined both in the academic literature and by you. This consideration demonstrates a number of points that provide an important context for considering human motivation.

- Definitions of motivation vary and, while this is not fundamentally problematic, it appears to make understanding the research challenging (Murphy and Alexander, 2000).

- Everyday use of motivation and related terms is likely to differ from the use of these terms in the academic literature.

- Researchers use the same terms to mean different things; examples are *motivation, motive, drive, urge, needs, goals, values,* and *standards* (Gable, 2006).

- Definitions are actually conceptualisations of the essence of human motivation.

Given these complex definitional issues, at this point we will define motivation in its broadest sense as *the reasons why people behave as they do.* This is consistent with other omnibus definitions of motivation, such as that of Baumeister et al. (2007, p2) who define motivation as *in essence . . . any sort of general drive or inclination to do something*. Similarly, according to Deci and Ryan (2000), motivation is something we are all concerned with because it is about *how to move ourselves or others to act*.

We will now clarify two further contextual issues about human motivation research. First, we will attempt to clarify what we mean when referring to human motivation as *self-regulation*. Then we will consider the conceptualisation of human motivation as a *state* as opposed to a *trait*.

Motivation as self-regulation

In Chapter 1 we clarified the nature and scope of individual differences psychology. In doing so we identified that currently researchers are conceptualising individual differences and the main aspects of such differences – such as personality and intelligence or intellect – as *self-regulation*. Likewise, contemporary research on human motivation frequently conceptualises human motivation as self-regulation. However, according to Baumeister et al. (2007, p1), despite the expansion of motivation research *Motivation is underappreciated in psychology generally . . . (and) Motivation's role in self-regulation has been similarly underestimated*. Nevertheless, the use of the term self-regulation to conceptualise human motivation is regarded as theoretically significant (Carver and Scheier, 2000a, 2000b) and as indicating a fundamental conceptual shift in motivation research (Caprara and Cervone, 2000). Furthermore, Caprara and Cervone (2000) argue that *classic theories of personality primarily are theories of motivation* (p339) and that the shift to conceptualising human motivation as self-regulation has also brought about an intellectual shift in motivation research. Namely, there appears to be a relative consensus in the academic literature about the sort of concept motivation actually is.

- Human motivation can be best conceptualised using *bottom-up* rather than *top-down* approaches.

- One consequence of this conceptual shift is that researchers should focus on the bottom-up *ingredients* (Baumeister et al., 2007) of human motivation.

According to Caprara and Cervone (2000) there are four components or ingredients common to contemporary bottom-up approaches to human motivation. These represent relative agreement among researchers about the main features of motivation, with researchers sharing concepts and ideas.

- *Standards:* motivation involves the use of these cognitive representations. Specifically, we decide to behave in a certain manner dependent upon whether this course of action is acceptable, and we have criteria or standards we use to compare this course of action against. Thus standards are not merely cognitive representations but also have an affective component.

- *Affective self-evaluation*: the experiencing of positive emotions also steers our motivated behaviour. In this sense motivation involves the evaluation of our affect, that is, affective self-evaluation.

- *Self-efficacy beliefs and perceived control*: beliefs that one can *control* both what one wants to achieve and the means, or behaviours, needed to achieve them – *self-efficacy* – also influence motivation. Consequently, beliefs about what one wants to achieve – outcomes – and one's ability to achieve these – behaviour – are important motivational ingredients. For example, believing that one's standards of behaviour are achievable and that one's behaviour can achieve these is likely to encourage such actions to be carried out.

- *Goals and self-regulation or the self-system*: more specifically, when we commit ourselves to achieving a relatively specific aim through planning and effort, we refer to this as a *goal*. The relationship between goals and *standards* appears complex given their use interchangeably by some researchers (Caprara and Cervone, 2000). However, to some extent they differ in terms of their specificity and functions. Standards can be relatively broad evaluative benchmarks that can function as relative aspirations that are not always achievable, such as standards of perfection in many actions or endeavours. In contrast, one's goals are likely to be more specific targets simply because, using Caprara and Cervone's (2000) conceptualisation, they involve effort, commitment and importantly *planning*. Goals and standards can *appear* conflicting or to lack coherency but the notion of *coherence* between these and all of the other motivational ingredients is central to many contemporary approaches to motivation. Goals and standards can also influence one another simply because they are part of how we regulate ourselves or self-regulation. When we reflect on how we are doing this entails thinking about one's self. Consequently, the self-system is called on when we engage in this self-reflection.

Therefore, according to Caprara and Cervone (2000), human motivation is about why we behave as we do or how we self-regulate, which they also refer to as the *self-system* (p339). In other words:

self-referent processes function as personal determinants of motivation. Through their capacity to set goals, develop strategies, reflect on themselves, and evaluate their performance, people are able to self-regulate their behaviour and emotional states.

According to this definition, human motivation is a uniquely human process of self-regulation involving affective, behavioural and cognitive processes. An overarching function of motivation is to achieve self-satisfaction as measured against our standards and made concrete through our goals. This means motivational processes are *guided in part by efforts to obtain positive feelings about oneself from oneself* (p341).

Task ⌐ Return to the first task you completed in this chapter and re-examine your uses of *motivation* and related terms. Consider whether any of your uses contain aspects of Caprara and Cervone's (2000) four components.

Comment

This task should help you make sure you understand some of the main features of contemporary bottom-up approaches to human motivation. It should also develop your awareness of the differences between top-down and bottom-up approaches that we will consider shortly. However, it is important not to oversimplify the nature of contemporary bottom-up approaches to human motivation or the degree of consensus among these sorts of approaches. First, Bandura and Locke (2003) are sceptical about the ways in which contemporary researchers appear to share concepts and develop theories of motivation by selecting from the menu of concepts on offer in the literature, a practice they describe as *cafeteria theorising*. Second, Carver and Scheier (2000a, 2000b) argue that although many researchers use the term self-regulation to conceptualise motivation, they may differ in what they mean by self-regulation. For example, in Carver and Scheier's research on motivation, self-regulation means goal-directed behaviour shaped by the use of feedback. However, Baumeister et al. (2007, p2) argue that self-regulation involves four *ingredients* (p3) and motivation is simply one of these. Furthermore, Baumeister et al. (2007) have a relatively narrow conceptualisation of self-regulation as a process of *self-stopping* (p11). Importantly, this narrow conceptualisation of self-regulation is criticised by Carver and Scheier (2000a, 2000b) as simplistic. However, despite this narrowness, Baumeister et al. (2006, p1773) regard self-regulation as a personality process (Baumeister et al., 2006, p1773) and acknowledge that self-regulation can mean many things. Finally, Murphy and Alexander (2000) found that some researchers in the field of motivation are actually reluctant to include self-regulation in their analysis of terminology used in research on academic motivation for an interesting reason (p7): *... the term crosses both the cognitive and motivation literature.*

The task ahead of you in this chapter, therefore, is challenging.

Motivational states and traits

The final contextual issue you need to be aware of is that researchers do not agree on whether motivation is a *state* or a *trait*. For example, Cooper (2002) differentiates motivation as a more enduring aspect of individual differences or as relatively dispositional in comparison to mood and emotion, which are states that can influence motivation. A major conceptual challenge here is that individual differences psychology focuses on enduring dispositions such as traits to describe and potentially explain inter-individual differences and intra-individual variation and coherence in behaviour, thoughts and feelings. Contemporary motivation research is, by and large, about why we behave as we do in *specific circumstances*. If you examine your answers to the first task in this chapter, you can perhaps notice that in your everyday uses of the term motivation and related terms, it is not always clear whether your uses denote states or traits.

Motivation as whole person psychology

The placing of the topic of motivation towards the end of this text is deliberate for a number of reasons. Contemporary research on human motivation is an amalgam of core topics and issues in individual differences psychology. Therefore, it is important that you have some prior knowledge and understanding of these issues. Furthermore, by this point you should have developed critical thinking skills that should help you understand a topic that is challenging and that is fundamentally a synthesis of many parts of individual differences and psychology in general. Importantly, at this point you should have awareness that individual differences psychology is concerned with how we regulate ourselves, and self-regulation is at the heart of contemporary conceptualisations of motivation.

In the next section we will consider how approaches to conceptualising human motivation have changed historically by focusing on some of the key questions asked in the research on motivation in the field, and by considering in more detail what is meant by *top-down* and *bottom-up* approaches to human motivation.

History of motivation research

Key questions

Certain key questions have dominated the history of motivation research, and these questions still shape contemporary research.

- What is motivation?

- What motivates humans, and can these be regarded as universal or relative?

- Why do individuals vary in their motivation (intra-individual variation and inter-individual differences)?

- What is the relationship between motivation, dispositions and contexts?

Interest in why we behave as we do is a central feature in the writings of ancient philosophers such as Aristotle (Reiss, 2004), and in the work of classic researchers in the discipline of psychology such as Freud (Caprara and Cervone, 2000) and William James (1890). The concept of instinct was important in this early work. For example, Allport (1937) in his classic paper 'The functional autonomy of motives', argued that psychology as a discipline and in particular personality psychology is essentially about motivation:

> *Any type of psychology that treats motives, thereby endeavouring to answer the question as to why men behave as they do, is called a dynamic psychology. By its very nature it cannot be merely a descriptive psychology, content to depict the what and the how of human behaviour.*

Allport (1937) went on to argue that human motivation could not be explained using concepts such as universal instincts or learnt habits and instead proposed nine functionally autonomous motives that *lie at the root of personal behaviour . . . thus* (forming) *the first step in establishing a basis for the more realistic study of unique and individual forms for personality.* To some extent, Allport's nine functionally autonomous motives do resemble a taxonomy comprised of other researchers' conceptualisations of motives. However, the key point here is that Allport (1937) was proposing that motivation is likely to be a *process* involving a range of psychological phenomena and processes that we can use to explain why we behave as we do and, furthermore, that motivation and personality are closely linked, a claim made by more contemporary researchers such as Rasmussen et al. (2006) who asserted that personality is all about *how behaviour happens.*

However, the key questions in motivation research have altered as conceptualisations of human motivation have changed. One question that has emerged as motivation has been reconceptualised as a process of self-regulation is whether we should examine human motivation using *top-down* or *bottom-up* approaches.

Top-down versus bottom-up approaches

One of the most important conceptual shifts in motivation research has been the rise in popularity of *process* accounts of motivation and the fall of *taxonomy* accounts. Caprara and Cervone (2000) describe this shift using slightly broader terms – the dominance of top-down approaches has been replaced by the rise of bottom-up approaches – see Figure 8.2 for a comparison of the two approaches.

Some of the features are either key questions themselves or they underpin one or more contemporary key questions in motivation research. The focus is now on self-regulation and the social (contextual), cognitive, biological, personality and developmental *determinants* of motivation. However, it would be simplistic to exaggerate the differences between these approaches using the terms *taxonomy* versus *process* accounts, as these are not mutually exclusive. We will use the terms bottom-up and top-down here because these are the terms used in the research, and their use should encourage you to think about how distinctive these accounts appear to be (Caprara and Cervone, 2000).

Figure 8.2: *Top-down and bottom-up approaches to motivation*

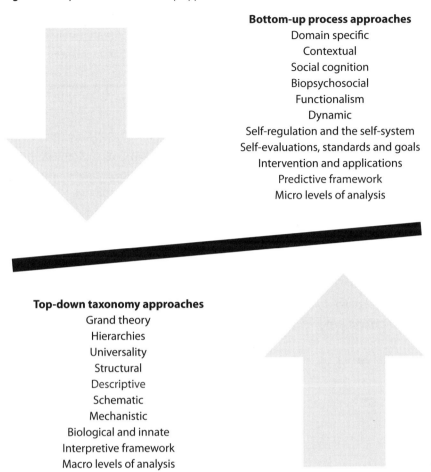

Bottom-up process approaches
Domain specific
Contextual
Social cognition
Biopsychosocial
Functionalism
Dynamic
Self-regulation and the self-system
Self-evaluations, standards and goals
Intervention and applications
Predictive framework
Micro levels of analysis

Top-down taxonomy approaches
Grand theory
Hierarchies
Universality
Structural
Descriptive
Schematic
Mechanistic
Biological and innate
Interpretive framework
Macro levels of analysis

To summarise, there has clearly been a conceptual shift in human motivation research. What is unclear is the *extent* of the shift from top-down to bottom-up approaches. Likewise, there appear to be important differences *between* bottom-up approaches, despite Caprara and Cervone's (2000) emphasis upon consensus in the field. Next, we will consider an example of each of these types of accounts of motivation.

Top-down approaches

Maslow's (1943, 1987) pyramid or *hierarchy of needs* is a well-known and widely used account of human motivation – see Figure 8.3. A defining feature of this account is the taxonomy of needs that Maslow argued could be applied *universally* to *describe the structure* of human motivation. In essence, this taxonomy of broad needs can be used to interpret the nature of human motivation: needs at the bottom of the hierarchy must be met before the individual moves on to satisfy the next higher-level need. Originally, Maslow identified five of the eight needs shown in Figure 8.3 – *transcendental*, *aesthetic* and *cognitive* needs were later additions to the theory. Maslow (1943) is, to some extent, a relatively prototypical top-down taxonomy account of human motivation. For example, the theory is a *schematic representation* or description of what motivates human behaviour universally, and the focus appears clearly on *listing* what motivates us. The needs that drive our actions are relatively general and provide a *macro-level framework* – it does not focus on the minutiae of motivational phenomena – and this is often *interpreted* as a mechanistic schematic representation of human motivation. Importantly, needs drive us and not vice versa, and fundamental needs at the base of the hierarchy are unconscious. However, in some respects Maslow's theory of motivation is more complex and less exclusively top-down than it appears to be. For example, a close reading of his original work suggests that Maslow (1943) did not intend his account to be a mechanistic list of must-have and must-satisfy needs. In fact, he identified 13 features that any theory of human motivation must meet, and he attempted to ensure that his theory conformed to these as (p.3):

> *[a] positive theory of motivation which will satisfy these theoretical demands and at the same time conform to the known facts, clinical and observational as well as experimental. It derives most directly, however, from clinical experience. This theory is, I think, in the functionalist tradition of*

Figure 8.3: *Maslow's pyramid of needs*

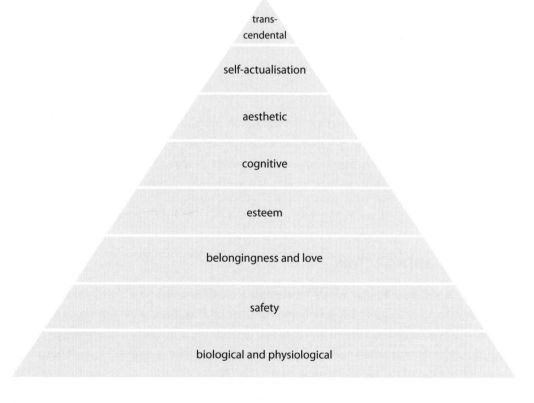

James and Dewey, and is fused with the holism of Wertheimer, Goldstein, and Gestalt Psychology, and with the dynamicism of Freud and Adler. This fusion or synthesis may arbitrarily be called a 'general-dynamic' theory.

Importantly, Maslow argued that his theory was not merely about listing drives and that it incorporated goals to form an integrated human-focused theory of motivation. In fact, his original descriptions of a number of the needs in the pyramid imply a level of interpretation, self-reflection, self-evaluation and agentic control within his model. For instance, he described self-actualisation as follows: *even if all these needs are satisfied, we may still often (if not always) expect that a new discontent and restlessness will soon develop, unless the individual is doing what he is fitted for* (1943, p10). This definition of self-actualisation does imply a level of subjective appraisal and processing within his theory of human motivation. These more subtle process aspects of Maslow have been incorporated into newer versions of his original theory, such as the work of Kenrick et al. (2010) who developed a renovation of the pyramid of needs using Maslow's original work integrated with evolutionary theory.

Bottom-up approaches

In contrast to top-down accounts of human motivation, bottom-up approaches tend to focus on *when, how* and *why* behaviour starts and stops. They also tend to focus more on the mechanisms involved in these, especially the role of feedback – its nature and use. In this sense, they use a more *micro-level of analysis* of motivation than their top-down counterparts.

Carver and Scheier's (2000b) control theory is in some respects a relatively prototypical bottom-up approach to human motivation. Figure 8.4 summarises its key elements. It uses what has been described as a *cybernetic computer metaphor* comprised of four components. Individual motivation is regulated by this system of components in which our goals, standards and reference values constitute a comparator mechanism – we monitor ourselves through the input function, and this input is then compared or judged against our goals and standards or reference values. This comparison process is performed by the comparator component. As a consequence of this comparator process an output is produced (output function) that has some impact on the environment. In cyclical fashion this impact on the environment then becomes a new input to the input function, and the process continues. Importantly, this theory proposes that the individual has a level of self-awareness or is conscious of these processes and that motivation is all about the recalibration or adjustment of motivated behaviour in response to feedback. Goal setting is a central feature of this theory and is a common feature of many bottom-up approaches to motivation (Locke et al., 1981), as is the premise that adaptive self-regulation involves using recalibration processes to change one's behaviour or engage in response shifts. For example, this theory of motivation suggests that we can use feedback to inform our motivational processes

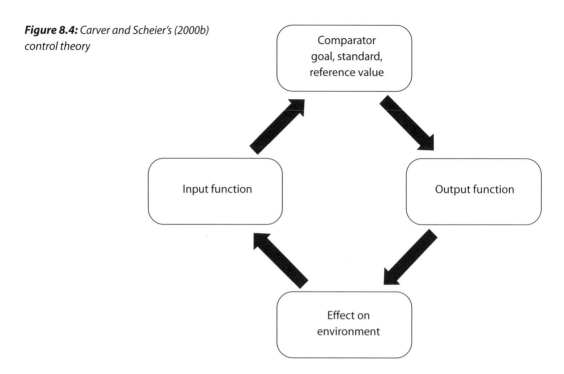

Figure 8.4: *Carver and Scheier's (2000b) control theory*

and in particular to judge when a goal is unattainable. In other words, we can use feedback from our own behaviour to judge when desisting in a course of action is good for us and perseverance is maladaptive (Carver and Scheier, 2000a, 2000b; Wrosch et al., 2003).

Task ⎯ An important part of control theory is *goal setting*. However, individuals vary is their ability to set realistic goals or standards. For example, some individuals typically set unrealistically high standards for themselves or *standards that are beyond reach or rationality, straining to reach those impossible goals, and defining one's worth by the accomplishment of those standards* (Bieling et al., 2003, p164).

Certain aspects of this *perfectionism* can be maladaptive. For this task think of different ways in which having unrealistic or unachievable personal goals can potentially disrupt the feedback loops central to Carver and Scheier's control theory of motivation.

Comment

This task should help you to think critically about the theoretical assumptions of control theory. Bandura and Locke (2003) argue that their research on self-efficacy theory demonstrates that desisting from a course of action or *giving up* is far from an adaptive part of self-regulation, and they challenge the notion that giving up is potentially adaptive and perseverance can be maladaptive – notions that are inherent in control theory. They also are critical of the notion that positive and negative feedback are equivalent, and of the ad hoc modifications that have been made to control theory. Bandura and Locke (2003) argue that control theory has developed using *cafeteria theorising* (p93) in which concepts have been added and removed to accommodate inconsistent results from research testing the theory. This criticism is not about theory modification per se but rather about the manner in which these modifications have been made (p93):

> that take different forms depending on the particular mix of socio-cognitive factors grafted on the negative feedback loop . . . The rich eclectic embellishment of the negative feedback loop is more akin to cafeteria theorising than to integrative theorising as claimed.

Other researchers have also found it difficult to replicate Carver and Scheier's original experiments, and Dahme et al. (2003) suggest that the predictions of control theory are dependent on the individual having a degree of *self-awareness* that enables them to monitor themselves.

Personality and human motivation

At the start of this chapter it was suggested that the links between motivation and individual differences are complex. However, it was also suggested that given these complexities, it is important to state *explicitly* the ways in which these constructs are potentially linked. Here, we are suggesting four such ways. These are far from exhaustive but they can be used as a rubric for trying to organise this complex literature.

- *Motivation and personality are all about self-regulation* and we considered this issue in Chapters 1 and 2, when we attempted to define the field, its scope and aims.

- *The FFT are all about how we manage ourselves* and we considered this in Chapter 4 when examining the links between atypical personality and mental health and mental disorder. Some researchers regard the FFT as implicitly focused on goals (Chulef et al., 2001), and there is evidence that the FFT of N and C are related to motivational constructions such as goal setting (Barrick, Mitchell and Stewart, 2001; Judge and Ilies, 2002).

- *Eysenck and Gray's biological theories of personality are all about self-regulation* or the approach and avoidance of certain stimuli. In this sense, they conceptualise personality as underpinned by the neurophysiological need to balance certain stimulus sensitivities (see Chapter 2). These biological theories of personality have been used to develop such constructs as appetitive motivation (Jackson and Smillie, 2004).

- *The big two of the FFT (E and N) influence approach-avoidance behaviour*, and we considered these issues in Chapter 4. Importantly, to some extent we can conceptualise motivation as about approach and avoidance behaviour and the processes underpinning such behaviour.

Critical thinking activity

Self-efficacy

Critical thinking focus: reflection

Key question: Is self-efficacy a general disposition?

Earlier in this chapter we identified self-efficacy as an important ingredient in bottom-up approaches to motivation. Self-efficacy theory draws on *Social cognitive theory* that is *rooted in an agentic perspective in which people function as anticipative, purposive, and self evaluating proactive regulators of their motivation and actions* (Bandura and Locke, 2003, p87). This has led researchers to focus on measuring self-efficacy using modifications of Bandura's measures (Bandura, 2006) or to develop activity and domain-specific self-efficacy measures, driven by Bandura's argument that self-efficacy should be considered in relation to *situational demands*. This *task-specific quality* has been supported by research showing that the predictive power of self-efficacy is greatest when it is used for specific tasks because this enables the specificity of the behaviour to match the specificity of the measure. Less attention has been given to the notion of general self-efficacy (GSE), which is the extent to which individuals *view themselves as capable of meeting task demands in a broad array of contexts* (Chen et al., 2001, p63). GSE can be considered both as a motivational trait and as a state known as state self-efficacy (SSE). The *plasticity hypothesis* predicts that high GSE and SSE protect against the influence of adverse external events (Brockner, 1988). However, measures of GSE are poor predictors of behaviour, and this is likely to be because GSE lacks specificity – it does not match the specificity or generality of the motivation being measured and the behaviour being predicted. However, Chen et al. (2001) attempted to develop a new general self-efficacy (NGSE) measure using the existing GSE scale items but testing more robustly for the scales construct validity. They produced the eight-item new general self-efficacy (NGSE) scale and this is shown in Figure 8.5. To complete the scale, individuals have to judge the extent to which they agree/disagree that each statement is an accurate description of themselves. This is done using a five-point scale where 1 = strongly disagree, 2 = disagree, 3 = undecided, 4 = agree, and 5 = strongly agree. The minimum score achievable on the NGSE is eight and the maximum is 40, with higher scores indicating stronger general self-efficacy.

Figure 8.5: *New general self-efficacy scale (NGSE)*

1.	I will be able to achieve most of the goals that I have set for myself	1	2	3	4	5
2.	When facing difficult tasks, I am certain that I will accomplish them	1	2	3	4	5
3.	In general, I think that I can obtain outcomes that are important to me	1	2	3	4	5
4.	I believe I can succeed at almost any endeavour to which I set my mind	1	2	3	4	5
5.	I will be able to successfully overcome many challenges	1	2	3	4	5
6.	I am confident that I can perform effectively on many different tasks	1	2	3	4	5
7.	Compared to other people, I can do most tasks very well	1	2	3	4	5
8.	Even when things are tough, I can perform quite well	1	2	3	4	5

The notion of general self-efficacy is contentious. Some researchers argue that the construct lacks predictive value and is inconsistent with the behaviour-specific nature of self-efficacy. In this activity you should reflect on these issues by measuring your own general self-efficacy using the NGSE and examine how this relates to your score on a more behaviour-specific measure of self-efficacy.

- First, calculate your NGSE score by completing the NGSE.

- Second, reflect on what this score actually indicates about your self-efficacy in general using the three questions:

   ○ *Does your GSE score suggest you have a high level of general self-efficacy or not?*

   ○ *What evidence do you have of this? Think of some examples.*

   ○ *How do you know when to give up or persevere with a behaviour or behaviours?*

- Third, complete one of the two specific self-efficacy measures given in Figures 8.6 and 8.7. One relates to physical activity and the other to how you manage physical pain.

- Finally, compare your score on the NGSE and the specific self-efficacy measure you chose to complete and ask yourself the following question: *how accurately does my NGSE score capture my self-efficacy on the specific measure?*

You should complete this activity individually, but you can discuss your reflections in a group once you have completed the activity.

Figure 8.6: *Self-efficacy to regulate exercise (Bandura, 2006)*

A number of situations are described below that can make it hard to stick to an exercise routine. Please rate in each of the blanks in the column how certain you are you can get yourself to perform your exercise routine regularly (three or more times a week).

Rate your confidence by recording a number from 0 to 100 using the scale given below:

| 0 | 10 | 20 | 30 | 40 | 50 | 60 | 70 | 80 | 90 | 100 |

| Cannot
do at all | Moderately
can do | Highly certain
can do |

	Confidence 0–100
When I am feeling tired	
When I am feeling under pressure from work	
During bad weather	
After recovering from an injury that caused me to stop exercising	
When I am feeling depressed	
When I am feeling anxious	
After recovering from an illness that caused me to stop exercising	
When I feel physical discomfort when I exercise	
After a vacation	
When I have too much work to do at home	
When visitors are present	
When there are other interesting things to do	
If I don't reach my exercise goals	
Without support from my family and friends	
During a vacation	
When I have other time commitments	
After experiencing family problems	

Figure 8.7: *Pain management self-efficacy (Bandura, 2006)*

People sometimes do things to reduce their pain without taking medication. Please rate how certain you are that you can *reduce* the different levels of pain described below.

Rate your confidence by recording a number from 0 to 100 using the scale given below:

0   10   20   30   40   50   60   70   80   90   100

| Cannot | Moderately | Highly certain |
| do at all | can do | can do |

	Confidence 0–100
Reduce a DULL PAIN: A small reduction A moderate reduction A large reduction	
Reduce an ACHING PAIN: A small reduction A moderate reduction A large reduction	
Reduce a PENETRATING PAIN: A small reduction A moderate reduction A large reduction	
Reduce an EXCRUCIATING PAIN: A small reduction A moderate reduction A large reduction	

Critical thinking review

This activity requires you to reflect both on your knowledge of self-efficacy theory and concepts and on your own self-efficacy. This involves making your self-efficacy beliefs explicit and quantifiable. It also requires you to think about your self-awareness and the evidence you use to persist or stop behaviours – or the nature and use of feedback.

Other skills likely to be used in this activity: this activity also requires you to use decision-making skills, critical and creative thinking, and your knowledge and understanding of self-efficacy theory.

Skill builder activity

Group self-efficacy

Transferable skill focus: teamwork

Key question: *What are the differences between the aggregate method and the group discussion method (Bandura, 2006) for assessing team internet self-efficacy?*

Eastin and LaRose developed an eight-item measure of internet self-efficacy. Although the scale was designed to measure individual self-efficacy, the following excerpt from Bandura (2006, pp316–17) suggests that the collective quality of self-efficacy is measurable. Please read this excerpt, paying particular attention to the difficulties Bandura (2006) identifies when trying to measure collective self-efficacy:

> *theorising and research on human agency has centered almost exclusively on personal influence exercised individually. People do not live their lives autonomously. Many of the outcomes they seek are achievable only through interdependent efforts. Hence, they have to work together to secure what they cannot accomplish on their own. Social cognitive theory extends the conception of human agency to collective agency. People's shared beliefs in their collective power to produce desired results is a key ingredient of collective agency . . . A group's attainments are the product not only of shared knowledge and skills of the different members, but also of the interactive, coordinative, and synergistic dynamics of their transactions. Therefore, perceived collective efficacy is not simply the sum of the efficacy beliefs of individual members. Rather, it is an emergent group-level property. A group operates through the behaviour of its members. It is people acting coordinatively on a shared belief, not a disembodied group mind that is doing the cognising, aspiring, motivating, and regulating. There is no emergent entity that operates independently of the beliefs and actions of the individuals who make up a social system. Although beliefs of collective efficacy include emergent aspects, they serve functions similar to those of persona efficacy beliefs and operate through similar processes . . . There are two main approaches to the measurement of a group's perceived efficacy. The first method aggregates the individual members' appraisals of their personal capabilities to execute the particular functions they perform in the group. The second method aggregates members' appraisals of their group's capability operating as a whole. The latter holistic appraisal encompasses the coordinative and interactive aspects operating within groups.*

You should imagine that you have been given the task of using a psychology electronic search engine, such as PsycINFO, to find at least ten high-relevance references that could be used in response to the following literature review question: *What contemporary evidence is there that supports Maslow's hierarchical theory of motivation (1987)?* You have been given 45 minutes to complete this task and must work as part of a team. One determinant of team performance on this task is the team's internet self-efficacy or their beliefs in their *capabilities to organise and execute courses of Internet actions required to produce given attainments* (Eastin and LaRose, 2000), and your team's internet self-efficacy is what you will focus on in this activity by completing the Internet Self-efficacy Scale (Figure 8.8) using Bandura's whole group aggregate method (2006) – that is, using a discussion to arrive at a single group-efficacy judgement. Complete the Internet Self-efficacy Scale in Figure 8.8 as part of a team that includes yourself and at least one other person. When working as a team to complete the scale please make a note of your answers to the following questions.

- How easy was it to reach a unanimous decision?

- How accurately do you believe your discussion-based collective judgement reflects each team members' internet self-efficacy?

- How might working as a team to complete the scale have influenced the collective judgement made?

- What are the advantages and disadvantages of working as a team to make collective judgements about the team's collective internet self-efficacy?

- How valid and reliable is your team judgement?

- What alternative methods could you use to complete the scale to reflect team internet self-efficacy?

Worked example

You might find that it is difficult to measure validly all group members' internet self-efficacy using this approach because you cannot easily reach a unanimous decision about your collective self-efficacy. You might also find that some members of your team have high levels of internet self-efficacy while others do not. Nevertheless, you believe that you should still record the team's self-efficacy as high in this instance because these individuals take the lead in the task you have to complete.

Figure 8.8: *Internet self-efficacy scale (Eastin and LaRose, 2000)*

Please rate how *confident you feel* that you can use the internet in each of the ways specified below, where 1 = strongly disagree and 7 = strongly agree

INTERNET SELF-EFFICACY SCALE

1.	. . . understanding words/terms relating to internet hardware	1	2	3	4	5	6	7
2.	. . . understanding words/terms relating to internet software	1	2	3	4	5	6	7
3.	. . . describing functions of internet hardware	1	2	3	4	5	6	7
4.	. . . troubleshooting internet problems	1	2	3	4	5	6	7
5..	. . . explaining why a task will not run on the internet	1	2	3	4	5	6	7
6.	. . . using the internet to gather data	1	2	3	4	5	6	7
7.	. . . confident learning advanced skills within a specific internet program	1	2	3	4	5	6	7
8.	. . . turning to an online discussion group when help is needed	1	2	3	4	5	6	7

Skill builder review

According to Bandura (2006, pp316–17):

Some researchers advocate that perceived collective efficacy be measured by having a group arrive at a single judgment of the group's capability . . . The discussion approach is methodologically problematic, however. Constructing unanimity about a Guide for Constructing Self-Efficacy Scales group's efficacy via group discussion is subject to the distorting vagaries of social persuasion by members who command power and other types of pressures for social conformity. Indeed, a group's collective judgment of its efficacy reflects mainly the personal judgments of higher status members rather than those of subordinate members . . . The discussion approach is likely to produce reactive effects in that persuasory efforts to reach consensus will alter members' views. Assessments that operate through social influence should be avoided. A method of measurement should not change what it is measuring. Moreover, no social system is a monolith with a unitary sense of efficacy . . . A forced consensus to a single judgment masks the variability in efficacy beliefs among the various factions within a social system and misrepresents their beliefs.

Group self-efficacy is central to Bandura's work; however, how this is measured can be challenging. This activity requires you to use teamwork skills to calculate your team's IT self-efficacy score, and to discuss the questions you must address about completing the activity (i.e. communication and collaboration).

Other skills likely to be used in this activity: this activity involves communication, reflection and decision-making skills when managing the team and recording your self-efficacy. You also have to analyse and evaluate data and think creatively about how to manage your group discussions.

Assignments

1. To what extent can contemporary approaches to human motivation be described as bottom-up rather than top-down?

2. *a quaint visual artefact without much contemporary theoretical importance* (Kenrick et al., 2010, p292). Critically examine this view in relation to Maslow's (1943) pyramid of needs.

3. A little bit of positive self-delusion does you good. Critically discuss this view in relation to the role of feedback in self-regulation.

4. Critically discuss whether evidence supports the view that personality and motivation processes are identical.

Summary: what you have learned

Research on human motivation has changed from focusing on describing motivations or top-down approaches to focusing on motivation as a self-regulation process. This means considering the bottom-up processes of self-regulation. However, these groups of approaches are not mutually exclusive. Among bottom-up approaches there is some degree of consensus about the nature of motivation, although these approaches themselves differ in how they specify and emphasise the ingredients of motivation processes. Finally, the tasks and activities should have drawn your attention to the conceptual and methodological challenges of conducting research on motivation.

Further reading

Bandura, A (1982) Self-efficacy mechanism in human agency. *American Psychologist,* 37(2): 22–147.

This is a readable overview of the key elements of self-efficacy theory. It is advisable to read this paper in conjunction with Carver and Scheier (2002), given the theoretical debate between these two theories.

Deci, EL and Ryan, RM (2000) The 'what' and 'why' of goal pursuits: human needs and the self-determination of behavior. *Psychological Inquiry*, 11(4): 227–68.

This is a substantial paper that although containing a number of complex issues, is an essential resource for understanding the concept of goals. In particular, these researchers take a different approach to motivational goals to that outlined in control theory and provide a detailed and contrasting example of a bottom-up approach.

Carver, CS and Scheier, MF (2002) Control processes and self-organizations as contemporary principles underlying behaviour. *Personality and Social Psychology Review*, 6(4): 304–15.

This is a helpful summary of the key elements of control theory and is best read in conjunction with Bandura (1982).

Covington, MV and Mueller, KJ (2001) Intrinsic versus extrinsic motivation: an approach/ avoidance reformulation. *Educational Psychology Review*, 13(2): 157–70.

This paper is useful for considering how motivation fits into individual differences psychology. It focuses on the issue of approach-avoidance behaviour and highlights the complex links between these literatures. This paper is a useful complement to Elliot and Thrash (2002).

Elliot, EJ and Thrash, TM (2002) Approach-avoidance motivation in personality: approach and avoidance temperaments and goals. *Journal of Personality and Social Psychology*, 82(5): 804–15.

This is another useful paper for considering how motivation fits into individual differences psychology. It also focuses on the issue of approach-avoidance behaviour but more explicitly links this to personality. This paper is a useful compliment to Covington and Mueller (2001).

Kenrick, DT, Griskevicius, SV, Neuberg, SL and Schaller, M (2010) Renovating the pyramid of needs: contemporary extensions built upon ancient foundations. *Perspectives in Psychological Science*, 5(3): 292–314.

These researchers' reworking of Maslow's work and integration with evolutionary theory are outlined in this paper. Their work is an important contribution to motivation research, making their paper a potential classic of the future.

Useful websites

www.psy.miami.edu/faculty/ccarver/

Charles Carver's Miami University homepage contains publications, overviews and scales available for use.

www.psych.rochester.edu/SDT/index.php (Self-determination theory: an approach to human motivation and personality)

Deci and Ryan's own website based at Rochester University in the USA provides details of their theory along with access to papers and research reports.

Chapter 9

Conclusions
The future of individual differences psychology

Learning outcomes

By the end of this chapter you should:

- *be able to consider, critically, contributions made by individual differences psychology to our understanding of variations in human behaviour;*

- *know and be able to discuss, critically, likely future challenges faced by individual differences psychology;*

- *develop critical thinking skills by considering how your implicit theoretical assumptions might influence both your analysis and evaluation of research data and your independent learning.*

Introduction

In this final chapter you will synthesise fundamental issues covered in previous chapters. This synthesis will focus on identifying how the field of individual differences psychology has contributed to our understanding of psychological variation. You will also speculate about the future of the field and, in particular, the challenges that are likely to shape its future landscape. The contributions of the field will be considered by returning to the question we first considered in Chapter 1, namely *how 3-d is contemporary individual differences psychology?* If you recall, the three dimensions or *ds* correspond to the *what*, *why* and *how* of human psychological individual differences. Specifically, in Chapter 1 we looked at:

- *what* human psychological variation looks like, and what structures best describe this;

- *why* this variation exists, and what its determinants are;

- *how* variation works or functions, and what processes underlie the variation we observe.

Judging the extent to which individual differences psychology is *3-d* means returning to issues that we covered in Chapter 1 about the purposes and scope of the field. There you were encouraged to conceptualise individual differences as central to how we manage ourselves in different life domains, a process we described as *self-regulation*. Importantly, it was argued that a full understanding of self-regulation processes requires understanding the *what, why* and *how* of a range of individual differences. We will therefore first examine, briefly, the extent to which individual differences psychology appears to be doing this. Then you will consider the future of individual differences psychology. You will consider the issues that potentially could and, according to some researchers, should be addressed by the field. You will attempt to do this by developing your own headlines drawn from the field. These headlines should capture your analysis and synthesis of what the evidence suggests are the unanswered questions and new issues that are emerging in individual differences psychology, and you will be encouraged to take an evidence-based approach to this task. However, you are also encouraged to take a considered, critical and creative approach when speculating about the headlines you develop. Doing this sort of synthesis involves analytical and evaluation skills. Therefore, the tasks and activities here are designed to develop these skills. You will analyse and evaluate your headlines and other literature from the field by identifying the broad explicit and implicit theoretical assumptions they contain. You will also attempt to make your own implicit theoretical assumptions about individual differences more explicit, and consider how these could potentially influence your independent learning.

Contributions: how 3-d is contemporary individual differences psychology?

Before attempting to answer this question, it is worth remembering why contemporary individual differences psychology needs to be *3-d*. The case for this was set out in Chapter 1.

In Chapter 1 we identified that early and more contemporary researchers argue that the field of individual differences psychology must be *3-d* because of the very nature of its subject matter. One consequence of this is that the field should take an *integrated* approach to theorising and studying individual differences. Our working definition of individual differences from Chapter 1 indicates clearly that individual differences psychology is about the *whole person*. It draws heavily on the work of Caprara and Cervone (2000, pp2–7) and states that the field is concerned with the study of the *structure and determinants of enduring psychological characteristics as perceived by the individual and those around them*. Specifically, these enduring characteristics are *collections of behaviours, feelings and thoughts* that *systematically typify how individuals and groups of individuals appear to be similar or different*. These psychological phenomena also have consequences for how individuals react and therefore *regulate themselves across a range of life domains*, and the relationship between these person and situation variables *is complex and reciprocal*.

In other words, if individual differences psychology is truly *whole person psychology*, this entails considering the *what, why* and *how* – the *3 dimensions* or *3-ds* – of individual differences. However, some researchers have noted that although *a new millennium marks a good time to examine the study of individual differences more holistically* (Lubinski, 2000, p407), this has yet to happen.

Task

You will start to consider how *3-d* the field is by developing an overview of the topics we have covered, and this is what the following task involves.

First, examine Figure 9.1. At the top of each column are the main topics we have covered here – *personality, intellect* and *motivation* – preceded by a *general* column to be used for your observations on the field in general. Underneath each of these are three cells and your task is to try to fill as many of these cells as possible with your observations of examples showing that individual differences psychology is addressing the *3-ds*. To help you do this, the *3-ds* have been translated into specific questions under the *general* column.

What does variation look like? In other words, in the field of individual differences psychology in *general*, can you find evidence that researchers have identified ways of describing psychological variation? How does individual differences psychology conceptualise psychological variation in general?

Then, please consider the two remaining questions.

Why is there variation?

How does variation *work*?

Your goal is to ask these questions about the field in *general*, and then to consider the main topic areas of the field we have considered individually and in more detail.

Figure 9.1: *Contributions of individual differences psychology*

General	Personality	Intellect	Motivation
What does variation look like?			
Why is there variation?			
How does variation *work*?			

Comment

This task should help you develop a rubric for identifying patterns and trends across the different topics we have considered. It can be used to form the basis of your synthesis of topics that you will need when developing your headlines. The task should also draw your attention to the different ways in which individual differences psychology is potentially whole person psychology.

Support for contemporary individual differences psychology as 3-d

The theory and evidence considered in Chapters 1–8 does provide some support for the notion that contemporary individual differences psychology is taking a relatively *3-d* approach to human psychological variation. Although the scientific study of individual differences is a relatively young field, it experienced rapid and global growth in the last part of the twentieth century (Boyle and Saklofske, 2004). Individual differences psychology is, more than ever, becoming an international field with emerging research frontiers in the Far East and eastern Europe (Boyle and Saklofske, 2004). To some extent this globalisation has encouraged researchers to consider, critically, the relevance of the concepts and methods they use for contexts outside the specific cultural contexts within which much mainstream research is conducted, namely the USA and UK. As seen in Chapter 5, this type of shift has drawn attention to a number of issues central to the *3-ds*, such as the nature of personality processes and the determinants of personality variation.

In their collection of key articles from 1984 to 2004 Boyle and Saklofske (2004) used four criteria to select papers that, they argued, captured important features of contemporary research in individual differences psychology.

- *Empirical research* is a dominant feature of contemporary work.

- *Research published from 1984 to 2004* is important to consider because, they argue, *classic papers in large part . . . have already served their intended purposes* (p4).

- The *citation impact* of this research across psychology indicates the impact of individual differences research on basic and applied areas of psychology and beyond.

- The increasing number of *critical literature reviews* indicates that the field is not merely dominated by test development. These publications suggest that the theoretical landscape is healthy in the sense that competing perspectives exist and are the source of intellectual debate.

Importantly, from their review of the field Boyle and Saklofske (2004) state that individual differences psychology now acknowledges that human psychological variation should be conceptualised in terms of *dynamic processes*:

Attempts to explain human behaviour only in terms of 'cold cognition' are doomed to failure from the outset (despite the cognitive revolution in psychology), and it is now widely recog-

Cold cognition is a reference to Metcalfe and Mischel's (1999) hot/cool framework, and it is important here because it signals that the researchers in the field are indeed considering conceptual frameworks outside the mainstream of psychometrics. In addition, Boyle and Saklofske (2004) suggest that the field *is* acknowledging that individual differences psychology should be about the *whole* person or *whole person psychology*, and the *dynamic processes* of personality. Deary et al. (2000, 2010) make a related point about research on intelligence. Although research on intellectual ability in the field has tended to focus on identifying the structure of intelligence and its measurement rather than intellectual processes, there has been a degree of change in how intelligence is *conceptualised*. As we considered in Chapters 6 and 7, interest in intellectual processes and types of intelligence other than the purely cognitive or intellectual has grown. This research has also led to the consideration of the multidimensional and at times counterintuitive nature of intelligence, such as Sternberg's notion that smart people can also be foolish (Sjoberg, 2004).

Boyle and Saklofske (2004) also draw attention to a more fundamental methodological shift in the field, one that supports the view that individual differences psychology is becoming increasingly *3-d* (2004, pp25–6):

> it appears that a complimentary [sic] relationship has been forged between both nomothetic and idiographic approaches . . . of research and practice, respectively, in relation to describing, explaining, predicting, and even changing human behaviour.

In fact, there is evidence that intellectual debate in the field has encouraged the development of alternative perspectives to those that characterise mainstream individual differences psychology and more fully developed responses to the question of how *3-d* the field actually is.

Task —— In the first task you started to evaluate the extent to which the field is *3-d* by identifying evidence of this from Chapters 1–8. In this task, you will use your answers to the first task, but here you will evaluate the evidence you have cited in terms of where there is *most evidence* that a *3-d* approach is being used using a *sorting task*. In Figure 9.2 each of the cells you completed in Figure 9.1 has been labelled from A to L. You should now sort these cells (A–L) into *groups*, ranging from cells where you judge there is the most substantial evidence of a *3-d* approach being used to those at the other end of the scale representing those cells where there is least evidence. You can sort the cells into as many piles as you want to, but each cell must be placed in only *one pile*.

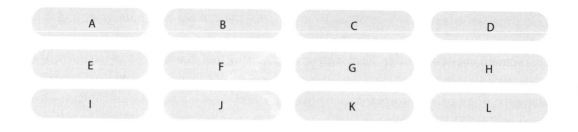

For example, you might sort all the cells into four groups where group 1 contains those where the greatest contributions have been made, group 2 the next greatest, group 3 the next and group 4 representing those where the least contribution has been made. This is shown in Figure 9.3. You might decide to place cell A in group 1 because your analysis and evaluation of the evidence suggests the greatest contributions have been made here. In contrast, you might judge that little progress has been made in explaining the underlying mechanisms of intellect in the field (CK in Figure 9.2) – in fact, so little that this is placed at the opposite end of the scale, in group 4.

Comment

This task should encourage you to start analysing and evaluating individual differences psychology research against specific criteria, namely, those fundamental to the 3-d approach.

Figure 9.3: Sorting task (continued)

Caveats

The extent to which individual differences psychology is taking a truly *3-d* approach to human psychological variation is questionable. For example, in the mid-1980s Pervin (1985, p104) in his review of personality psychology over the preceding 20 years of research stated: *My own sense is that progress is being made, but not as much as some might expect.* Pervin's (1985) point is that there was a *sense of progress* but also evidence of that in other ways, the field's progress had been limited. First, there was evidence of a *chasm* between the nature of some theories in the field and the actual nature of the psychological phenomena they claimed to be theories of. Second, many of the theoretical and empirical debates in the field could be described as *face-off debates* that kept intellectual ideas segregated often by the use of simplistic *for versus against* argument structures. Finally, and to some extent as a consequence of the use of face-off debates, insufficient attention was given to developing integrated approaches within the field.

Ironically, it could be said that 25 years later, these doubts remain relevant. Boyle and Saklofske (2004) raise similar doubts about the individual differences research from 1984 to 2006.

- *Scientific psychology must often compete with 'pop-psychology', as well as pseudosciences such as astrology, and other such introspective speculations* (Boyle and Saklofske, 2004, p3). Unfortunately the distinction between pseudoscience and psychology remains at times *grey* (p4). Arkes (2003) makes a related point about the underuse of psychology. To some extent, there has been some misuse and misunderstanding of individual differences research, and the expansion of research in the field has not necessarily been matched by an enhanced quality in research (Landy, 2005).

- There is a bias in publications, especially against null findings, and this makes challenging mainstream ideas difficult.

- It is not clear that individual differences psychology has really embraced *theory*. Boyle and Saklofske (2004, p7) themselves state: *All too often, psychological research into individual differences has not effectively discriminated between competing theories and models, due to failure to obtain quantitative measurement data needed to test hypotheses.*

- The ubiquity of testing remains, leading to the burden of ensuring test validity, reliability, and ethical use and score interpretation. Ensuring the quality of our measures is, quite rightly, of *critical importance* (Boyle and Saklofske, 2004, p7). However, there is and should be more to individual differences psychology than these issues. Moreover, the power of test publishers and their financial imperatives mean that they control substantial databases. One potential consequence of this control is that some aspects of academic development that could be fostered by access to such data are outside of the control of the academic community.

- Individual differences research remains heavily reliant on self-report tests and statistical modelling.

- Interpretations of psychological variation tend to examine links or correlates rather than pro-cesses.

- Many tools are still used despite being problematic (Boyle and Saklofske, 2004; see Chapter 7). For example, to some extent there is an overuse of tests of general intelligence, and many key questions about such tests remain unanswered (Ceci, 2000).

The future of individual differences psychology: identifying the headlines

In the 1980s and towards the approach of the new millennium, the twenty-first century agenda for individual differences psychology was debated (Deary et al., 2000; Kenrick and Funder, 1988; Kruglanski, 2001). The issue here is whether the headlines of contemporary individual differences psychology demonstrate that the field is meeting this agenda.

Researchers differ in the specific details of their future agenda for individual differences psy-chology. However, those suggested for the field in the twenty-first century have tended to include two issues.

- The need for a more *integrated approach* to human psychological variation.

- The need to consider, critically, the *methods* and *tools* – in particular, psychometric tests – that dominate the field and how we apply these outside academia.

In essence, these issues represent the headlines and therefore the *future challenges* of the field. Drawing on the topics considered in Chapters 1–8, it is possible to identify a number of headlines for the field in general, and for the main topic areas covered, namely *personality*, *intellect* and *motivation*. These are summarised in Figure 9.4. These issues are selective – far from exhaustive – but nevertheless provide a starting point from which you can develop your *own* headlines.

There are a number of *general headlines* that we can draw from the field. An issue that has recurred across all the topics we have considered is the social policy implication of much of the work of individual differences psychology, along with the professional and ethical responsibilities of those in the field to ensure their work is neither misrepresented nor misused. Unfortunately, some policies driven by individual differences research have had some negative consequences, such as the controversy surrounding the impact of positive discrimination policies in education (Boyle and Saklofske, 2004, p14). In this case, such policies have been in some respects evidence-based, drawing on research and theory from the field demonstrating the multidimensional nature of intelligence and the flaws inherent in the use of explicit standardised tests of intellectual ability (see Chapters 6 and 7). However, such policies have not met with either universal support or success (Boyle and Saklofske, 2004). The issue here is a more general one for the field, namely that there is little sign that such uses of individual differences research are diminishing. In fact, the

Figure 9.4: *Future challenges in individual differences psychology*

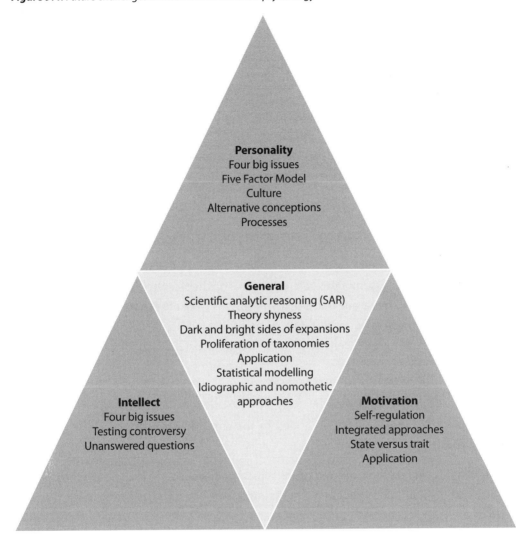

growth of the field could actually increase the use of the field's research by those outside of academia for social and political purposes. This contemporary trend suggests that the social policy implications of individual differences psychology headline the field and present professional and ethical challenges for those working within it.

Another recurring issue across the topics we have considered is whether there is a *crisis in psychology* (Goertzen, 2009). One aspect of this debate is whether the discipline of psychology has become *segregated* (Vertue, 2003), a tendency that some researchers regard as damaging for its intellectual development (e.g. Cacioppo et al., 2000). In Chapter 1 we alluded to these more general issues when we considered what is meant specifically by individual differences psychology. It was suggested that this field should be whole person psychology because this would provide us with the fullest understanding of individual differences, and that such an approach meant considering the *3-ds* of individual differences by critically and creatively integrating or synthesising research from across the field. Consequently, the *segregated or integrated crisis in psychology* is a *headline* with especial relevance to individual differences psychology. The *3-d* approach you have been encouraged to take in this book aligns with the *integrated* approach, and entails the future challenge of thinking critically and creatively about how we evaluate and use individual differences theory and empirical evidence. The *3-d* approach is also consistent with Yanchar et al.'s approach to critical thinking (2008). They argue that the development of psychology as a discipline is likely to depend on consideration of implicit theoretical assumptions, of which there are two types.

- *Prosaic* or lay or everyday theoretical assumptions.

- *Theoretical* or formal scientific theoretical assumptions.

They argue that the future development of psychology as a discipline requires the consideration of such implicit theoretical assumptions *before* the use of method-centred evaluations or scientific analytic reasoning (SAR). They argue that SAR dominates the work of both researchers and student learning and teaching activities. Importantly, as identified in Chapter 1, individual differences psychology is especially method-centred and, as Yanchar et al. (2008) suggest, this makes sense given that:

- the field is set apart from other fields in psychology by its methods;

- the credibility of the field is currently tied to the credibility of its methods, in particular, psychometrics.

However, it is this very method-centred characteristic of individual differences psychology that make the need to think critically about the field's implicit theoretical assumptions more pressing. Yanchar at al (2008) argue that this is not achievable using SAR alone. This issue is a particularly important future challenge for the field because, as we have seen, the use of psychometrics and statistical modelling are being challenged. Whole person psychology that conceptualises individual differences as self-regulatory processes implies that we will need to think critically about whether psychometrics alone are fit for this purpose.

In Chapter 1 we considered how individual differences psychology is dominated by psycho-metrics, and this dominance is regarded by many as appropriate because such methods and measures are *objective* and *rigorous, systematic* and *replicable.*

However, Yanchar et al. (2008) argue that these are implicit theoretical assumptions that rely on the fallacy of *positionless critical analysis* (p267). Clearly, a future challenge for the field is to think critically about the implicit theoretical assumptions in its methods, data and concepts. For example, in Chapter 1, we considered the psychometric approach and challenges to mainstream individual differences psychology. This involved asking questions about the assumptions of the approach, and the consequences of these assumptions for our knowledge of individual differences. The appropriateness of the psychometric approach for considering the *3-ds* of individual differences was questioned. As Yanchar et al. (2008) argue, research *methods that may be counterproductive or problematic in some sense will not be recognised as such because they have not been examined with a form of critical thinking designed to inquire into such a possibility* (p270). Throughout this text you have been encouraged to think critically about the implicit theoretical assumptions of the field, and your own prosaic theoretical assumptions about human psychological variation. You should therefore have already started to engage in the sort of critical thinking that, according to Yanchar et al. (2008), the field requires for its future development.

Task — In this task you should now go on to develop your *own* evidence-based headlines for the more specific topics we have considered in Chapters 2–8, namely personality, intellect and motivation, using the issues shown in Figure 9.4, Future challenges in individual differences psychology. These headlines should be clear and concise statements that capture the following sorts of issues.

Overlooked issues – questions and issues as yet unaddressed despite being identified as part of the twenty-first century agenda.

New issues – questions and issues that have emerged from research that should be addressed.

Shattered myths – well-established ideas that have now been challenged.

Comment

This should encourage you to start synthesising theory and empirical research across individual differences psychology. It should also draw your attention to a number of unanswered questions that headline the field, as well as the longevity of a number of perennial debates in the field. For example, four questions or the big four issues perpetually headline personality research: what is its *structure*? What *methods* should we use to study it? How should we *measure* it? Do measures of personality *predict* actual behaviour? Finally, this task should demonstrate that you are studying individual differences psychology at an interesting time in the development of the field. Hopefully, considering the extent to which the field is *3-d* will help you develop a critical and creative perspective to this challenging aspect of psychology.

Critical thinking activity

Theoretical assumptions in research on personality and intellect

Critical thinking focus: analysis and evaluation of data

Key question: *How can we identify implicit theoretical assumptions?*

Earlier, we discussed Yanchar et al's (2008) approach to critical thinking that involves identifying implicit theoretical assumptions by examining broad theoretical assumptions in the literature to foster intellectual debate, the development of fields and critical thinking among academics and students. This approach can also be used to encourage students to examine the theoretical assumptions they bring with them to psychology, and how this influences their analysis and evaluation of the literature, and their independent learning decisions and motivation. In this activity, you will examine the implicit theoretical assumptions in a specific theory of personality, intelligence or motivation.

First, select a specific theory of *personality, intelligence* or *motivation*. Make sure you select one that you feel confident in discussing. Then ask yourself the questions shown in Figure 9.5 about the theory you have chosen, and use the diagram to list your answers:

Then, ask yourself the following questions.

- How easy/difficult did you find this analysis and evaluation?

- How explicit are the theoretical assumptions you have identified in the theory you selected?

Worked example

If you selected a theory of personality, you might consider how the theory explains what determines personality variation. It might be determined by biological mechanisms over which the individual has little or no free will. The theory might not explicitly consider the issue of whether individuals have free will; however, you might identify the consequences of the theory for this issue. For example, even though a theory might refer to the biological determinants of psychological variation, the theory might also refer to the role of environmental factors in shaping variation and, therefore, use social rather than biological determinism. However, you might consider whether the theory is both biologically and environmentally deterministic – with the individual having little power to influence the impact of these factors.

Critical thinking review

This activity requires you to analyse and evaluate a theory of your choice but to think critically and creatively beyond the explicit content. This activity should also demonstrate that analysis and evaluation using the SAR provides a partial but necessary part of critical thinking.

Other skills likely to be used in this activity: the activity involves using your knowledge and understanding of psychological theory and reflection skills to ensure you have considered the theory of your choice in sufficient detail. The activity also involves thinking independently about issues not routinely considered in the literature.

Skill builder activity

Your theoretical assumptions about personality and intellect

Transferable skill focus: independent learning

Key question: *Can your implicit theoretical assumptions influence your learning?*

In the previous activity you attempted to identify the implicit theoretical assumptions of a specific theory of personality, intelligence or motivation. In this activity you should try to identify *your own* implicit theoretical beliefs about the topic you selected for the previous activity – personality, intellect or motivation. Ask yourself the questions about your beliefs about your chosen topic set out in Figure 9.6. Then ask yourself the following questions.

Do your implicit assumptions match those of the specific theory that you analysed and evaluated in the previous activity?

Do you think your implicit theoretical assumptions have any implications for how you learn independently, e.g. the effort and attention you give to certain topics?

Worked example

You might believe that personality, intellect or motivation are affected by the environment, but that the individual has some degree of free will in shaping this aspect of their psychology. You might also find that the extent to which your implicit theoretical assumptions match those in your chosen theory influences your approach to *that particular* named theory. For example, you might have chosen a named theory that contains implicit theoretical assumptions similar to your own.

Figure 9.5: *Implicit theoretical assumptions*

determinism or free will?	active or passive mind?	affected by environment or not?	selfish or altruistic?	personal responsibility?	therapy and damage?	education?

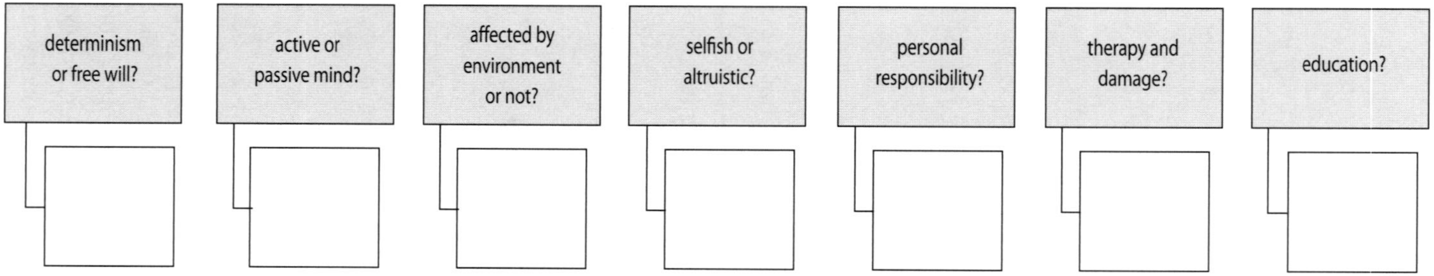

Figure 9.6: *Your implicit theoretical assumptions*

determinism or free will?	active or passive mind?	affected by environment or not?	selfish or altruistic?	personal responsibility?	therapy and damage?	education?

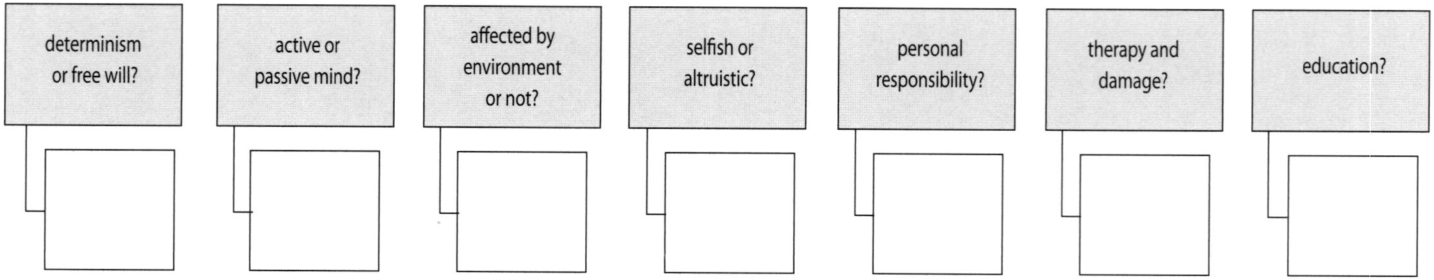

You might also consider theories that you have avoided and whether this might be because you do not share the implicit theoretical assumptions of these theories.

Skill builder review

As with the previous activity, you are required to analyse and evaluate a theory of your choice but to think critically and creatively beyond the explicit content. This activity should also demonstrate that analysis and evaluation using the SAR provides a partial but necessary part of critical thinking. However, in addition, this activity focuses on your independent learning and how this is potentially shaped by your implicit theoretical assumptions that are not explicitly acknowledged using the method-focused approach.

Other skills likely to be used in this activity: this activity also requires you to use data analysis and evaluation skills, as well as skills of reflection.

Assignments

1. Critically discuss the extent to which contemporary individual differences psychology remains the study of psychological *structures* rather than *processes*.

2. The distinction between pseudoscience and scientific psychology is at times *grey* (Boyle and Saklofske, 2004, p4). Critically evaluate the accuracy of this view in relation to individual differences research on *either* personality *or* intelligence.

3. To what extent is contemporary individual differences psychology dominated by outmoded implicit theoretical assumptions about the nature of human variation?

Summary: what you have learned

Individual differences psychology is a diverse field in psychology that is, to some extent, meeting its twenty-first-century agenda. However, some elements of this agenda are reminiscent of those discussed by early twentieth-century individual differences researchers. Moreover, despite a number of developments in the field, many of the headlines that can be drawn from the contemporary research suggest that progress is *partial*. By considering the extent to which the field takes a *3-d* approach to individual differences, and by completing the tasks and activities in this chapter, you should have started to develop your own independent but nevertheless evidence-based critical thinking about the future of the field.

Further reading

Arkes, HR (2003). The nonuse of psychological research at two federal agencies. *Psychological Science*, 14(1): 1–6.

This is a readable discussion of why USA governmental agencies are reluctant to use psychological research when making decisions that have psychological relevance. It is a good illustration of the challenges psychologists face when attempting to address social issues.

Boyle, GJ and Saklofske, DH (2004) Editors' introduction: contemporary perspectives on the psychology of individual differences, in Boyle, G.J. and Saklofske, D.H. (eds) *Sage benchmarks in psychology: psychology of individual differences*. London: Sage.

This includes an invaluable review of individual differences research from 1984 to 2004 that provides an excellent synthesis of the headlines that have emerged across that period. It is also a relatively balanced account of both the substantial and rather less substantial progresses made in the field.

Ceci, SJ (2000). So near and yet so far: lingering questions about the use of measures of general intelligence for college admissions and employment screening. *Psychology, Public Policy, and Law*, 6(1): 233–52.

Although this paper is a decade old, the issues it raises about the uses and misuses of explicit standardised tests of intellectual ability remain pertinent.

Deary, IJ, Austin, EJ and Caryl, PG (2000) Testing versus understanding human intelligence. *Psychology, Public Policy, and Law*, 6(1): 180–90.

This focused paper is a useful outline of the ways in which much research on intellectual ability has mistaken the contributions of the testing movement for accounts of intellectual ability processes.

Nesselroade, JR and Ram, N (2004) Studying intraindividual variability: what we have learned that will help us understand lives in context. *Research in Human Development*, 1(1 and 2): 9–29.

This paper provides a much needed contrast to individual differences research that focuses on inter-individual variation. This is an account of the developments in theory and research on intra-individual variation. Consequently, it is especially pertinent to the question of how 3-d the field actually is.

Yanchar, SC, Slife, BD, Warne, R. (2008). Critical thinking as disciplinary practice. *Review of General Psychology*, 12(3): 265–81.

This paper is essential reading because it attempts to deconstruct the nature of critical thinking that shapes contemporary psychology, including individual differences. Importantly, it also deconstructs the type of critical thinking students of psychology are typically encouraged to take (the scientific analytic reasoning (SAR) approach), and outlines the case for a shift towards using an implicit theoretical assumptions approach. This paper is a vital primer for critical thinking per se in the discipline, and you should find it useful across all your studies in psychology.

Useful websites

All of the following websites are useful for the same reason: they will give you access to the international dimension of the field, as well as access to current research projects on cultural psychology related to the field and online journals and papers.

www.apa.org/about/division/div8.aspx (APA Division 8 Personality and Social Psychology)

www.bps.org.uk/networks/networks_home.cfm (BPS Members Network – note that there is no division, section or special interest group on individual differences)

http://issid.org/ (International Society for the Study of Individual Differences)

www.isspd.com/ (International Society for the Study of Personality Disorders)

www.personality.org/ (Society for Personality Assessment)

www.spsp.org/ (Society for Personality and Social Psychology)

Glossary

agentic approach to personality refers to Bandura's (1999) social cognitive theory of personality. This describes individuals as *Agentic . . . self-organizing, proactive, self-reflecting, and self-regulating, not just reactive organisms shaped and shepherded by external events* (Bandura, 1999, p2). Consequently, personality emerges as the result of this interplay between the individual and their situation.

alcohol dependence refers to a dependency syndrome or collection of symptoms in which the use of alcohol becomes the central and overpowering focus of the individual's life over and above other behaviours (*ICD-10* [World Health Organization, 2007]).

androgens male sex hormones.

angina pectoris chest pain resulting from an inadequate flow of blood in the heart.

anxiety a term used to describe behaviours, feelings and thoughts that reflect an uneasy sense of apprehension – typically apprehension about the future or anticipated events and circumstances.

ascending reticular activating system (ARAS) a collection of neuro-anatomical structures in the brainstem and brain, stretching from the brainstem through the midbrain to the cerebral cortex.

blood clotting the thickening or coagulation of the blood.

concept the term used to describe an abstract idea/s or notion/s. Some researchers use the term interchangeably with the term *construct* although their meanings are distinct. In psychology *construct* is typically used to describe some psychological entity/entities or phenomenon/phenomena. For example, individual differences are enduring dispositions that can be described using the construct of *personality* and this can be described more specifically using the concept of *traits*. The term concept is an idea from which we can draw principles or conceptual *principles*. In contrast, a construct is a way of describing psychological phenomena and we are unlikely to refer to it having constructual principles. However, tredistinctions between concepts and constructs are not always clear or agreed upon by researchers.

conditionability the ease with which a conditioned response can be established.

construct a term used in psychology typically to describe some psychological entity/entities or phenomenon/phenomena (see *concept*).

coronary artery disease (CAD) the gradual blockage of coronary arteries as a result of a build-up of hard fatty deposits or plaques from cholesterol.

differential psychology	another term used to refer to individual differences psychology. However, the term has a broader meaning. It tends to be used to refer to the study of both human and animal psychological variation, rather than simply the psychometric assessment of human personality, intelligence and motivation.
economic psychology	the study of the economic behaviour of both consumers and entrepreneurs. It encompasses research on a range of issues and phenomena including individuals' decision making, consumer attitudes, beliefs and expectancies, as well as co-operation, competition and government policy (Kirchler and Holzl, 2006).
emotions	the term used for experiences that arise as a result of the conscious aware-ness of a change in state following the appraisal or evaluation of an event or stimulus, leading to a motivational state that drives behaviour. This is underpinned by physiological changes that are appraised, and this appraisal can be described, broadly, as the emotion (Frijda, 2009). This sequence of events can be described as the emotion process, and emotions that individuals experience tend to differ in their valence (positive or negative). Emotions tend to be of short duration compared to moods and they have some focus or source.
field of psychology	a specific distinct area of study or enquiry within the discipline of psychology. Typically it denotes the subject matter of this area of study. To some extent, such a field might also have distinct aims, scope and methods.
grey matter	the nerve cell bodies in the cortex of the brain.
heuristic	a rule of thumb, device or strategy that serves some particular purpose.
hypertension	a clinical term used to describe consistently elevated levels of blood pressure.
idiographic	a term used in psychology to refer to *specific, particular or relatively unique* principles, laws or statements. Approaches to developing such laws typically draw on research principles, paradigms and methods that will enable the evaluation of such individualistic phenomena. This term is usually contrasted with *nomothetic*.
inter-individual processes	the psychological mechanisms involved in interaction between individuals. The term is typically used in individual differences psychology to describe the mechanisms that underlie how individual differences, such as personality, influence how people interact and vice versa.
inter-individual variability	a phrase that can be used to describe enduring or stable differences between individuals – how they vary on some measure of individual differences. When

making such a comparison between groups of individuals this can be described as *inter-individual variation between groups*, and such comparisons are typically made by aggregating each group's scores on a measure and comparing the groups' typical score (e.g. mean).

intra-individual processes
the psychological mechanisms that underlie observable psychological phenomena, such as behaviour, and expressions of emotion and thought. The term is typically used in individual differences psychology to describe the processes that underlie personality, intelligence and motivation.

intra-individual variability
the term used to describe the variability in an individual's behaviour across situations.

job strain
the level of measurable stressors in the work environment that can trigger the onset of disease. Although researchers disagree on the specific components and processes involved in this, generally this term is used to refer to the existence of psychosocial stressors in the workplace that impact adversely on the individual's health, such as high job demands and low control over the working environment.

life course
a term used to describe an approach to considering ways in which the individual's development across the lifespan is shaped by the dynamic context that they experience. It is sometimes used interchangeably with *lifespan* but for some researchers the term *life course* has a more specific theoretical meaning. The term was developed in child development research in the USA in the 1920s and 1930s, and focused on the ways in which an individual's developmental pathway, or trajectory, can be shaped by a range of psychosocial variables. In this sense, the term draws attention to the dynamic and multidimensional nature of human development as a process (Elder, 1998).

limbic system
five neuro-anatomical structures in the mid-brain: the amygdala, hippocampus, hypothalamus, septal area and cingulated cortex.

mind–body dualism a term used to describe the notion that the mind has no physical substance and is thus separate from the body, which has a physical or material quality. However, there is some debate about both the origins of the notion and its original meaning (Duncan, 2000).

mood
a term used to describe a relatively low level and non-specific feeling that one has. In comparison with emotions, moods have a longer duration and are unlikely to have a focus or be related to a specific object or event.

morbidity	disease or illness.
mortality	loss of life, or death.
myocardial infarction (MI)	the sudden blockage of a coronary artery. When the blockage is sudden and total, this is known as an *acute MI* or what is commonly known as a heart attack.
nomothetic	a term used in psychology to refer to principles, laws or statements about psychological phenomena that can be applied to individuals *in general*. Approaches to developing such general laws are typically those drawing on scientific principles, paradigms and methods that we can describe as nomothetic in their approach. This term is usually contrasted with *idiographic*.
pan-cultural	a term used to describe a phenomenon that can be found or observed across *all* cultural contexts.
pathophysiological processes	physiological processes that are known to underpin the onset of a disease.
principles	rules, premises, implications or propositions that are drawn typically from other broader frameworks of ideas or knowledge, such as a theory.
reflective critical thinking	a term used here to describe the process of thinking critically about academic theory and research by considering the epistemological and ontological assumptions in this work, and how they are constructed. Here, this is contrasted with the scientific analytic reasoning (SAR) approach to thinking critically that focuses primarily (but not exclusively) on thinking critically about the methods used by researchers. *Reflective self-criticality* involves the same processes but applied to one's own assumptions as a student, academic and researcher or practitioner. However, terms such as *criticality* are used differently by researchers.
research paradigm	the general principles and structure underlying a research method. An experimental research paradigm uses the principle of reductionism to test the effects a variable or variables have on some outcome. The principle of reductionism is then used to structure the actual methods a researcher employs. For example, a controlled environmental context is likely to be used so that the effects caused by the variable or variables being manipulated can be measured.
resilience	broadly refers to the extent to which the individual is protected against the effects of adverse life events and experiences, and is thus able to remain adapted positively to their circumstances.

semantics	the study of the meaning of language and the systems that we use to express such meanings.
serum cholesterol	levels of cholesterol – a mixture of fat (lipid) and steroid – found in the blood-stream.
sociodemographic information	general biographical and social information that can be used to describe the characteristics of a large number of individuals such as their age, sex, racial identity and social class.
taxonomy	a term used in psychology to refer to a list, system or framework that describes particular psychological phenomena.
theory	an organised framework of principles used to explain observed phenomena.
veridical	a term used to describe the truthfulness of an observation or measurement.
white matter	the myelinated nerve fibres in the brain.
whole person psychology	the term used by researchers such as Caprara and Cervone (2000) to describe what they argue individual differences psychology should encompass, namely, the holistic and integrated study of psychological phenomena – *affects*, *behaviours*, *cognitions* and *desires* or *whole person psychology*.
zygosity	a term that refers to whether individuals have identical genotypes, as is the case with MZ twins, or have different genotypes, as is the case with DZ twins.

References

Achat, H, Kawachi, I, Byrne, C, Hankinson, S and Colditz, G (2000) A prospective study of job strain and risk of breast cancer. *International Journal of Epidemiology*, 29: 622–28.

Ackerman, PL (1997) Personality, self-concept, interests, and intelligence: which construct doesn't fit? *Journal of Personality*, 65(2): 171–204.

Ackerman, PL and Heggestad, ED (1997) Intelligence, personality, and interests: evidence for overlapping traits. *Psychological Bulletin*, 121(2): 219–45.

Al-Halabí, S, Herrero, R, Saiz, PA, Garcia-Portilla, MP, Corcoran, P, Bascaran, MT, Errasti, JM, Lemos S and Bobes, J (2010) Sociodemographic factors associated with personality traits assessed through the TCI. *Personality and Individual Differences*, 48: 809–14.

Allport, FH and Allport, GW (1921) Personality traits: their classification and measurement. *Journal of Abnormal and Social Psychology*, 16: 6–40. http://psychclassics.yorku.ca/Allport/Traits/

Allport, GW (1927) Concepts of trait and personality. *Psychological Bulletin*, 24: 284–93.

Allport, GW (1937) The functional anatomy of motives. *American Journal of Psychology*, 50: 141–56.

Allport, GW and Odbert, HS (1936) Trait names: a psycho-lexical study. *Psychological Monographs*, 47(1, Whole Number 211).

Amelang, M (1997) Using personality variables to predict cancer and heart disease. *European Journal of Personality*, 11: 319–42.

American Psychiatric Association (1994) *Diagnostic and Statistical Manual of Mental Disorders* (4th edn). Washington, DC: American Psychiatric Association.

Ames, DR, Rose, P and Anderson, CP (2006) The NPI-16 as a short measure of narcissism. *Journal of Research in Personality*, 40: 440–50.

Anastasi, A (1937) *Differential Psychology: Individual and group differences in behaviour*, New York: Macmillan.

Arkes, HR (2003) The nonuse of psychological research at two federal agencies. *Psychological Science*, 14(1): 1–6.

Axelrod, S R, Widiger, TA, Trull, TJ and Corbitt, EM (1997) Relations of Five-Factor Model antagonism facets with personality disorder symptomatology. *Journal of Personality Assessment*, 69(2): 297–313.

Backstrom, M, Larsson, MR and Maddox, RE (2009) A structural validation of an inventory based on the Abridged Five Factor Circumplex Model (AB5C). *Journal of Personality Assessment*, 91(5): 462–72.

Bandura, A (1999) A social cognitive theory of personality, in Pervin, L and John, O (eds) *Handbook of Personality* (2nd edn, pp154–96). New York: Guilford Publications.

Bandura, A (1982) Self-efficacy mechanism in human agency. *American Psychologist,* 37(2): 22–147.

Bandura, A (2006) Guide for constructing self-efficacy scales, in Pajares, F and Urdan, TC (eds) *Self-efficacy Beliefs of Adolescents* (pp307–37). Charlotte, NC: Information Age Publishing.

Bandura, A and Locke, EA (2003) Negative self-efficacy and goal effects revisited. *Journal of Applied Psychology*, 88(1): 87–99.

Barab, S and Squire, K (2004) Design-based research: putting a stake in the ground. *The Journal of the Learning Sciences*, 13(1): 1–14.

Barnard, L, Burley, H, Olivarez, A and Crooks, S (2008) Measuring vulnerability to stereotype threat. Department of Educational Psychology, Texas Tech University. Unpublished.

Barrick, MR, Mitchell, TR and Stewart, GL (2001) Situational and motivational influences on trait-behaviour relationships, in Barrick, MR and Ryan, AM (eds) *Personality and Work: Reconsidering the role of personality in organisations* (pp60–82). San Francisco, CA: Jossey-Bass.

Barrington, E (2004) Teaching to student diversity in higher education: how multiple intelligence theory can help. *Teaching in Higher Education*, 9(4): 421–34.

Bartram, D and Lindley, P (2005) *Psychological Testing: The BPS Test Administration (Occupational) Open Learning Programme.* Oxford: BPS Blackwell. www.psychtesting.org.uk/download$.cfm?file_uuid=A1FBEA7D-1143-DFDO-7EAB-C510B9DIDCIA&siteName=ptc

Batty, GD and Deary, IJ (2004) Early life intelligence and adult health: associations, plausible mechanisms, and public health importance are emerging. *British Medical Journal*, 329(7466): 585–86.

Baum, A and Posluszny, DM (1999) Health psychology: mapping biobehavioural contributions to health and illness. *Annual Review of Psychology*, 50: 137–63.

Baumeister, RF, Gailliot, M, DeWall, CN. and Oaten, M (2006) Self-regulation and personality: how interventions increase regulatory success, and how depletion moderates the effects of traits on behaviour. *Journal of Personality*, 74(6): 1773–802.

Baumeister, RF, Vohs, KD and Tice, DM (2007) The strength model of self-control. *Current Directions in Psychological Science*, 16(6): 351–5.

Beauchaine, TP, Klein, DN, Crowell, SE, Derbidge, C and Gatzke-Kopp, L (2009) Multifinality in the development of personality disorders: a biology sex environment interaction model of antisocial and borderline traits. *Development and Psychopathology*, 21: 735–70.

Beedie, CJ, Terry, PC and Lane, AM (2005) Distinctions between emotion and mood. *Cognition and Emotion*, 19 (6): 847–78.

Beidel, DC, Turner, SM and Morris, TL (1995) A new inventory to assess childhood social anxiety and phobia: the social phobia and anxiety inventory for children. *Psychological Assessment,* 7(1): 73–79.

Belsky, J (2008) War, trauma and children's development: observations from a modern evolutionary perspective. *International Journal of Behavioural Development,* 32(4): 260–71.

Belsky, J, Steinberg, L and Draper, P (1991) Childhood experience, interpersonal development, and reproductive strategy: an evolutionary theory of socialisation. *Child Development,* 62: 647–70.

Bem, SL (1974) The measurement of psychological androgyny. *Journal of Consulting and Clinical Psychology,* 42(2): 155–62.

Bem, SL (1975) Sex role adaptability: one consequence of psychological androgyny. *Journal of Personality and Social Psychology,* 31(4): 634–43.

Bem, SL (1977) On the utility of alternative procedures for assessing psychological androgyny. *Journal of Consulting and Clinical Psychology,* 45(3): 196–205.

Benning, SD, Patrick, CJ, Blonigen, DM, Hicks, BM and Iacono, WG (2005) Estimating facets of psychopathy from normal personality traits: a step toward community epidemiological investigations. *Assessment,* 12(1): 3–18.

Bergeman, CS, Chipuer, HM, Plomin, R, Pedersen, NL, McClearn, GE, Nesselroade, JR, Costa JP.T and McCrae, RR (1993) Genetic and environmental effects on openness to experience, agreeableness, and conscientiousness: an adoption/twin study. *Journal of Personality* 61(2): 159–79.

Bieling, PJ, Israeli, A, Smith, J and Antony, MM (2003) Making the grade: the behavioural consequences of perfectionism in the classroom. *Personality and Individual Differences,* 35(1): 163–78.

Biesanz, JC and West, SG (2000) Personality coherence: moderating self-other profile agreement and profile consensus. *Journal of Personality of Social Psychology,* 79(3): 425–37.

Binet, A (1905) New methods for the diagnosis of the intellectual level of subnormals. First appeared in Kite, ES. (1916) *The Development of Intelligence in Children.* Vineland, NJ: Publications of the Training School at Vineland. http://psychclassics/yorku.ca/Binet/binet1.htm

Blackwell, LS, Trzesniewski, KH and Dweck, CS. (2007) Implicit theories of intelligence predict achievement across an adolescent transition: a longitudinal study and an intervention. *Child Development,* 78(1): 246–63.

Boggs, CD Morey, LC, Skodol, AE, Shea, MT, Sanislow, CA, Grilo, CM, McGlashan, TH, Zanarini, MC and Gunderson, JG (2009) Differential impairment as an indicator of sex bias in *DSM–IV* criteria for four personality disorders. *Personality Disorders: Theory, Research, and Treatment,* 5(1): 61–8.

Boorsboom, D (2006) The attack of the psychometricians. *Psychometrika*, 71(3): 425–40.

Boorsboom, D, Mellenbergh, GJ and van Heerden, J (2004) The concept of validity. *Psychological Review*, 111(4):1061–71.

Booth-Kewley, S and Friedman, HS (1987) Psychological predictors of heart disease: a quantitative review. *Psychological Bulletin*, 101(3): 343–62.

Borrell-Carrió, F, Suchman, AL and Epstein, RM (2004) The biopsychosocial model 25 years later: principles, practice, and scientific inquiry. *Annals of Family Medicine*, 2(6): 576–82.

Boyce, WT and Ellis, BJ (2005) Biological sensitivity to context: I. An evolutionary–developmental theory of the origins and functions of stress reactivity. *Development and Psychopathology*, 17: 271–301.

Boyle, GJ and Saklofske, DH (2004) (eds) *Sage Benchmarks in Psychology: Psychology of individual differences*. London: Sage.

Brand, RJ, Rosenman, RH, Sholtz, RI and Friedman, M (1976) Multivariate prediction of coronary heart disease in the Western Collaborative Group Study compared to the findings of the Framingham study. *Circulation,* 53: 348–55.

British Psychological Society (2007) *Code of Good Practice for Psychological Testing*. Leicester: British Psychological Society.

British Psychological Society (2008) *Generic Professional Practice Guidelines* (2nd edn). London: British Psychological Society.

British Psychological Society (2009) *Code of Ethics and Conduct Guidance Published by the Ethics Committee Of the British Psychological Society*. London: British Psychological Society.

Brockner, J (1988) *Self-esteem at Work: Research, theory, and practice*. Lexington, MA: Lexington Books.

Brown, AL (1992) Design experiments: theoretical and methodological challenges in creating complex interventions in classroom settings. *The Journal of the Learning Sciences*, 2(2): 141–78.

Brown, AL (1997) Transforming schools into communities of thinking and learning about serious matters. *American Psychologist*, 52(4): 399–413.

Brown, JS, Collins, A and Duguid, P (1989) Situated cognition and the culture of learning. *Educational Researcher*, January–February: 32–42.

Buss, DM (1991) Evolutionary personality psychology. *Annual Review of Psychology*, 42: 459–91.

Buss, DM (2009) How can evolutionary psychology successfully explain personality and individual differences? *Perspectives on Psychological Science*, 4: 359–66.

Butow, PN, Hiller, JE, Price, MA, Thackway, SV, Kricker, A and Tennant, CC (2000) Epidemiological evidence for a relationship between life events, coping style, and personality factors in the development of breast cancer. *Journal of Psychosomatic Research* (49):169–81.

Byrne, RW. (1996) Machiavellian intelligence. *Evolutionary Anthropology*, 5(5): 172–80.

Cacioppo, JT, Berntson, GG, Sheridan, JF and McClintock, MK (2000) Multilevel integrative analyses of human behaviour: social neuroscience and the complementing nature of social and biological approaches. *Psychological Bulletin*, 126(6): 829–43.

Calvin, CM, Fernandes, C, Smith, P, Visscher, PM and Deary, IJ (2010) Sex, intelligence and educational achievement in a national cohort of over 175,000 11-year-old schoolchildren in England. *Intelligence*, 38: 424–32.

Campbell, WK, Goodie, AS and Foster, JD (2004) Narcissism, confidence, and risk attitude. *Journal of Behavioural Decision Making*, 17: 297–311.

Cantor, N (1990) From thought to behaviour: 'Having' and 'doing' in the study of personality. *American Psychologist*, 45(6), 735–50.

Caprara, GV and Cervone, D (2000) *Personality Determinants, Dynamics, and Potentials*. New York: Cambridge University Press.

Carver, CS and Scheier, MF (2000a) Autonomy and self-regulation. *Psychological Inquiry*, 11(4): 284–91.

Carver, CS and Scheier, MF (2000b) Scaling back goals and recalibration of the affect system are processes in normal adaptive self-regulation: understanding 'response shift' phenomena. *Social Science & Medicine*, 50: 1715–22.

Carver, CS and Scheier, MF (2002) Control processes and self-organizations as contemporary principles underlying behaviour. *Personality and Social Psychology Review*, 6(4): 304–15.

Caspi, A, Roberts, BW and Shiner, RL (2005) Personality development: stability and change. *Annual Review of Psychology*, 56: 1–17.

Cattell, J McKeen (1890) Mental tests and measurements. *Mind,* 15: 373–81.

Cattell, RB (1943) The description of personality. II: Basic traits resolved into clusters. *Journal of Abnormal and Social Psychology*, 38: 476–507.

Cattell, RB (1971) *Abilities: Their structure, growth and action*. New York: World Book Company.

Ceci, SJ (2000) So near and yet so far: Lingering questions about the use of measures of general intelligence for college admission and employment screening. *Psychology, Public Policy, and Law*, 6(1): 233–52.

Cervone, D (2005) Personality architecture: within-person structures and processes. *Annual Review of Psychology*, 56: 423–52.

Chamorro-Premuzic, T and Arteche, A (2008) Intellectual competence and academic performance: preliminary validation of a model. *Intelligence*, 36: 564–73.

Chamorro-Premuzic, T and Furnham, T (2004) A possible model for understanding the personality–intelligence interface. *British Journal of Psychology*, 95: 249–64.

Chapman, BP, Duberstein, PR, Sorensen, S and Lyness, JM (2007) Gender differences in Five Factor Model personality traits in an elderly cohort: extension of robust and surprising findings to an older generation. *Personality and Individual Differences*, 43(06): 1594–603.

Chen, G, Gully, SM and Eden, D (2001) Validation of a new general self-efficacy scale. *Organisational Research Methods*, 4(1): 62–83.

Chida, Y and Steptoe, A (2009) The association of anger and hostility with future coronary heart disease: a meta-analytic review of prospective evidence. *Journal of the American College of Cardiology*, 53(11): 936–46.

Chien, L-L, Ko, HLC and Wu, JY.-W (2007) The five-factor model of personality and depressive symptoms: one-year follow-up. *Personality and Individual Differences*, 43: 1013–23.

Chorney, MJ, Chorney, K, Seese, N, Owen, MJ, Daniels, J, McGuffin, P, Thompson, LA, Detterman, DK, Benbow, C, Lubinski, D, Eley, T and Plomin, R (1998) A quantitative trait locus associated with cognitive ability in children. *Psychological Science*, 9(3): 159–66.

Christopher, AN, Jones, JR (2004) Affluence cues and first impressions: the moderating impact of the Protestant work ethic. *Journal of Economic Psychology*, 25: 279–92.

Christopher, AN and Schlenker, BR. (2000) The impact of perceived material wealth and perceiver personality on first impressions. *Journal of Economic Psychology*, 21: 1–19.

Christopher, AN, Morgan, RD, Marek, P, Troisi, JD, Jones, JR, and Reinhart, DF (2005) Affluence cues and first impressions: does it matter how the affluence was acquired? *Journal of Economic Psychology*, 26: 187–200.

Chulef, AS, Read, SJ and Walsh, DA (2001) A hierarchical taxonomy of human goals. *Motivation and Emotion*, 25(3): 191–232.

Church, AT, Katigbak, K, Ortiz, FA, del Prado, AM, Vargas-Flores, J de J, Ibanez-Reyes, J, Reyes, JAS, Pe-Pua, R and Cabrera, HF (2005) Investigating implicit trait theories across cultures. *Journal of Cross-Cultural Psychology*, 36(4): 476–96.

Church, AT, Katigbak, MS, Miramontes, LG and del Prado, AM (2007) Culture and the behavioural manifestations of traits: an application of the act frequency approach. *European Journal of Personality*, 21(4): 389–417.

Church, AT, Katigbak, MS, Reyes, JAS, Salanga, MGC, Miramontes, LA and Adams, NB (2008) Prediction and cross-situational consistency of daily behaviour across cultures: testing trait and cultural psychology perspectives. *Journal of Research in Personality*, 42: 1199–215.

Collins, A, Joseph, D and Bielaczyc, K (2004) Design research: theoretical and methodological issues. *Journal of the Learning Sciences*, 13(1): 15–42.

Conway, ARA, Kane, MJ and Engle, RW (2003) Working memory capacity and its relation to general intelligence. *TRENDS in Cognitive Sciences*, 7(12): 547–52.

Cooper, C (2002) *Individual differences* (2nd edn). Malta: Hodder Arnold.

Corr, PJ and Perkins, AM (2006) The role of theory in the psychophysiology of personality: from Ivan Pavlov to Jeffrey Gray. *International Journal of Psychophysiology,* 62: 367–76.

Costa, PT and McCrae, RR (1976) Age differences in personality structure: a cluster-analytic approach. *Journal of Gerontology*, 31: 564–70.

Costa, PT and McCrae, RR (1985) *The NEO Personality Inventory Manual.* Odessa, FL: Psychological Assessment Resources.

Costa, PT and McCrae, RR (1992a) 4 ways 5 factors are basic. *Personality and Individual Differences,* 13: 653–65.

Costa, PT and McCrae, RR (1992b) *Neo-PI(R) Professional Manual.* Odessa, FL: Psychological Assessment Resources.

Costa, PT, McCrae, RR and Dye, DA (1991) Facet scales for agreeableness and conscientiousness: a revision of the NEO Personality Inventory. *Personality and Individual Differences*, 12: 887–98.

Covington, MV and Mueller, KJ (2001) Intrinsic versus extrinsic motivation: an approach/avoidance reformulation. *Educational Psychology Review*, 13(2), 157–70.

Craft, A, Cremin, T, Burnard, P and Chappell, K (2007) Teacher stance in creative learning: a study of progression. *Thinking Skills and Creativity*, 2: 136–47.

Cronbach, LJ (1957) The two disciplines of scientific psychology. *American Psychologist*, 12: 671–84. http://psychclassic.yorku.ca/Cronbach/Disciplines/

Cronbach, L J and Meehl, P E (1955) Construct validity in psychological tests. *Psychological Bulletin,* 52: 281–302.

Crosby, FJ, Iyer, A and Sincharoen, S (2006) Understanding affirmative action. *Annual Review of Psychology*, 57: 585–611.

Dahme, G, Eichstadt, J and Rudolph, U (2003) Experiments important to Carver and Scheier's self-regulation theory are not replicable. *Swiss Journal of Psychology*, 62(1): 53–65.

Dalton,SO, Mellemkjær, L, Olsen, JH, Mortensen, PB and Johansen, C (2002) Depression and cancer risk: a register-based study of patients hospitalized with affective disorders, Denmark, 1969–1993. *American Journal of Epidemiology*, 155(12): 1088–95.

D'Amato, CP and Denney, RL (2008) The diagnostic utility of the Rarely Missed Index of the Wechsler Memory Scale Third Edition in detecting response bias in an adult male incarcerated setting. *Archives of Clinical Neuropsychology*, 23: 553–61.

Deary, IJ and Batty, GD (2007) Cognitive epidemiology. *Journal Epidemiological Community Health*, 61: 378–84.

Deary, IJ, Austin, EJ and Caryl, PG (2000) Testing versus understanding human intelligence. *Psychology, Public Policy, and Law*, 6(1): 180–90.

Deary, IJ Johnson, W and Houliham, LM (2009) Genetic foundations of human intelligence. *Human Genetics*, 126: 215–32.

Deary, IJ, Penke, L and Johnson, W (2010) The neuroscience of human intelligence differences. *Nature Reviews Neuroscience*, 11: 201–11.

Deci, EL and Ryan, RM (2000) The 'what' and 'why' of goal pursuits: human needs and the self-determination of behavior. *Psychological Inquiry*, 11(4): 227–68.

Deffenbacher, JL (1993) General anger: characteristics and clinical implications. *Psicologia Conductual*, 1(1): 49–67.

Del Rosario, PM and White, RM (2005) The Narcissistic Personality Inventory: test–retest stability and internal consistency. *Personality and Individual Differences*, 39: 1075–81.

De Moor, MM, Distel, MA, Trull, TJ and Boomsma, DI (2009) Assessment of borderline personality features in population samples: is the personality assessment inventory–borderline features scale measurement invariant across sex and age? *Psychological Assessment*, 21(1): 125–30.

Denollet, J (2005) DS14: Standard assessment of negative affectivity, social inhibition, and Type D personality. *Psychosomatic Medicine*, 67: 89–97.

Denollet, J, Sys, SU and Brutsaert, D L (1995) Personality and mortality after myocardial infarction. *Psychosomatic Medicine*, 57: 582–91.

Denollet, J, Sys, SU, Stroobant, N, Rombouts, H, Gillebert, TC and Brutsaert DL (1996) Personality as independent predictor of long-term mortality in patients with coronary heart disease. *The Lancet*, 347: 417–21.

Department of Health (2009) *Recognising Complexity: Commissioning guidance for personality disorder services*. London: Department of Health.

Diener, E and Scollon, CN. (2002) Our desired future for personality psychology. *Journal of Research in Personality*, 36: 629–37.

Diener, E, Lucas, RE and Scollon, CN (2006) Beyond the hedonic treadmill: revising the adaptation theory of well-being. *American Psychologist,* 61(4): 305–14.

Dixon, JA and Mahoney, B (2003) The effect of accent evaluation and evidence on a suspect's perceived guilt and criminality. *Journal of Social Psychology,* 144(1): 63–73.

Dixon, JA, Mahoney, B and Cocks, R (2002) Accents of guilt effects of regional accent, race, and crime type on attributions of guilt. *Journal of Language and Social Psychology,* 21(2): 162–68.

Duckworth, AL (2009) (Over and) beyond high-stakes testing. *American Psychologist*, May–June: 279–80.

Duncan, G (2000) Mind-body dualism and the biopsychosocial model of pain: what did Descartes really say? *Journal of Medicine and Philosophy*, 25(4): 485–513.

Duncan, LA, Schaller, M and Park, JH (2009) Perceived vulnerability to disease: development and validation of a 15-item self-report instrument. *Personality and Individual Differences*, 47: 541–46.

Dweck, CS and Leggett, EL (1988) A social-cognitive approach to motivation and personality. *Psychological Review*, 95(2): 256–73.

Dweck, CS, Chiu, C-Y and Hong, Y-Y (1995) Implicit theories and their role in judgments and reactions: a world from two perspectives. *Psychological Inquiry*, 6(4): 267–85.

Eastin, MS and LaRose, R (2000) Internet self-efficacy and the psychology of the digital divide. *Journal of Computer-Mediated Communication*, 6(0).

Eckhardt, CI and Deffenbacher, JL (1995) Diagnosis of anger disorders, in Kassinove, H (ed.) *Anger Disorders: Definition, diagnosis, and treatment* (pp27–48). Washington, DC: Taylor & Francis.

Eckhardt, C, Norlander, B and Deffenbacher, J (2004) The assessment of anger and hostility: a critical review. *Aggression and Violent Behaviour*, 9: 17–43.

Edwards, JR and Baglioni Jr, AJ (1991) Relationship between Type A Behaviour Pattern and mental and physical symptoms: a comparison of global and component measures. *Journal of Applied Psychology*, 76(2): 276–90.

Elder, GH (1998) The life course as developmental theory. *Child Development*, 69(1): 1–12.

Elliot, EJ and Thrash, TM (2002) Approach-avoidance motivation in personality: approach and avoidance temperaments and goals. *Journal of Personality and Social Psychology*, 82(5): 804–15.

Emmons, RA (1987) Narcissism: theory and measurement. *Journal of Personality and Social Psychology*, 52(1): 11–17.

Engel, GL (1977) The need for a new medical model: a challenge for biomedicine. *Science*, 196(4286): 129–36.

Evans, DL, Herbert, JD, Nelson-Gray, RO and Gaudiano, BA (2001) Determinants of diagnostic prototypicality judgments of the personality disorders. *Journal of Personality Disorders*, 16(1): 95–106.

Eysenck, HJ (1992) Four ways five factors are not basic. *Personality and Individual Differences*, 13: 667–73.

Eysenck, HJ, Barrett, P, Wilson, G and Jackson, C (1992) Primary trait measurement of the 21 Components of the P-E-N System. *European Journal of Psychological Assessment*, 8(2): 109–17.

Facione, PA (2000) The disposition toward critical thinking: its character, measurement, and relationship to critical thinking skill. *Informal Logic*, 20(1): 61–84.

Fincher, CL, Thornhill, R, Murray, DR. and Schaller, M (2008) Pathogen prevalence predicts human cross-cultural variability in individualism/collectivism. *Proceedings of the Royal Society B*, 275: 1279–85.

Fiske, DW (1949) Consistency of factorial structures of personality ratings from different sources. *Journal of Abnormal and Social Psychology*, 44: 329–44.

Fleeson, W (2001) Toward a structure- and process-integrated view of personality: traits as density distributions of states. *Journal of Personality and Social Psychology*, 80(6): 1011–27.

Fleeson, W (2004) Moving personality beyond the person situation debate: the challenge and the opportunity of within person variability. *American Psychologist*, 13(2): 83–87.

Foster, JD and Campbell, WK (2007) Are there such things as 'Narcissists' in social psychology? A taxometric analysis of the Narcissistic Personality Inventory. *Personality and Individual Differences*, 43: 1321–32.

Frederickson, N and Petrides, KV (2008) Ethnic, gender, and socio-economic group differences in academic performance and secondary school selection: a longitudinal analysis. *Learning and Individual Differences*, 18: 144–51.

Freud, S (1936) *The Ego and the Mechanisms of Defense*. Madison, CT: International Universities Press.

Friedman, HS and Booth-Kewley, S (1987) Personality, Type A Behavior, and coronary heart disease: the role of emotional expression. *Journal of Personality and Social Psychology*, 53(4): 783–92.

Friedman, M and Rosenman, RH (1957) Comparison of fat intake of American men and women: possible relationship to incidence of clinical coronary artery disease. *Circulation*, 16: 339–47.

Friedman, M and Rosenman, RH (1959) Association of specific overt behaviour pattern with blood and cardiovascular findings: blood cholesterol level, blood clotting time, incidence of arcus senilis, and clinical coronary artery disease. *Journal of the American Medical Association*, 169: 1286–96.

Frijda, NH (2009) Emotion experiences and its varieties. *Emotion Review*, 1(3): 264–71.

Funder, DC (2009) Persons, behaviours and situations: an agenda for personality psychology in the postwar era. *Journal of Research in Personality*, 43: 120–26.

Furmack, T, Tillfors, M, Everz, P-O, Marteinsdottir, I, Gefvert, O and Fredrikson, M (1999) Social phobia in the general population: prevalence and sociodemographic profile. *Social Psychiatry Psychiatric Epidemiology*, 34: 416–24.

Furmack, T, Tillfors, M, Stattin, H, Ekselius, L and Fredrikson, M (2000) Social phobia subtypes in the general population revealed by cluster analysis. *Psychological Medicine*, 30: 1335–44.

Furr, RM (2009) Profile analysis in person–situation integration. *Journal of Research in Personality*, 43: 196–207.

Gabbard, GO. (2005) Mind, brain, and personality disorders. *American Journal of Psychiatry*, 162: 648–55.

Gable, SL (2006) Approach and avoidance: social motives and goals. *Journal of Personality*, 74(1): 175–222.

Gallo, LC and Matthews, KA (2003) Understanding the association between socioeconomic status and physical health: do negative emotions play a role? *Psychological Bulletin*, 129(1): 10–51.

Galton, F (1865) Heredity talent and character. *Macmillan's Magazine*, 12: 157–66, 318–27.

Galton, F (1875) History of twins. *Inquiries into Human Faculty and its Development*, 155–73.

Galton, F (1876) The history of twins as a criterion of the relative powers of nature and nurture. *Royal Anthropological Institute of Great Britain and Ireland Journal,* 6: 391–406.

Galton, F (1883) *Inquiries into Human Faculty and its Development*. London: Macmillan.

Gardner, FL and Moore, ZE (2008) Understanding clinical anger and violence: the anger avoidance model. *Behaviour Modification*, 32(6): 897–912.

Gardner, H (1993) *Frames of Mind*. London: HarperCollins.

Gardner, H and Hatch, T (1989) Multiple intelligences go to school: educational implications of the theory of multiple intelligences. *Educational Researcher*, 18(8): 4–10.

Garrett, HE (1946) A developmental theory of intelligence. *American Psychologist*, 1: 372–78.

Goertzen, JR (2009) On the possibility of unification: the reality and nature of the crisis in psychology. *Theory and Psychology*, 18(6): 829–52.

Goetz, AT and Shackleford, TK (2006) Modern application of evolutionary theory to psychology: key concepts and clarifications. *American Journal of Psychology*, 119(4): 567–84.

Goldberg, LR (1981) Language and individual differences: the search for universals in personality lexicons, in Wheeler, L (ed) *Review of personality and social psychology* (volume 2), pp141–65. Beverley Hills, CA: Sage.

Goldberg, LR (1990) The development of markers for the Big-Five factor structure. *Psychological Assessment*, 4: 26–42.

Goldberg, LR (1993) The structure of phenotypic personality traits. *American Psychologist* 48(1): 26–34.

Gosling, SD (2001) From mice to men: what can we learn about personality from animal research? *Psychological Bulletin*, 127(1): 45–86.

Gottfredson, LS (1986) Societal consequences of the g factor in employment. *Journal of Vocational Behaviour*, 29: 379–410.

Graham, J, Ramirez, A, Love, S, Richards, M and Burgess, C (2002) Stressful life experiences and risk of relapse of breast cancer: observational cohort study. *British Medical Journal,* 324: 1420–24.

Gray, JA (1970) The psychophysiological basis of introversion-extraversion. *Behaviour Research and Therapy*, 8: 249–66.

Gray, JA (1979) Is there any need for conditioning in Eysenck's conditioning model of neurosis? *Behavioural and Brain Sciences*, 2: 169–71.

Gray, JA (1987) *The psychology of fear and stress*. New York: Cambridge University Press.

Gray, JA (1990) Brain systems that mediate both emotion and cognition. *Cognition and Emotion*, 4: 269–88.

Grossarth-Maticek, R, Eysenck, HJ and Boyle, GJ (1995) Method of test administration as a factor in test validity: the use of a personality questionnaire in the prediction of cancer and coronary heart disease. Humanities and Social Sciences papers, Bond University.

Groth-Marnat, G (2003) *Handbook of Psychological Assessment* (4th edn). New York: Wiley.

Gudonis, LC, Miller, DJ, Miller, JD and Lynam, DR. (2008) Conceptualizing personality disorders from a general model of personality functioning: antisocial personality disorder and the five-factor model. *Personality and Mental Health*, 2: 249–64.

Guilford, JP (1967) *The Nature of Human Intelligence*. New York: McGraw-Hill.

Hakstian, AR. and Cattell, RB (1978) Higher-stratum ability structures on a basis of twenty primary abilities. *Journal of Educational Psychology*, 70(5): 657–69.

Hale, JB, Fiorello, CA, Kavanagh, JA, Holdnack, JA and Aloe, AM (2007) Is the demise of IQ interpretation justified? A response to special issue authors. *Applied Neuropsychology*, 14(1): 37–51.

Hankin, BL and Abramson, LY (2001) Development of gender differences in depression: an elaborated cognitive vulnerability-transactional stress theory. *Psychological Bulletin*, 127(6): 773–96.

Hansen, PE, Floderus, B, Frederiksen, K and Johansen, C (2005) Personality traits, health behaviour, and risk for cancer: a prospective study of a Swedish twin cohort. *Cancer,* 103: 1082–91.

Hawthorne. G, Mouthaan, J, Forbes, D and Novaco, RW. (2006) Response categories and anger measurement: do fewer categories result in poorer measurement? Development of the DAR5. *Social Psychiatry and Psychiatric Epidemiology*, 41: 164–72.

Hayes, N and Joseph, S (2003) Big 5 correlates of three measures of subjective well-being. *Personality and Individual Differences*, 34: 723–27.

Haynes, S, Feinleib, M and Kennel, WB (1980) The relationship of psychosocial factors to coronary heart disease in the Framingham Study. III. Eight-year incidence of coronary heart disease. *American Journal of Epidemiology*, 111(1): 37–58.

Hebb, DO (1949) *The Organisation of Behaviour*. New York: Wiley.

Hecker, MHL, Chesney, MA, Black, GW. and Frautschi, N (1988) Coronary-prone behaviours in the Western Collaborative Group Study. *Psychosomatic Medicine*, 50: 153–64.

Hellman, CM and Caselman, TD (2004) A psychometric evaluation of the Harvey Imposter Phenomenon Scale. *Journal of Personality Assessment*, 83(2): 161–66.

Hernandez, OJ, Parga, MX.F and Aznar, CM (2007) Illness behaviour: prediction by symptoms, the Grossarth-Maticek and Eysenck Personality Types, neuroticism, life events, coping, health locus of control, social support, and attribution style. *The Spanish Journal of Psychology*, 10(2): 388–98.

Herrmann, E, Call, J, Hernández-Lloreda, MV, Hare, B and Tomasello, M (2007) Humans have evolved specialized skills of social cognition: the cultural intelligence hypothesis. *Science*, 317: 1360–66.

Hofstede, G and McCrae, RR (2004) Personality and culture revisited: linking traits and dimensions of culture. *Cross-Cultural Research*, 38(1): 52–88.

Hofstee, WKB, De Raad, B and Goldberg, LR. (1992) Integration of the Big Five and circumplex approaches to trait structure. *Journal of Personality and Social Psychology*, 63: 146–63.

Horn, JL and Cattell, RB (1966) Refinement and test of the theory of fluid and crystallised intelligence. *Journal of Educational Psychology*, 57: 253–70.

Houts, AC (2001) Harmful dysfunction and the search for value neutrality in the definition of mental disorder: response to Wakefield, part 2. *Behaviour Research and Therapy*, 39: 1099–32.

Hoyle, RH (2006) Personality and self-regulation: trait and information-processing perspectives. *Journal of Personality*, 74(6): 1507–26.

Ingram, RE and Loxton, DD (2005) Vulnerability-stress models, in Hankin, BL and Abela, JZR (eds) *Development of Psychopathology: A vulnerability-stress perspective* (pp32–46). New York: Sage.

Jackson, CJ and Smillie, LD (2004) Appetitive motivation predicts the majority of personality and an ability measure: a comparison of BAS measures and a re-evaluation of the importance of RST. *Personality and Individual Differences*, 36: 1627–36.

Jacobwitz, S and Egan, V (2006) The dark triad and normal personality traits. *Personality and Individual Differences*, 40: 331–39.

James, W (1890) *The Principles of Psychology*. London: Penguin Books.

Jenkins, CD, Rosenman, RH and Friedman, M (1968) Replicability of rating the coronary-prone behaviour pattern. *British Journal of Preventative & Social Medicine*, 22: 16–22.

Jenkins, CD, Zysanski, SJ and Rosenman, RH (1976) Risk of new myocardial infarction in middle-aged men with manifest coronary heart disease. *Circulation*, 53: 342–47.

John, OP and Srivastava, S (1999) The Big Five trait taxonomy: history, measurement, and theoretical perspectives, in Pervin, LA and John, OP (eds) *Handbook of Personality: Theory and research* (2nd edn), pp102–39. New York: Guilford Press.

Johns, LC and van Os, J (2001) The continuity of psychotic experiences in the general population. *Clinical Psychology Review*, 21(8): 1125–41.

Judge, TA and Ilies, R (2002) Relationship of personality to performance motivation: a meta-analytic review. *Journal of Applied Psychology*, 87(4): 797–807.

Kandler, C, Bleidorn, W, Riemann, R, Spinath, FM, Thiel, W and Angleitner, A (2010) Sources of cumulative continuity in personality: a longitudinal multiple-rater twin study. *Journal of Personality and Social Psychology*, 98(6): 995–1008.

Kassinove, H and Sukhodolsky, DG (1995) Anger disorders: basic science and practice issues, in Kassinove, H (ed.) *Anger disorders: definition, diagnosis, and treatment* (pp1–27). Washington, DC: Taylor & Francis.

Kendell, RE (2002) The distinction between personality disorder and mental illness. *British Journal of Psychiatry*, 180: 110–15.

Kenrick, DT and Funder, DC (1988) Profiting from controversy lessons from the person-situation debate. *American Psychologist*, 43(1): 23–34.

Kenrick, DT, Griskevicius,V, Neuberg, SL and Schaller, M (2010) Renovating the pyramid of needs: contemporary extensions built upon ancient foundations. *Perspectives on Psychological Science*, 5(3): 292–314.

Keyes, CLM (2002) The mental health continuum: from languishing to flourishing in life. *Journal of Health and Behaviour Research,* 43: 207–22.

Keyes, CLM (2005) Mental illness and/or mental health? Investigating axioms of the Complete State Model of Health. *Journal of Consulting and Clinical Psychology,* 73(3): 539–48.

Keyes, CLM (2007) Promoting and protecting mental health as flourishing: a complementary strategy for improving national mental health. *American Psychologist,* 62(2), 95–108.

Keyes, CLM, Shmotkin, D and Ryff, CD (2002) Optimizing well-being: the empirical encounter of two traditions. *Journal of Personality and Social Psychology,* 82(6): 1007–22.

Kihlstrom, JF (2004) To honor Kraepelin . . . : from symptoms to pathology in the diagnosis of mental illness, in Beutler, LE and Mallik, ML (eds) *Alternatives to DSM* (pp279–303). Washington, DC: American Psychological Association.

Kimbrel, NA (2008) A model of the development and maintenance of generalised social phobia. *Clinical Psychology Review,* 28: 592–612.

Kirchler, E and Holzl, E (2006) Twenty-five years of *the Journal of Economic Psychology* (1981–2005): a report on the development of an interdisciplinary field of research. *Journal of Economic Psychology,* 27: 793–804.

Kissen, DM and Eysenck, HJ (1962) Personality in male lung cancer patients. *Journal of Psychosomatic Research,* 6: 123–27.

Kline, P (1991) *Intelligence: The psychometric view*. London: Routledge.

Kornstein, SG, Schatzberg, AF, Thase, ME, Yonkers, KA, McCullough, JP, Keitner, GI, Gelenberg, AJ, Ryan, CE, Hess, AL, Harrison, W, Davis, SM and Keller, MB (2000) Gender differences in chronic major and double depression. *Journal of Affective Disorders,* 60: 1–11.

Korotkov, D and Hannah, TL (2004) The Five-Factor Model of personality: strengths and limitations in predicting health status, sick-role and illness behaviour. *Personality and Individual Differences,* 36: 187–99.

Kotov, R (2006) Extension of the hierarchical model of anxiety and depression to the personality domain. Unpublished PhD thesis, The University of Iowa.

Krueger, RF (2005) Continuity of Axes I and II: toward a unified model of personality, personality disorders, and clinical disorders. *Journal of Personality Disorders,* 19(3): 233–61.

Krueger, RF and Tackett, JL (2003) Personality and psychopathology: working toward the bigger picture. *Journal of Personality Disorders,* 17(2): 109–28.

Kruglanski, AW (2001) That 'vision thing': the state of theory in social and personality psychology at the edge of the new millennium. *Journal of Personality and Social Psychology,* 80(6): 871–75.

Kubarych, TS, Deary, IJ and Austin, EJ (2004) The Narcissistic Personality Inventory: factor structure in a non-clinical sample. *Personality and Individual Differences*, 36: 857–72.

Kuehn, M (2001) *Kant: A Biography*. New York: Cambridge University Press.

Kuhn, D (2000) Metacognitive development. *Current Directions in Psychological Science*, 9(5): 178–81.

Kuncel, NR and Hezlett, SA (2007) Standardised tests predict graduate students' success. *Science*, 315(5815): 1080–81.

Lachar, BL (1993) Coronary-prone behaviour Type A Behaviour revisited. *Texas Heart Institute Journal*, 20(3): 143–51.

Lamiell, JT (2007) On sustaining critical discourse with mainstream personality investigators. *Theory and Psychology*, 17(2): 169–85.

Landy, FJ (2005) Some historical and scientific issues related to research on emotional intelligence. *Journal of Organisational Behaviour*, 26: 411–24.

Lazarus, RS (1993) From psychological stress to the emotions: a history of changing outlooks. *Annual Review of Psychology*, 44: 1–21.

Leary, MR (1983) A brief version of the fear of negative evaluation scale. *Personality and Social Psychology Bulletin*, 9(3): 371–75.

Lee, K and Ashton, MC (2004) Psychometric properties of the HEXACO Personality Inventory. *Multivariate Behaviour Research*, 39(2): 329–58.

Li, S-C, Lindenberger, U, Hommell, B, Aschersleben, G, Prinz, W, Baltes, P B (2004) Transformations in the couplings among intellectual abilities and constituent cognitive processes across the life span. *Psychological Science*, 15(3): 155–63.

Lichtenberger, EO. (2005) Mental retardation and developmental disabilities. *Research Reviews*, 11: 197–208.

Lindau, S, Laumann, EO, Levinson, W and Waite, LJ (2003) Synthesis of scientific disciplines in pursuit of health: the interactive biopsychosocial model. *Perspectives in Biology and Medicine*, 46 (3 Suppl): S74–S86.

Lippa, RA (2010) Sex differences in personality traits and gender-related occupational preferences across 53 nations: testing evolutionary and social-environmental theories. *Archives of Sexual Behavior*, 39: 619–36.

Locke, EA, Shaw, KN, Saari, LM. and Latham, GP (1981) Goal setting and task performance: 1969–1980. *Psychological Bulletin*, 90(1): 125–52.

Loehlin, JC, Horn, JM and Willerman, L (1990) Heredity, environment, and personality change: evidence from the Texas Adoption Project. *Journal of Personality*, 58: 221–43.

Loehlin, JC, McCrae, RR and Costa Jr, PT (1998) Heritabilities of common and measure-specific components of the Big Five personality factors. *Journal of Research in Personality*, 32: 431–53.

Lubinski, D (2000) Scientific and social significance of assessing individual differences: "Sinking Shafts at a Few Critical Points". *American Review of Psychology*, 51: 405–44.

Lubinski, D (2004) Introduction to the special section on cognitive abilities: 100 years after Spearman's (1904) 'General intelligence objectively determined and measured'. *Journal of Personality and Social Psychology*, 86(1): 96–111.

Lubinski, D, Benbow, CP, Webb, RM and Bleske-Rechek, A (2006) Tracking exceptional human capital over two decades. *Psychological Science*, 17(3): 194–99.

Lynam, DR. and Widiger, TA (2001) Using the Five-Factor Model to represent the *DSM-IV* personality disorders: an expert consensus approach. *Journal of Abnormal Psychology*, 110(3): 401–12.

Lynn, R, Meisenberg, G, Mikk, J and Williams, A (2007) National IQs predict differences in scholastic achievement in 67 countries. *Journal of Biosocial Science*, 39: 861–74.

Lyubomirsky, S, King, L and Diener, E (2005) The benefits of frequent positive affect: does happiness lead to success? *Psychological Bulletin*, 131(6): 803–55.

Markon, KE, Krueger, RF and Watson, D (2005) Delineating the structure of normal and abnormal personality: an integrative hierarchical approach. *Journal of Personality and Social Psychology*, 88(1): 139–57.

Maslow, AH (1943) A theory of human motivation. *Psychological Review*, 50: 370–96.

Maslow, AH (1987) *Motivation and Personality* (3rd edn). New York: Harper & Row.

Matthews, G and Gilliland, K (1999) The personality theories of HJ Eysenck and JA Gray: a comparative review. *Personality and Individual Differences*, 26: 583–626.

Matud, MP (2004) Gender differences in stress and coping styles. *Personality and Individual Differences*, 37: 1401–15.

May, R (2007) Working outside the diagnostic frame. *The Psychologist*, 20: 300–1.

Mayer, DM and Hanges, PJ (2003) Understanding the stereotype threat effect with 'culture-free' tests: an examination of its mediators and measurement. *Human Performance*, 16(3): 207–30.

Mayr, E (1982) *The Growth of Biological Thought*. Cambridge, MA: Harvard University Press.

McAdams, DP (1996) Personality, modernity, and the storied self: a contemporary framework for studying persons. *Psychological Inquiry,* 7(4), 295–321.

McAdams, DP and Pals, JL (2006) A new Big Five fundamental principles for an integrative science of personality. *American Psychologist*, 61(3): 204–17.

McClelland, DC (1973) Testing for competence rather than for 'intelligence'. *American Psychologist*, January: 1–14.

McCrae, RR (2001) Trait psychology and culture: exploring intercultural comparisons. *Journal of Personality*, 69(6): 819–46.

McCrae, RR (2004) Human nature and culture: a trait perspective. *Journal of Research in Personality*, 38: 3–14.

McCrae, RR, Lockenhoff, CE and Costa, PT (2005a) A step toward *DSM-V*: cataloguing personality-related problems in living. *European Journal of Personality*, 19: 269–86.

McCrae, RR, Terracciano, A and 78 members of the Personality Profiles of Cultures project (2005b) Universal features of personality traits from the observer's perspective: data from 50 cultures. *Journal of Personality and Social Psychology*, 88(3): 547–61.

McCrae, RR, Terracciano, A, De Fruyt, F, De Bolle, M, Gelfand, MJ, Costa, Jr, PT and 42 collaborators of the Adolescent Personality Profiles of Cultures Project (2010) The validity and structure of culture-level personality scores: data from ratings of young adolescents. *Journal of Personality*, 78(3): 815–38.

McGue, M, Bacon, S and Lykken, DT (1993) Personality stability and change in early adulthood: a behavioural genetic analysis. *Developmental Psychology*, 29: 96–109.

McGuffin, P, Riley, B and Plomin, R (2001) Genomics and behaviour: toward behavioural genomics, *Science*, 291(5507): 1232–49.

McHugh, PR (2005) Striving for coherence: psychiatry's efforts over classification. *Journal of the American Medical Association*, 293(20): 2526–28.

McNaughton, N, Gray, JA (2002) 'The neuropsychology of anxiety' as it really is: a response to O'Mara (2001). *Neuropsychological Rehabilitation*, 12: 363–67.

Meehl, PE (1962) Schizotaxia, schizotypy, schizophrenia. *American Psychologist*, 17: 827–38.

Mehta, PH and Gosling, SD (2008) Bridging human and animal research: a comparative approach to studies of personality and health. *Brain, Behaviour, and Immunity*, 22: 651–61.

Metcalfe, J and Mischel, W (1999) A hot/cool system analysis of delay of gratification: dynamics of willpower. *Psychological Review*, 106(1): 3–19.

Michalski, RL and Shackelford, TK (2010) Evolutionary personality psychology: reconciling human nature and individual differences. *Personality and Individual Differences*, 48: 509–16.

Miller, TQ, Smith, TW, Turner, CW, Guijarro, ML and Hallet, AJ (1996) A meta-analytic review of research on hostility and physical health. *Psychological Bulletin*, 119: 322–48.

Mischel, W (1968) *Personality and Assessment*. New York: Wiley.

Mischel, W (2004) Toward an integrative science of the person. *Annual Review of Psychology*, 55: 1–22.

Mischel, W and Shoda, Y (1995) A cognitive-affective system theory of personality: reconceptualising situations, dispositions, dynamics, and invariance in personality structure. *Psychological Review*, 102(2): 246–68.

Mischel, W, Shoda, Y and Mendoza-Denton, R (2002) Situation-behaviour profiles as a locus of consistency in personality. *Current Directions in Psychological Science*, 11(2): 50–54.

Moffitt, TE, Arseneault, L, Jaffee, SR, Kim-Cohen, J, Koenen, KC, Odgers, CL, Slutske, WS and Viding, E (2008) Research review: *DSM-V* conduct disorder: research needs for an evidence base. *Journal of Child Psychology and Psychiatry*, 49(1): 1–42.

Monroe, SM and Simons, AD (1991) Diathesis-stress theories in the context of life stress research implications for the depressive disorders. *Psychological Bulletin*, 110(3): 406–25.

Mooradian, TA and Swan, KS (2006) Personality-and-culture: the case of national extraversion and word-of-mouth. *Journal of Business Research*, 59: 778–85.

Morf, CC and Rhodewalt, F (2001) Unraveling the paradoxes of narcissism: a dynamic self-regulatory processing model. *Psychological Inquiry,* 12(4):177–96.

Mortensen, CR, Vaughn Becker, D, Ackerman, JM, Neuberg, SL and Kenrick, DT. (2010) Infection breeds reticence: the effects of disease salience on self-perceptions of personality and behavioral avoidance tendencies. *Psychological Science*, 21(3): 440–47.

Movahedi, B (1975) Loading the dice in favor of madness. *Journal of Health and Social Behaviour*, 16(2): 192–97.

Murphy, KP and Alexander, PA (2000) A motivated exploration of motivation. *Contemporary Educational Psychology*, 25: 3–53.

Murray, DM and Schaller, M (2010) Historical prevalence of infectious diseases within 230 geopolitical regions: a tool for investigating origins of culture. *Journal of Cross-Cultural Psychology*, 41(1): 99–108.

Musek, J (2007) A general factor of personality: evidence for the Big One in the five-factor model. *Journal of Research in Personal*ity, 41: 1213–33.

Myrtek, M (1995) Type A Behaviour Pattern, personality factors, disease, and physiological reactivity: a meta-analytic update. *Personality and Individual Differences*, 18(4): 491–502.

Nabi, H Kivimaki, M, Zins, M, Elovainio, M, Consoli, SM, Cordier, SP, Ducimetiere, P, Goldberg, M and Singh-Manoux, A (2008) Does personality predict mortality? Results from the GAZEL French prospective cohort study. *International Journal of Epidemiology*: 1–11.

Nakaya, N, Hansen, PE, Schapiro, IR, Eplov, LF, Saito-Nakaya, K, Uchitomi, Y and Johansen, C (2006) Personality traits and cancer survival: a Danish cohort study. *British Journal of Cancer*, 95: 146–52.

Neisworth, JT and Bragnato, SJ (2004) The mismeasure of young children: the authentic assessment alternative. *Infants and Young Children*, 17(3): 198–212.

Nettle, D (2006) The evolution of personality variation in humans and other animals. *American Psychologist*, 61(6): 622–31.

Noble, D (2008) Genes and causation. *Philosophical Transactions of the Royal Society A*, 366: 3001–15.

Norman, WT (1967) 2800 personality trait descriptors: normative operating characteristics for a university population. Department of Psychology, University of Michigan, Ann Arbor, MI.

Norton, L (n.d.) *Psychology Applied Learning Scenarios (PALS): a practical introduction to problem-based learning using vignettes for psychology lecturers*. LTSN Psychology. Available online at www.psychology.heacademy.ac.uk/docs/pdf/p20040422_pals.pdf (accessed 24 February 2011).

Nunnally, JC (1975) Psychometric theory – 25 years ago and now. *Educational Researcher*, 4(10): 7–19.

O'Connor, MC and Paunonen, SV (2007) Big Five personality predicts of post-secondary academic performance. *Personality and Individual Differences*, 43: 971–90.

Paisey, TJH and Mangan, GL (1982) Neo-Pavlovian temperament theory and the biological bases of personality. *Personality and Individual Differences*, 3: 189–203.

Parker, I (1999) Critical psychology: critical links. *Annual Review of Critical Psychology*, 1: 3–18.

Paulhus, DL and Williams, KM. (2002) The Dark Triad of personality: narcissism, Machiavellianism, and psychopathy. *Journal of Research in Personality*, 36: 556–63.

Paunonen, SV and Jackson, DN (2000) What is beyond the Big Five? Plenty! *Journal of Personality*, 68(5): 821–35.

Paunonen, SV, Lönnqvist, J-E, Verkasalo, M, Leikas, S and Nissinen, V (2006) Narcissism and emergent leadership in military cadets. *The Leadership Quarterly*, 17: 475–86.

Pavlov, IP (1927) *Conditioned Reflexes*. Oxford: Oxford University Press.

Pavlov, IP (1935) *Conditioned Reflexes and Psychiatry*. New York: International Publishers.

Pea, RD (1993) Practices of distributed intelligence and designs for education, in Salomon, G (ed.) *Distributed cognitions: psychological and educational considerations* (pp47–87). New York: Cambridge University Press.

Pea, RD (2004) The social and technological dimensions of scaffolding and related theoretical concepts for learning, education, and human activity. *The Journal of the Learning Sciences*, 13(3): 423–51.

Pedersen, SS and Denollet, J (2006) Is Type D Personality here to stay? Emerging evidence across cardiovascular disease patient groups. *Current Cardiology Reviews*, 2: 205–13.

Pederson, AK, King, JE and Landau, VI (2005) Chimpanzee (Pan troglodytes) personality predicts behaviour. *Journal of Research in Personality*, 39: 534–49.

Pelle, AJ, Pedersen, SS, Szabo, BM. and Denollet, J (2009a) Beyond Type D personality: reduced positive affect (anhedonia) predicts impaired health status in chronic heart failure. *Quality Life Research,* 18: 689–698

Pelle, AJ, Schiffer, AA, Smith, OR, Widdershoven, JW. and Denollet, J (2009b) Inadequate consultation behaviour modulates the relationship between Type D personality and impaired health status in chronic heart failure. *International Journal of Cardiology*, 142(1): 65–71.

Penke, L, Denissen, JJA and Miller, GF (2007) Evolution, genes, and inter-disciplinary personality research. *European Journal of Personality*, 21: 639–65.

Perkins, D, Tishman, S, Ritchhart, R, Donis, K and Andrade, A (2000) Intelligence in the wild: a dispositional view of intellectual traits. *Educational Psychology Review,* 12(3): 269–93.

Persky, VW, Kempthorne-Rawson, J and Shekelle, RB (1987) Personality and risk of cancer: 20-year follow-up of the Western Electric Study. *Psychosomatic Medicine,* 49: 435–49.

Pervin, LA (1985) Personality: current controversies, issues, and directions. *Annual Review of Psychology*, 36: 83–114.

Pezdek, K, Berry, T and Renno, PA (2002) Children's mathematics achievement: the role of parents' perceptions and their involvement in homework. *Journal of Educational Psychology*, 94(4): 771–77.

Pilgrim, D (2002) The biopsychosocial model in Anglo-American psychiatry: past, present and future? *Journal of Mental Health,* 11(6): 585–94.

Plomin, R and Caspi, A (1999) Behavioural genetics and personality, in Caspi, A and Roberts, BW (eds) *Handbook of Personality: Theory and research* (pp251–76). New York: Guilford Press.

Plomin, R and Spinath, FM (2004) Intelligence: genetics, genes, and genomics. *Journal of Personality and Social Psychology*, 86(1): 112–29.

Psychologist (2007) Special issue on diagnosing mental disorders. *The Psychologist*, 20(5). Available at www.thepsychologist.org.uk/archive/archive_home.cfm?volumeID=20&editionID=147.

Putnam, KM and Silk, KR (2005) Emotion dysregulation and the development of borderline personality disorder. *Development and Psychopathology*, 17: 899–925.

Quinn, DM and Spencer, SJ (2001) The interference of stereotype threat with women's generation of mathematical problem-solving strategies. *Journal of Social Issues*, 57(1): 55–71.

Raskin, R and Hall, H (1979) A narcissistic personality inventory. *Psychological Reports*, 45: 590.

Raskin, R and Terry, H (1988) A principal-components analysis of the Narcissistic Personality Inventory and further evidence of its construct validity. *Journal of Personality and Social Psychology*, 54(5): 890–902.

Rasmussen, HN, Wrosch, C, Scheier, MF and Carver, CS (2006) Self-regulation processes and health: the importance of optimism and goal adjustment. *Journal of Personality*, 74(6): 1721–48.

Reidy, DE, Zeichner, A, Foster, JD and Martinez, MA (2008) Effects of narcissistic entitlement and exploitativeness on human physical aggression. *Personality and Individual Differences*, 44: 865–75.

Reiss, S (2004) Multifaceted nature of intrinsic motivation: the theory of 16 basic desires. *Review of General Psychology*, 8(3): 179–93.

Reisenzein, R and Weber, H (2007) Personality and emotion, in Corr, PJ and Matthews, G (eds) *The Cambridge Handbook of Personality* (pp54–71). Cambridge: Cambridge University Press.

Revelle, W and Scherer, KR (2009) Personality and emotion, in Sandler, D and Scherer, K (eds) *Oxford Companion to the Affective Sciences*. Oxford: Oxford University Press.

Revelle, W, Wilt, J and Condon, DM (2010) Individual differences and differential psychology: A brief history and prospect, in Chamorro-Premuzic, T, Furnham, A and von Stumm. S (eds) *Handbook of Individual Differences* (pp1–28). Chichester: Wiley-Blackwell.

Roberts, BW, Kuncel, N, Shiner, RN, Caspi, A and Goldberg, LR. (2007) The power of personality: the comparative validity of personality traits, socio-economic status, and cognitive ability for predicting important life outcomes. *Perspectives in Psychological Science*, 2: 313–45.

Roberts, LJ and Duffy, DL (1995) A psychometric evaluation of the Short Interpersonal Reactions Inventory (SIRI) in an Australian twin sample. *Personality and Individual Differences*, 18(3): 307–20.

Rosenman, RH and Friedman, M (1961) Association of specific behaviour pattern in women with blood and cardiovascular findings. *Circulation*, 24: 1173–84.

Rosenman, RH, Brand, RJ, Jenkins, CD, Friedman, M, Straus, R and Wurm, M (1975) Coronary heart disease in the Western Collaborative Group Study: final follow-up of 81/2/2 years. *Journal of the American Medical Association*, 233(8): 872–77.

Ross, SR, Lutz, CJ and Bailley, SE (2004) Psychopathy and the Five Factor Model in a non-institutionalised sample: a domain and facet level analysis. *Journal of Psychopathology and Behavioural Assessment*, 26(4): 213–23.

Ruch, W (1992) Pavlov's types of nervous system, Eysenck's typology and the Hippocrates-Galen temperaments: an empirical examination of the asserted correspondence of three temperament typologies. *Personality and Individual Differences*, 13(12): 1259–71.

Rushton, JP and Jensen, AR (2005) Wanted: more race realism and less moralistic fallacy. *Psychology, Public Policy, and Law*, 11(2): 328–36.

Ryff, C (1989) Happiness is everything, or is it? Explorations on the meaning of psychological well-being. *Journal of Personality and Social Psychology*, 57(6), 1069–82.

Sackett, PR and Lievens, F (2008) Personnel selection. *Annual Review of Psychology*, 59:16.1–16.32.

Sackett, PR, Borneman, MJ and Connelly, BS (2008) High-stakes testing in higher education and employment appraising the evidence for validity and fairness. *American Psychologist,* 63(4): 215–27.

Sackett, PR, Kuncel, NR, Arneson, JJ, Cooper, SR and Waters, SD (2009) *Socioeconomic status and the relationship between SAT and freshman GPA: an analysis of data from 41 colleges and universities.* Research Report No. 2009–1. New York: The College Board.

Saucier, G (1994) Mini-markers: a brief version of Goldberg's unipolar Big Five Markers. *Journal of Personality Assessment*, 63(3): 506–16.

Saucier, G (2003) Factor structure of English-language personality type-nouns. *Journal of Personality and Social Psychology*, 85(4): 695–708.

Saucier, G and Goldberg, LR (1996) The language of personality: lexical perspectives on the five-factor model, in Wiggins, J (ed.) *The Five-Factor Model of Personality* (pp21–50). New York: Guilford Press.

Saupe, JL and Eimers, MT (2010) Correcting correlations when predicting success in college. Presented at the 50th Anniversary Forum of the Association for Institutional Research Charting our Future in Higher Education May 29–June 2, 2010. Chicago, IL Unpublished.

Schaller, M and Murray, DM (2008) Pathogens, personality, and culture: disease prevalence predicts worldwide variability in sociosexuality, extraversion, and openness to experience. *Journal of Personality and Social Psychology*, 95(1): 212–21.

Schapiro, IR, Ross-Petersen, L, Sælan, H, Garde, K, Olsen, JH and Johansen, C (2001) Extroversion and neuroticism and the associated risk of cancer: a Danish cohort study. *American Journal of Epidemiology*, 153(8): 757–63.

Scheier, MF and Bridges, MW (1995) Person variables and health: personality predispositions and acute psychological states as shared determinants for disease. *Psychosomatic Medicine*, 57: 255–68.

Schlinger, HD (2003) The myth of intelligence. *The Psychological Record*, 53: 15–32.

Schmitt, DP, Realo, A, Voracek, M and Allik, J (2008) Why can't a man be more like a woman? Sex differences in big five personality traits across 55 cultures. *Journal of Personality and Social Psychology*, 94(1): 168–82.

Schmitz, PG (1992) Personality, stress reactions and disease. *Personality and Individual Differences*, 13(6): 683–91.

Schraw, G and Moshman, D (1995) Metacognitive theories. *Educational Psychology Review*, 7(4): 351–71.

Shavelson, RJ, Phillips, DC, Towne, L and Feuer, MJ (2003) On the science of education design studies. *Educational Researcher*, 32(I): 25–28.

Shedler, J and Westen, D (2004) Dimensions of personality pathology: an alternative to the Five-Factor Model. *American Journal of Psychiatry*, 161: 1743–54.

Shekelle, RB, Hulley, SB, Neaton, JD, Billings, JH, Borhani, NO, Gerace, TA, Jacobs, DR, Lasser, NL, Mittlemark, MB and Stamler, J (1985). The MRFIT behaviour pattern study. II. Type A behaviour and incidence of coronary heart disease. *American Journal of Epidemiology*, 122: 559–70.

Sjoberg, L (2004) Commentaries on Robert J Sternberg's 'Why smart people can be so foolish'. *European Psychologist,* 9(3): 151–53.

Smedslund, G (1995) Personality and vulnerability to cancer and heart disease: relations to demographic and life-style variables. *Personality and Individual Differences*, 19(5): 691–97.

Smith, BM (1961) 'Mental health' reconsidered: a special case of the problem of values in psychology. *American Psychologist*, 16(6): 299–306.

Smith, TW and Ruiz, JM (2002) Psychosocial influences on the development and course of coronary heart disease: Current status and implications for research and practice. *Journal of Consulting and Clinical Psychology*, 7: 548–68.

Smith, TW, Glazer, K, Ruiz, JM and Gallo, JC (2004) Hostility, anger, aggressiveness, and coronary heart disease: an interpersonal perspective on personality, emotion, and health. *Journal of Personality*, 72(6): 1217–70.

Smith, WD (2002) *The Hippocratic Tradition*. Ithaca, NY: Cornell University Press.

Sparrow, SS and Davis, SM (2000) Recent advances in the assessment of intelligence and cognition. *Journal of Child Psychology and Psychiatry*, 41(1): 117–31.

Spearman, C (1904) 'General intelligence,' objectively determined and measured. *American Journal of Psychology*, 15: 201–92.

Spielberger, CD (1988) *Manual for the State Trait Anger Expression Inventory*. Odessa, FL: Psychological Assessment Resources.

Srivastava, S, John, OP, Gosling, SD and Potter, J (2003) Development of personality in early and middle adulthood: set like plaster or persistent change. *Journal of Personality and Social Psychology*, 84(5): 1041–53.

Stelmack, RM (1997) Toward a paradigm in personality: comment on Eysenck's (1997) view. *Journal of Personality and Social Psychology,* 73(6): 1238–41.

Sternberg, RJ (1985) *Beyond IQ: A triarchic theory of human intelligence.* New York: Cambridge University Press.

Sternberg, RJ (1986) *Intelligence Applied.* Orlando, FL: Harcourt Brace College.

Sternberg, RJ (2003) What is an 'expert student'? *Educational Researcher*, 32(8): 5–9.

Sternberg, RJ (2005) The theory of successful intelligence. *Interamerican Journal of Psychology*, 39(2): 189–202.

Sternberg, RJ and Grigorenko, EL (2001) Unified psychology. *American Psychologist*, 56(12): 1069–79.

Sternberg, RJ, Conway, BE, Ketron, JL and Berstein, M (1981) People's conceptions of intelligence. *Journal of Personality and Social Psychology*, 4(1): 37–55.

Sternberg, RJ, Grigorenko, EL and Kalmar, DA (2001) The role of theory in unified psychology. *Journal of Theoretical and Philosophical Psychology*, 21(2): 99–117.

Sternberg, RJ, Grigorenko, EL and Kidd, KK (2005) Intelligence, race, and genetics. *American Psychologist*, 60(1): 46–95.

Szasz, T S (1974). The myth of mental illness: foundations of a theory of personal conduct (revised edition). New York: Harper & Row.

Tackett, JL, Balsis, S, Oltmanns, TF and Krueger, RF (2009) A unifying perspective on personality pathology across the life span: developmental considerations for the fifth edition of the *Diagnostic and Statistical Manual of Mental Disorders. Development and Psychopathology*, 21: 687–713.

Terracciano, A, Abdel-Khalak, AM, Adam, N, Adamovova, L, Ahn, C-k, Ahn, H-n. et al. (2005) National character does not reflect mean personality trait levels in 49 cultures. *Science*. 310: 96–100.

Thorndike, EL (1920) Intelligence and its uses. *Harpers Magazine,* 140: 227–35.

Thorndike, EL and Woodworth, RS (1901) The influence of improvement in one mental function upon the efficiency of other functions (I). *Psychological Review*, 8: 247–61.

Thurstone, LL (1934) The vectors of mind. *Psychological Review*, 41: 1–32.

Thurstone, LL (1935) *The Vectors of the Mind: Multiple-factor analysis for the isolation or primary traits.* Chicago, IL: University of Chicago Press.

Thurstone, LL (1938) Primary mental abilities. *Psychometric Monographs*, No. 1.

Tiliopoulos, N, Pallier, G and Coxon, AP.M (2010) A circle of traits: a perceptual mapping of the NEO-PI-R *Personality and Individual Differences*, 48: 34–39.

Tupes, EC and Christal, RC (1961) Recurrent personality factors based on trait ratings. Technical report, USAF, Lackland Air Force Base, TX.

Twenge, JM, Konrath, S, Foster, JD, Campbell, WK and Bushman, BJ (2008) Egos inflating over time: a cross-temporal meta-analysis of the Narcissistic Personality Inventory. *Journal of Personality*, 76(4): 875–901.

Vernon, PA, Villani, VC, Vickers, LC and Harris, JA (2008) A behavioural genetic investigation of the Dark Triad and the Big 5. *Personality and Individual Differences*, 44: 445–52.

Vertue, FM. (2003) From adaptive emotion to dysfunction: an attachment perspective on social anxiety disorder. *Personality and Social Psychology Review*, 7(2): 170–91.

Vul, E, Harris, C, Winkielman, P and Pashler, H (2009) Puzzlingly high correlations in fMRI studies of emotion, personality, and social cognition. *Perspectives in Psychological Science*, 4(3): 274–90.

Wakefield, JC (1992) The concept of mental disorder: on the boundary between biological facts and social values. *American Psychologist*, 47(3): 373–88.

Wallwork, J, Mahoney, B and Mason, S (2007) Watching people do stuff: an analysis of newly recruited students' accounts of doing a psychology degree. *Psychology Learning and Teaching*, 6(2): 139–49.

Watson, D and Friend, R (1969) Measurement of social-evaluative anxiety. *Journal of Consulting and Clinical Psychology*, 33: 448–57.

Watson, D, Gamez, W and Simms, LJ (2005) Basic dimensions of temperament and their relation to anxiety and depression: a symptom-based perspective. *Journal of Research in Personality*, 39: 46–66.

Watson, G and Glaser, EM. (2008) *Watson-Glaser Critical Thinking Appraisal Short Form Manual.* Upper Saddle River, NJ: Pearson Education.

Webster, GD (2009) Evolutionary theory's increasing role in personality and social psychology. *Evolutionary Psychology*, 5(1): 84–91.

Weinberg, RA (1989) Intelligence and IQ landmark issues and great debates. *American Psychologist*, 44(2): 98–104.

Wellisch, DK and Yager, J (1983) Is there a cancer-prone personality? *CA: A Cancer Journal for Clinicians,* 33: 145–53.

Westen, D (1998) The scientific legacy of Sigmund Freud toward a psychodynamically informed psychological science. *Psychological Bulletin,* 124(3): 333–71.

White, J (2008) Intelligence testing in education. *Educational Journal,* 97: 15.

Widiger, TA and Trull, TJ (2007) Plate tectonics in the classification of personality disorder shifting to a dimensional model. *American Psychologist,* 62(2): 71–83.

Wiggins, JS. (1979) A psychological taxonomy of trait-descriptive terms: the interpersonal domain. *Journal of Personality and Social Psychology,* 37: 395–412.

Williams, JE, Paton, CC, Siegler, IC, Eigenbrodt, ML, Nieto, J and Tyroler, HA (2000) Anger proneness predicts coronary heart disease risk: prospective analysis from the Atherosclerosis Risk in Communities (ARIC) Study. *Circulation,* 101: 2034–39.

Williams, PG, O'Brien, CD and Colder, CR. (2004) The effects of neuroticism and extraversion on self-assessed health and health-relevant cognition. *Personality and Individual Differences,* 37: 83–94.

Wittchen, H-U and Fehm, L (2003) Epidemiology and natural course of social fears and social phobia. *Acta Psychiatrica Scandinavica,* 108 (Suppl. 417): 4–18.

Wolf, H, Spinath, FM, Riemann, R and Angleitner, A (2009) Self-monitoring and personality: a behavioural-genetic study. *Personality and Individual Differences,* 47: 25–29.

Wood, D, Nye, CD and Saucier, G (2010) Identification and measurement of a more comprehensive set of person-descriptive trait markers from the English lexicon. *Journal of Research in Personality,* 44: 258–72.

World Health Organization (2007) *The ICD-10 Classification of Mental and Behavioural Disorders: Clinical Descriptions and Diagnostic Guidelines.* Geneva: World Health Organization.

Wrosch, C, Scheier, MF, Carver, CS and Schulz, R (2003) The importance of goal disengagement in adaptive self-regulation: when giving up is beneficial. *Self and Identity,* 2: 1–20.

Yamagata, S, Suzuki, A, Ando, J, Ono, Y, Kijima, N, Yoshimura, K, Ostendorf, F, Angleitner, A, Riemann, R, Spinath, FM, Livesley, WJ and Jang, KL (2006) Is the genetic structure of human personality universal? A cross-cultural twin study from North America, Europe, and Asia. *Journal of Personality and Social Psychology,* 90(6): 987–98.

Yanchar, SC and Slife, BD (2004) Teaching critical thinking by examining assumptions, *Teaching of Psychology,* 31(2): 85–90.

Yanchar, SC, Slife, BD and Warne, R (2008) Critical thinking as disciplinary practice. *Review of General Psychology*, 12(3): 265–81.

Yik, MSM and Russell, JA (2001) Predicting the Big Two of affect from the Big Five of personality. *Journal of Research in Personality*, 35: 247–77.

Young, SM and Pinsky, D (2006) Narcissism and celebrity. *Journal of Research in Personality*, 40: 463–71.

Index

Page references in *italic* type indicate relevant figures and tables.